Edited by
JEREMY CHERFAS &
ROGER LEWIN

Not Work Alone

A cross-cultural
view of activities
superfluous to
survival

 SAGE PUBLICATIONS • Beverly Hills, California

For information address:

SAGE PUBLICATIONS, INC.
275 South Beverly Drive
Beverly Hills, California 90212

Printed in Great Britain
International Standard Book Number 0-8039-1394-X
Library of Congress Catalog Card No. 79-3805

First published in the United Kingdom by
Maurice Temple Smith Ltd

FIRST PRINTING

Contents

Preface

PERHAPS BECAUSE, as Alexander Pope wrote, the proper study of mankind is man, anthropology grips the common imagination. We want to know about other peoples, to marvel at our similarities and wonder at our differences, but the picture many have of so-called primitive people, those who are not as dependent on technology as we are, is often a false one. By and large they view the 'savage' much as Thomas Hobbes did, as eking out a miserable existence and leading a life 'solitary, poor, nasty, brutish, and short'.

Proper study of these peoples reveals that they lead rather easy lives, spending much of the day in pursuits that apparently confer no advantage for survival. They play games, tell stories, decorate themselves. There is no strict need for these activities and yet people invest a great deal of time in them. Despite this, discussion of such 'non-serious' behaviour is often tucked away in weighty tomes.

We began to think of collating some of these findings in one place, and were encouraged by the anthropologists we talked to. This book is the result. It is not an exhaustive catalogue of pastimes, and it is not a whimsical selection. We hope, rather, that this collection of articles makes the point that work and play are equally important, and not always distinguishable.

JEREMY CHERFAS
ROGER LEWIN

An Introduction to Affluence

ROGER LEWIN

FOR MILLENNIA upon millennia, customs, traditions, myths and beliefs were essential elements in the social pattern within which our ancestors lived and – through time – evolved. The human mind is therefore a product of culture as well as a source of it. And it is culture – the *way* we do things rather than *what* we do – that makes *Homo sapiens* a very special kind of animal. For humans, the business of surviving in the interval between birth and death is more than simply ensuring an adequate supply of food and safety from hazards in the outside world: it is concerned with the repeated experience of activities that have absolutely nothing to do with economic subsistence.

Not that all other members of the animal kingdom are mechanistic automata directed solely to the job of surviving and reproducing. Many young animals play, for instance, apparently for the fun of it (although there are important functional facets to play); and some of the higher primates display behaviours that come close to being cultural creations, having nothing to do with subsistence needs (the Gombe Stream chimpanzees' 'rain dance' is a good example). But the art of engaging in activities unrelated to survival has been raised to a ridiculously high level in humans. Being so very much a creature of culture, man runs riot with the creative energy that this unmatched medium of social organisation proffers. The way in which we build our homes, the shape in which we form our furniture, the clothes we wear, the songs we sing, the games we play, the stories we tell and the myths in which we believe – all are threads in the rich fabric that is human culture.

Bushmen of the Kalahari (Alan Hutchison Library)

The force that enables these threads to be spun in the first place, and then to be woven into a complex fabric is of course language, the means by which we frame our thoughts and communicate them to each other. Without the power of language, culture could not be the potent social organiser that it is. Language evolved because it produced an unequalled degree of social cohesion. It was the key to new heights of social organisation, an essential step on the evolutionary road to modern Man. The social structures in non-human primates are complex indeed, but with the radical departure in economic activity taken by our ancestors millions of years ago, when they developed a 'hunting and gathering' way of life, the demands for an even tighter social order became fierce. The emergence of human culture somewhere along the road was the evolutionary response to those intense pressures of selection.

Slowly, over the past two or so million years, the interaction between an evolving brain and an emerging culture produced the human mind. The American anthropologist Clifford Geertz describes this interaction – and its consequence – graphically and stylishly.

> The Pleistocene period, with its rapid and radical variations in climate, land formations, and vegetation, has long been recognised to be a period in which conditions were ideal for the speedy and efficient evolution of man; now it seems also to have been a period in which a cultural environment supplemented the natural environment in the selection process so as to further accelerate the rate of hominid evolution to an unprecedented speed. The Ice Age appears to have been not merely a time of receding brow ridges and shrinking jaws, but a time in which were forged nearly all those characteristics of man's existence which are most graphically human: his thoroughly encephalated nervous system, his incest-taboo-based social structure, and his capacity to create and use symbols.
>
> The fact that these distinctive features of humanity emerged together in complex interaction with one another rather than serially as for so long supposed, is of exceptional importance in the interpretation of human mentality, because it suggests that man's nervous system does not

merely enable him to acquire culture, it positively demands that he do so if it is going to function at all. Rather than culture acting only to supplement, develop, and extend organically-based capacities logically and genetically prior to it, it would seem to be ingredient to those capacities themselves.

A cultureless human being would probably turn out to be not an intrinsically talented though unfulfilled ape, but a wholly mindless and consequently unworkable monstrosity. Like the cabbage it so much resembles, the *Homo sapiens* brain, having arisen within the framework of human culture, would not be viable outside of it. (Geertz 1975 p 55.)

In other words, culture is not just one of the clever things that human beings do. It is not something extra added to a rather bright animal. Because it was an integral part of *becoming* human, culture is an integral part of *being* human.

Manifestations of culture come in all forms, from the magnificence of the Taj Mahal to a simple story told by one child to another; some of our culture is tangible, but much of it is a simple construct of the mind, passed from individual to individual. Very often, songs, stories and myths are the richest element of a people's culture, particularly nomadic people to whom material possessions are an unwelcome burden. This essentially evanescent nature of cultural activity provides prehistorians with a daunting and frustrating task. How do you peer into the minds of our ancestors when all they left behind were a few stone tools? Are we to infer a simple mind from a simple technology? Just as language makes no tangible impression on the fossil record, so cultural creations must also have faded rapidly from our ancestors' past lives. Only when paintings and crude carvings are preserved – such as those in France, Spain and Africa from thirty thousand years ago – do we get a hint of what went on in their creators' minds.

No, simple technology does not betray limited intellectual horizons: it is merely the hallmark of the hunting and gathering way of life, a way of life that began at least two million years ago and continued until the agricultural revolution ten thousand years ago. This distinctly human way of making a living was extraordinarily successful; it brought our ancestors through the evolutionary steps of *Homo habilis* to *Homo erectus* to *Homo sapiens*; and it took the human stock from the lush tropics to every corner of the globe, no matter how physically hostile. When, eventually, hunting and gathering gave way to agriculture as the new economic order, the sedentary existence permitted the accumulation of possessions and the creation of material wealth. Whereas wealth to a hunter-gatherer is a burden, to the city dweller it is often the *raison d'être*.

Brought up in the business economy of the industrial world, anthropology has viewed the life of the hunter-gatherer as dismal and hopeless. In attacking this bourgeois ethnocentric view, Marshall Sahlins has written: 'Almost universally committed to the proposition that life was hard in the Paleolithic, our textbooks compete to convey a sense of impending doom, leaving one to wonder not only how hunters managed to live, but whether, after all, this was living. The spectre of starvation stalks the stalker through these pages. His technical incompetence is said to enjoin continuous work just to survive, affording neither respite nor surplus, hence not even the leisure to build a culture. . . . And in treatises on economic development he is condemned to play the role of bad example: the so-called 'subsistence economy'. (Sahlins 1962, p. 1.)

The bourgeois ethnocentric view of the hunting and gathering way of life is a classic case of one culture failing totally to understand another. The values of one society are assumed to hold in the other. So, as Sahlins says, 'Having equipped the hunter with bourgeois impulses and Paleolithic tools, we judge his situation hopeless.' If modern man still has to strive to attain the 'natural' rewards of life, what chance has the naked savage with his spear, or puny bow and arrow? And does not the endless trek from camp to camp imply the continuous flight from starvation? No wonder, the traditional argument runs, the hunter-gatherer has no culture. Certainly, Melville Herskovits would have agreed with Thomas Hobbes: in 1952 he said that the people of the Kalahari desert and the Australian aborigines were 'a classic illustration of a people whose economic resources are of the scantiest . . . so that only the most intense application makes survival possible.'

The apparent indolence of 'the savage' was also a source of amazement to many. Hunters and gatherers never lay down food stores and frequently feast on the spoils of the day with no thought for future prospects. They have 'not the slightest thought of, or care for, what the morrow might bring,' wrote two bewildered Victorian observers. Speaking of the Montagnais Indians, an earlier commentator said that they behaved as if 'the game they were to hunt were locked up in a stable'. There are, as Sahlins points out, two interpretations of the hunters' attitude: either the people are fools, or they are not worried. Hunting and gathering is a highly skilled and demanding business, and to exploit this way of life successfully requires a deep understanding of the physical and animal world. With that understanding there comes, in the words of Rodney Needham, 'a confidence in the capacity of the environment to support them, and in their own ability to extract their livelihood from it'. Hunters and gatherers are not fools, and, as recent studies show, their unique economy gives them all the time they need in which to build culture.

When, ten thousand years ago, agriculture first developed, there were perhaps ten million people in the world, all practising some form of hunting and gathering. They occupied the most fertile areas of the globe as well as the most demanding. As the number of agriculturalists began to rise, they slowly but surely took over the land most suitable for farming, leaving the marginal areas to the diminishing number of hunter-gatherers. Now, with upwards of 4,000 million people based on agricultural and industrial economies (about two-thirds of whom are starving), there are less than 300,000 hunter-gatherers remaining, and inevitably, they live in some of the most inhospitable parts of the world. Once again, this factor influenced anthropologists' views on the nature of this form of ancient economy, and many of them concentrated their studies on the hunters and gatherers who were bewildered by the advance of agriculture. As the enlightened Victorian anthropologist, Sir George Grey, wrote: 'the anthropology of hunters is largely an anachronistic study of ex-savages – an inquest into the corpse of one society presided over by members of another'.

The question that anthropologists have recently being trying to answer is, how hard a life is hunting and gathering in reality? Is it constant toil on the brink of starvation? Richard Lee, a Canadian, did an eighteen-month study on the !Kung San

(Bushmen) of the north-west Kalahari, a semi-arid area that regularly suffers drought. Lee was interested in !Kung subsistence, both in their food, and in how much effort was involved in getting it. The results were striking.

The !Kung live in bands of about twenty-five people congregating at waterholes in the dry season, and spreading out into the surrounding desert when more water is available. Following traditional hunting and gathering patterns, the women collect plant foods while the men direct most, but not all, of their efforts to hunting animals. The !Kung are fortunate in having a constant supply of highly nutritious mongongo nuts. The women collect many other vegetables in addition, so that the overall diet for the !Kung is a mixture of meat, mongongo nuts, and other plant foods.

This mixed diet gives the !Kung ten per cent more calories than that set out in the US Food and Drug Administrations Recommended Daily Allowances (RDA), and fifty per cent more protein. Now, the first striking result of the dietary analysis is that plant foods supply two-thirds of the calories needed as against those supplied by meat, and close to sixty per cent of the protein. This distinct bias in favour of plant versus animal foods came as a surprise to many anthropologists, as it seemed to relegate hunting to a minor role in a society in which the quest for meat was seen as paramount. Some hunter-gatherers eat more meat than the !Kung, some less. The difference depends on the availability of plant food; people living near the equator, where plant foods are plentiful throughout the year, have a strong preference for these foods; only where plants are unreliable as a steady food source, such as in more temperate and colder climates, do hunters and gatherers concentrate on meat and on fish. The world average comes close to the pattern followed by the !Kung.

What is more, the effort in obtaining meat is far greater than for plants. In !Kung life, one hour of hunting produces eight hundred edible calories, whereas !Kung women collect two thousand calories of plant food in the same time. Hunting turns out to be a highly unpredictable business: most of the time hunters returning empty-handed. Overall, hunting is a high-risk, low-return activity whereas collecting plant foods is low-risk, high-return.

The most striking figure of all to come out of this analysis, however, is that for the effort expended in the total food quest. On average the !Kung work two and a half days a week, and since their working day is just six hours long, the weekly tally is fifteen hours – and this is for a diet that well exceeds recommended dietary allowances set by western standards! Moreover, youngsters usually begin working when they are about twenty, and the retiring age is about sixty. The young have time and encouragement to play and enjoy themselves, and the old are valued for their experience and knowledge of the world around them. When Lee was visiting the camps he recorded the number of 'retired' people in the community: it came to about ten per cent of the total population, a proportion comparable to that in the industrialised world. Such an existence, which is not atypical of hunter-gatherers the world over, can hardly be described as 'nasty, brutish and short'.

Of their working life, the !Kung spend roughly one-third working, one-third visiting relatives and friends at the other camps, and one-third entertaining visitors. 'This rhythm of steady work and steady leisure is maintained throughout the year,' says Lee. Such a large slice of leisure time leaves ample opportunity for 'building culture', which, in the case of the !Kung means singing, trance dances, and telling stories. Storytelling is a favourite occupation of the older members of the community and they usually draw an enthusiastic and participatory audience. As with most peoples, their stories are often parables, explanations of how they were created and by whom. The !Kung, like most hunter-gatherers, carry much of their culture in their heads, not on their backs.

As I said earlier, the prime function of culture is to bind people together, whether it is by strict rules of kinship or a mythology that gives everyone a common origin and a common cause. Although many of the things we do have no function in the strict subsistence sense, they are just some of a countless number of activities that are created in the context of cultural interactions. And it is somewhat ironic that culture – the unifying feature of all mankind – is the means by which one people is separated from another – their different languages, their beliefs and ideals, and even their style of dress. Thus culture makes man a variable animal. As Geertz says: 'One of the most significant facts about us may finally be that we all begin with the natural equipment to live a thousand kinds of life but in the end having lived only one.' (Geertz 1975, p. 45.) The games we play, the stories we tell, and the things we wear determine which one it will be.

YOUNG PLAY

Three chapters examine the part of games and play in the lives and growth of the young. Dorothy Einon reviews the evidence on the purpose of play, drawing on observations of children incidentally deprived of play and young animals experimentally subjected to similar deprivations. Colwyn Trevarthen and Fiona Grant restrict themselves to the human infant, and ask whether fun and games do not have a fundamental importance for the human species. Jeremy Cherfas looks at the more obviously organised games of the older child, speculating on the forces that keep games going through history.

The Purpose of Play

DOROTHY EINON

TO AN OBSERVER watching a young kitten getting tangled up in a piece of string, or two young puppies wrestling, it is natural to say that these young animals are indulging in 'play'. Of course, it is notoriously difficult to *define* or explain 'play' and 'games' even in the human species, and these difficulties are enormously magnified when we consider other animals, who cannot communicate about their basic motivations. It would appear, however, that the young of many, but not all, mammalian species indulge in activities which seem to have no obvious survival value, to be less serious than adult activities, and to be in many cases highly enjoyable to the animals engaging in them. These 'playful' activities cease as the animal gets older and are replaced by more obviously functional behaviour. For example, juvenile rats spend a great deal of their time, under no obvious provocation, wrestling, standing on their hind legs and 'boxing', and carrying out many other types of adult aggressive behaviour; but they hardly ever injure one another. If adult rats carry out such activities they do so with less restraint, and injury results.

The adaptive value of play is not immediately apparent; one might almost say that it is its maladaptive nature which is more readily observed. Although rodents make up a significant proportion of the diet of many animals, the young rat, in chasing and wrestling, makes a considerable amount of noise which could attract the attention of predators; nevertheless, play does not occur until after weaning at twenty-one days when, in the normal course of events, the mother will have a new litter of young. While the young rat is to some extent protected by other members of its social group, young badgers and foxes have been observed playing away from the home site

Seven month old orang-outangs (Keystone Press Agency)

without parental protection. Why should the young put themselves at risk? From the point of view of the social group they are the most easily replaced investment, in terms of food and experience, so it matters least that the *young* play. But what advantage does the society gain from the play of its young?

One suggestion is that play produces social cohesion at a time when the young are dependent upon the mother and must of necessity live together. However, play is not as prevalent in social groups of adult animals, where cohesion is also necessary, nor is it necessarily found in social groups of young animals; young mice and guinea pigs do not play, and rats and hamsters only begin to play at about the time of weaning when the absolute necessity of remaining as a social group has passed.

Another suggestion often made is that the young might, through play, introduce novel behaviour into the social group. If some of this behaviour is an advantage the group will gain; if unsuccessful, the individual and other young animals will probably be lost, but the investment loss for the society is small. There is some evidence that young primates introduce new behaviour into a social group. Instances of tool use, for example, have been traced to one inventive young individual, but there is a notable paucity of evidence to support this general contention.

Over the years there have been two recurring explanations of play. The first view, the 'excess energy' explanation, does not admit any functional significance for play. This theory is normally attributed to Herbert Spencer, but in a modified form, it has been put forward on a number of occasions. Basically, the idea as advanced by Spencer is as follows: higher animals 'having faculties more efficient and more numerous' find that 'time and strength are not wholly absorbed in providing for immediate needs. Better nutrition gained by superiority, occasionally yields a surplus vigour'. In addition we find in the more advanced animals 'many powers adjusted to many requirements [which] cannot all act at once . . . and some may remain unexercised for considerable periods.' Spencer suggests that when mental powers are not used they become 'unusually ready to act . . . it happens that a simulation of these activities is easily fallen into, when circumstances offer it in place of real activities. Hence play of all kinds.'

While we may dismiss the idea that higher species are necessarily better nourished, the idea that play is a bubbling over of
energy which activates under-used behaviour patterns is a
recurring theme in ethology. Although it is possible to initiate
some behaviour patterns which have not occurred for some
time in response to normally inadequate stimuli (which we can
interpret as a lowering of threshold) or even without any
stimuli (so-called vacuum activities) it is not clear that we can
place play in this category.

One of the most striking aspects of social play in animals is its
similarity across species. It involves wrestling, chasing, jump-
ing and leaping onto or at playmates and, in some species,
boxing with the forepaws. Why is it these *particular* activities
which are released by excess energy in so many species? One
might argue that fighting is inhibited in the young, hence the
outlet into play, but fighting is also inhibited in the stable social
group where it is replaced by posturing and signals between
more and less dominant individuals and between old and young.
The fighting pattern remains for the most part unexpressed,
yet it does not break out as play fighting. In the guinea pig
and mouse, aggression between adult individuals is common
(in my experience much more common than between rats) yet
play fighting is *not* observed in the young. Even when kept in the
safety and sterility of the laboratory cage with abundant food
and water the 'excess energy' of the well-nourished young
guinea pig does not result in play.

The excess energy view of play has a final problem, to explain
how play, with its obvious disadvantages to the animal, has
survived if there are no compensating advantages.

The other predominant view of play was put forward by Karl
Groos in 1898 and can be summarised in one word – practice.
To quote Groos: 'Animals cannot be said to play because they
are young and frolicsome, *but rather that they have a period of youth
in order to play*; for only by so doing can they supplement the
insufficient heredity endowment with individual experience'.
Thus one may view social play as a form of practice – a means
by which the organism 'tests' different behavioural patterns
and learns to integrate its behaviour with that of other members of its species. This view is particularly compelling when
one sees young animals in play making many of the responses

found in adult aggressive or sexual behaviour. Harry Harlow and his colleagues at Wisconsin have shown that monkeys isolated for the first year of life do not play, nor do they develop normal social and sexual relationships. Even monkeys raised with their mothers may show many of these abnormalities if they are not allowed to play with their peers. Isolation at later ages does not have these effects.

Although Harlow's work may seem forceful evidence for the practice function of play, closer examination makes the idea less tenable. The effects of isolation on aggression are most easily demonstrated in the mouse. Male mice kept in social isolation will, when placed together, fight, often to the death, while such behaviour is less readily observed in rats after isolation. Yet rats spend long periods engaged in play fighting and wrestling as juveniles, while mice do not play. Thus it is *the species which does not normally 'practise' fighting* which is most disturbed by juvenile isolation. Depriving the rat of these 'practice fights' does not appear to have any gross effects upon aggression, although there could be more subtle effects.

Aggressive play is in any case an unpromising context in which to learn or practise antagonistic signals. These signals are not observed in play, and those that do occur are restricted to play and are inappropriate to adult aggression. The appropriate response to a young monkey with a play face is to reply with a play face, to approach and to playfight. The appropriate response to an open mouth threat, a very similar expression seen more in adults, is to flee or to make a submissive gesture.

A similar case can be made for sexual behaviour. When watching young animals at play one is frequently aware of sexual elements to their play. At about thirty-five days the young rat will incorporate mounting, genital sniffing and lordosis (the receptive posture of the willing female) into bouts of chasing and wrestling. Deprivation of social contact in the juvenile male rat retards but does not normally prevent sexual behaviour; however, sexual behaviour is similarly affected by juvenile isolation in the guinea pig, a species in which social play is absent.

Robert Goy's observations of monkeys also suggest that although some aspect of early social contact is important for later sexual behaviour, social play is not a necessary component.

He found that isolated monkeys given half-hour social sessions with groups of young monkeys of similar age, showed many sexual deficiencies as adults in spite of intensive play during the social sessions, a finding we have recently replicated in the rat.

Perhaps the most striking evidence against the 'practice' function of play is provided by John and Janice Baldwin's study of a group of squirrel monkeys in Barqueta in south-west Panama. In 261 hours of observation of two small troops of monkeys not a single instance of play was recorded, yet the reproductive success rate was normal for the species. Aggressive interactions between individuals were lower than normal for the species, and fighting was never observed. The troop survived as a social group in spite of adverse conditions; food was scarce and ninety-five per cent of the animals' time was spent in food gathering.

When comparing the behaviour of adults at Barqueta to adults in other environments, the Baldwins suggest that the most outstanding difference is that social behaviours were very simple and infrequent in the Barqueta troops. However, a simple basic repertoire can be adequate for survival, at least in an environment which affords little free time.

Thus there is little evidence that play serves any direct practice role for later aggressive or sexual behaviour. Does it have any influence on adult learning? There are some indications that it may. Occasionally children raised in social isolation are discovered; so-called wild or feral children, and individuals raised in isolated rooms or cupboards. Like rats, dogs, cats, monkeys and chimpanzees, these isolated children are reported to be very excitable and to show stereotyped head and body movements. They are also classified as being severely subnormal. Although there appears to be nothing wrong with their sense organs, they do not respond to noxious or painful stimuli, turning to a ticking clock yet barely flinching at a gun fired a few feet from their head. Ronald Melzack has reported similar behaviour in isolated dogs. Although the behaviour of these children improves when they are returned to a normal social environment, with rare exceptions they remain severely impaired. It is these rare exceptions which are of particular interest. In all cases the children were under the age of seven when discovered, and had been removed to a normal social setting where they could interact with both children and adults.

'Alex' and 'Isabelle' were both discovered at about six years of age; Alex in England in the 1920s, Isabelle in Chicago in the 1940s. At this time they were reported to have poor coordination and to be incontinent, and were classified as severe mental defectives. Neither was able to speak, and Alex could not walk. Isabelle had been confined to a room with her deaf mute mother. Alex, who suffered from eczema, had been tied to a bed to stop him scratching. When discovered, both children were returned to normal social conditions and given additional attention and individual language tuition. For Isabelle this continued until she was able to attend school. By the age of fourteen she had reached grade six, and was considered by her teachers to be normal in every way. For Alex the tutoring lasted less than a year, nevertheless he showed considerable improvement, and the last reports, made at eight years of age, showed that he was mastering language and interacting with his environment. His teachers thought he was not mentally deficient.

Two recent cases have been reported by Koluchova in Czechoslovakia. The first concerns twin boys who lived for their first six years in a small unheated closet with intermittent periods in a cellar. When discovered at seven years of age they could barely walk and were thought to be seriously retarded. Their play was limited to simple manipulation of objects. A second case involved a girl with a similar history. All three children were placed with the same family. Seven years later the twin boys showed normal development and average intelligence, while the girl is able to attend a normal school. There is other evidence that children returned to normal social life may show considerable improvement, but no evidence that children of twelve or more ever become wholly normal. Although social play continues throughout man's life it is very much reduced after puberty. Thus it appears that recovery from early isolation may only occur if the child has a period of socialisation at a time when it would normally play. Of course children discovered at twelve years old or more will have been in isolation for very much longer, but this may not be a crucial variable; in a case known to the author a child was isolated from the age of about seven until late middle age, a period of over forty years, with no obvious intellectual impairment.

It would be foolish to maintain that these children became mentally defective solely because they had no chance to play. They were deprived of all social interaction – analogous to Harlow's socially deprived monkeys rather than the Barqueta monkeys observed by the Baldwins.

The point I wish to make is that early *social* deprivation can influence more than adult social behaviour; it can also have severe effects upon intellectual ability – or to turn the argument on its head: *early social interactions facilitate later learning.*

In the past few years we have been examining the effects of early social deprivation on the adult learning abilities of the rat. We have used tests that might be used by psychologists interested in animal learning abilities: tests of habituation, exploration, general activity, and memory. We have also attempted to assess the flexibility of the isolated rat by examining its ability to inhibit a previously learned response when reward is withheld, and the learning and reversal of a complex motor task. The rats had to remove a ball from a tube in order to enter a box which contained sugar. Initially the ball could be removed only by pulling it out of the tube. When this had been learned the pulling response was blocked and the rats now had to *push* it out. On all these tests we found that rats isolated for twenty days in their lives – between twenty-five and forty-five days of age – show large and permanent deficiences. Rats isolated for up to 150 days from fifty days of age have no difficulties with these tasks.

Isolated rats are very active, slow to habituate and have difficulties on some memory tasks. They are also very inflexible, taking much longer to stop or reverse a response than the normal rat. In the rat, social rough and tumble play commences at about seventeen days, increases over the next twenty days and then declines. By fifty days of age it has virtually ceased. The period during which isolation is effective in disrupting behaviour development coincides with the period during which the rat normally plays.

The involvement of play was further made clear to us in some very early experiments in which we attempted to delineate the sensitive period for the development of this behavioural inflexibility. We had isolated rats for a particular number of days, and after testing their behaviour, they were to be temporarily held in a large sawdust-filled gang cage in the corridor outside the testing room, before returning to the animal-keeping room in another part of the building. I tested two animals and placed them together in the gang cage, and was about to test the third when I noticed a great deal of shuffling and squeaking coming from the gang cage. On investigation I discovered that the air in the corridor was rapidly filling with sawdust. The two young rats I had placed together were racing about, rolling over one another, leaping, bouncing and generally engaging in rough and tumble play. The play continued without a break for almost an hour. When at a later stage in the experiment I regrouped the animals after forty-five days of age, they simply sniffed at each other, and there was no sign of play. In later formal testing we isolated rats for various periods between fifteen and forty-five days and then regrouped them. We were able to show that whenever regrouped rats played, the effects of earlier isolation disappeared, while if they did not play the effects of isolation were permanent.

Total isolation almost certainly does more than deprive the animal of play. Our next step therefore was to show that the learning difficulties experienced by our rats did not occur if the rats were allowed short periods of daily play. We raised three groups of rats: a socially-housed group, a group housed in isolation, and a group housed in isolation but allowed one hour of social play a day between twenty-five and forty-five days of age. We found that the rats allowed to play for one hour for twenty days behaved on our later tests very like socially reared rats, even though they lived in complete isolation from forty-five days of age.

During the hour of play the young rats also received exercise and bodily contact, and generally learned the smell and feel of another rat. All, or any one of these factors, could influence later behaviour. We have attempted to implicate the social nature of the play experience by manipulating its quality. With the help of Christopher Kibbler we raised three groups of rats as in the previous experiment, but we added two further control groups. These two groups were allowed one hour of daily social contact with 'stooge' rats that did not play. The stooge rats were other isolated rats who were drugged just before the playing session. One group received the depressant drug chlorpromazine, which made them drowsy, and they tended to sit in a corner, and could only occasionally be roused to play. A second group of stooge rats received d. amphetamine, a stimulant, which makes rats very active; it also induces stereotyped behaviour. In the rat this stereotype takes the form of repetitive sniffing and following. Thus the stooge rat followed the undrugged rat about the cage sniffing incessantly, but was very unresponsive to all the undrugged rats' play invitations. In both of the control groups and the group that played normally, the amount of time that the two rats spent in contact with each other was very similar. Nevertheless the one hour play sessions were of very little benefit to either of the control groups. When tested as adults, only the rats which had played with undrugged rats behaved like the socially-housed animals.

If the behavioural deficits, which occur when young rats and dogs are isolated, are due to play deprivation and not to other forms of social deprivation, then mice, and other animals which do not play, should not show these permanent abnormalities following early isolation.

We have recently completed a comparative study of the effects of isolation on mice, guinea pigs and rats. The preliminary work was done in Cambridge by two students, Sarah Field and Vivienne Naylor. They raised three groups of rats and mice: a social group, an isolated group, and a group which lived in isolation but was allowed one hour of play each day. The rats and mice were tested for activity and habituation, and underwent two timidity tests: eating a novel food, and emerging from a small enclosure into a novel environment. On the activity and the habituation tests the rats that had been allowed to play behaved like social rats. On the timidity tests they behaved more like isolated rats. On all tests the 'playing' mice behaved like isolated mice. The isolated mice were more timid and less active. After a short period of social housing the timidity differences disappeared in both rats and mice, but the activity and habituation differences remained in the rats. We have replicated these findings using guinea pigs, with similar results.

We started by asking what function play might serve. We believe play is not simply practice for later social interactions, but that it affects adult flexibility and the animals' ability to learn; that because it plays the young rat becomes a more intelligent adult. At present Anne Humphreys and I are looking at the play of young rats under a variety of conditions in an attempt to discover just which aspects of play are necessary for the normal development of the adult non-social behaviours. Our aim is to predict the quality of the play sessions which are necessary to protect the animals from the ill effects of social isolation. So far we have found two important factors: first we cannot exclude the importance of physical rough and tumble, and second a degree of reciprocity appears to be important. When a young rat initiates a response it is essential that on most occasions its partner makes some answering response.

The young of many, but not all, mammalian species engage in social play. Perhaps the answer to the question of why animals play can be found by answering another question – why do some animals play while others do not? If one wished to categorise the behavioural differences between socially-reared and isolated rats, one would be forced to use very general words and statements such as flexibility, plasticity and the degree of elaboration of their behavioural repertoire. These are also the kinds of words and statements which the Baldwins used to characterise the differences between the Barqueta monkeys and troops of squirrel monkeys living elsewhere. While these descriptions are admittedly vague they are also the sort of description one would use to characterise the difference between guinea pigs and rats. One explanation of why social play may induce behavioural flexibility may be that social play induces *social* flexibility, and that behavioural flexibility is secondary to this.

In short, animals play because they are young and frolicsome, but because they play the intense social interactions they experience may have benefits both to the individual by increasing its capacity to learn, and to the society by increasing the flexibility of the individual's interaction with its environment and with its social group. Let us conclude with a quotation from Konrad Lorenz:

The Raven can live just as well as a parasite of sea bird colonies in the north like a Skua, as a carrion-eater in the desert like a vulture, or as a hunter of small animals in Middle Europe. Into each habitat he fits as if he were specifically adapted for it while, in reality, the adaptation is only individually acquired. . . . Besides the Raven, the Norwegian Rat and Man are the most striking examples of this type.

One other characteristic shared by the Raven, the Norwegian Rat, and Man is their playfulness. The Raven plays more than other birds, the Norwegian Rat plays more than other rodents, and Man plays more than any other animal.

Infant Games
and the Creation of Culture

COLWYN TREVARTHEN and
FIONA GRANT

NEWBORN BABIES are completely innocent. They can have no
idea of the culture into which they are born, nor can they know
of the symbols adults use in society. In trying to understand this
early state, psychologists have often compared infants with
animals, driven by instinct. But animals are never able to share
conscious awareness with us by describing and explaining what
they are doing. In contrast, even very young children are able
to surprise adults with their reflective and perceptive comments about what is happening. Conscious awareness is shared
between human adults in societies throughout the world, and
everyone lives with a culture in which their understanding is
dominated by experience, skills and beliefs fashioned over
thousands of years. Is it not possible that human babies are
born with a predisposition for this particularly human way of
living?

Recent research with young infants leads to a completely
new view of the complexity of their minds, and most important,
a new interpretation of how understanding arises between
them and other people. First, babies act as if they have intentions. Secondly, they react differently to people and to inani-
mate things. They are passionately interested in people who
show them affection, and face-to-face reactions soon become
subtle and complex. Babies respond brightly to the friendly
attentions of any kind person they know well. Even a new-born
baby is beginning to develop a relationship with his mother,
soon recognising her as different from other people. As early as
two months after birth, the play between a mother and her
baby starts to show remarkable similarities to conversations

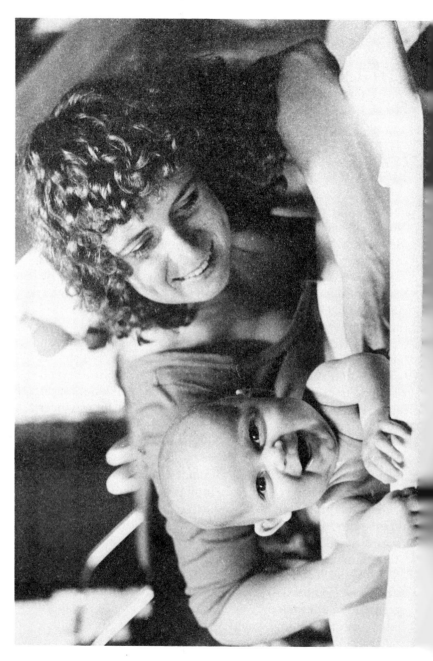

(Photo: Bob Bray)

between adults. Each takes turns in listening and gazing attentively at the lively gesturing and changing facial expressions of the other. Laughter, excitement and involvement are shared between the two, and each is sharply aware of times when the other's attention wanders. Then mutual interest is lost and an apparently bored or annoyed baby may become unresponsive, restless or irritable, frequently turning away from its mother. In such ways, babies are highly successful in influencing the feelings and reactions of other people, and they show strong preferences for people who are sensitive to this human kind of need.

We wonder how this precocious response to others may influence the development of more complete understanding of the world as the infant becomes a toddler, a user of language and master of many objects. We think that most theories on how children learn to be contributing members of their society underestimate the role of their spontaneous actions and feelings.

Despite the obvious role of the child itself, anthropologists interested in the origins of culture and cultural transmission, educational policy-makers, and sociologists, all find it convenient to play down the role of self-motivation in directing the development of infants and children. The unavoidable problem for all these theories would seem to be the lack of an adequate psychological description of how infants gain their understanding of other people's purposes, their culture and society.

Up to now studies in developmental child psychology have focused on the models that children of different ages construct of the world, and on the features of the environment or experience that influence the model. The studies tend to see the child's development as something to be measured, something that is added to the child by the outside environment. The investigators are assuming that knowledge is clearly separable from the way in which it is learned, and they see the world of nature and adults as the source of all knowledge. Even when admitting that the child can actively seek to know, they ignore its highly structured motivation to seek experience with others.

The typical experimental tests – asking the child whether a tall, narrow glass contains more water than a short, squat one, for example – simply tell us about how children 'work' towards the goal we impose. They tell us nothing about how children 'play' with, or joke about, the problems they themselves seek out. Because of this, conventional tests can tell us nothing about man's incomparable ability to create his own environment. What we need are careful observations of children going about their everyday activities, studies which would describe how the child's spontaneous behaviour fits the context in which it occurs. Different children may have a great variety of different strategies of behaviour, but a full and complete study of this kind should give us insight into the kinds of experience all children themselves seek.

The necessary activities of child care – eating, bathing, dressing or whatever – do not allow much scope for the baby's imagination, and so tell us little about how babies search for knowledge. On the other hand, playing with another person is an enjoyable activity for babies of all cultures; it always involves shared imagination, with little or no shape imposed on the action from outside. People who play make up the action. Even games with stated rules and objectives are played because players can freely choose which rule to use, and when to apply which strategy. The essence of the enjoyment lies in this freedom, and the thrill of playing a game with someone else is in trying to enter into the other player's imagination and guess what his intentions and strategies might be. Children, even babies, spend much time in apparently useless social play, but because of the attempt to see inside another's mind, play makes use of the most complex social abilities, and we think it entirely likely that the essential function of play in childhood is to practise these abilities.

Play is not vital for the biological survival of the body as are eating and sleeping, but it is vital for psychological survival in society. Society operates from a basis of negotiated rules and conventions that govern what people do. In social play, an opportunity is provided for children to practise and develop the elementary skills of negotiation implied in giving and taking food, a toy, or even a joke.

Karl Groos suggested that play had evolved to help to develop intellectual abilities and other skills needed in more serious activity, by allowing practice without risk of immediate, possibly harmful consequences (see Dorothy Einon's chapter).

The Swiss psychologist, Jean Piaget, went further, and added the idea that children play to discover the meaning of their own actions and then to incorporate these discoveries into their models of the world. Groos and Piaget, and their followers, emphasise individual learning and understanding, and as a result tend to evaluate the benefits of play by the study of children playing on their own.

In human society, learning how to cope with and eventually participate in the cultural roles of other people is important for a child if it is ever to take part in the immensely complicated cooperative enterprises that go to make up life in that society. If, instead of looking at the child playing alone, we concentrate on the child playing with other people, we can examine the benefits of play for cooperation. How does the child learn to work with others through play? As the Soviet psychologist Lev Vygotsky emphasised, 'what children can do with the assistance of others might be in some sense more indicative of their mental development than what they can do alone.'

Our own work is based on these ideas, but we do not look solely at the content or result of human learning. Rather, we focus on the motivational processes that are part of learning, that are especially important for the kinds of social learning that allow the child to find out about language and the conventions of its society. We are interested in what encourages children to communicate – how they share meaning with other people and how they express their intentions – and we find that playing with others is an ideal activity for our study. When playing, a child creates an imaginary situation where the activities and rules of play are much freer than when the child works towards a specified goal. The rules can be varied by one player and negotiated between the players, depending on what each wants to do in the game. The internal desires of each player shape the game, rather than external factors, and when a child plays with another person he is trying to find out as much as possible about what the other will do next.

As the child grows up, his understanding, both of himself and of the people and the society in which he lives, increases, and as it does, so the way he plays changes. Some of these changes in play appear to be related to age, which suggests that changes in the child's thoughts about the world may come by regulation

from within. One could almost say that any behaviour that a
society considers appropriate for a child of a given age must be
a reflection of the way in which a child normally develops at
that time. Central to this concept of the process is the notion
that, rather than being 'developed' by the society around them,
children 'develop' themselves as a result of changes in their own
motivation. As he grows older the child's interest in other
people changes in a characteristic way, and as this motivation
changes so too do the things that the child is ready to learn
about culture, convention and communication. All these
changes in turn affect the way that children play at different
ages.

Mothers interpret the lively responses of two-month-olds as
excitement and enjoyment, and as a request for more playful
teasing. Often a mother may use some aspect of her infant's
behaviour to develop the game; if her baby puts out its tongue,
she may switch from saying 'boo' to putting out her own
tongue, and so on. When a mother imitates her baby's actions
and joins in the fun of a game, she may be helping her baby to
recognise that another person can share his own feelings and
intentions.

As the baby grows older its responses to mother's play
become more comical and witty. At six months, happy babies
are exceedingly playful. The baby takes turns more often, and
begins to make a real contribution to the game. Jerome Bruner
and V. Sherwood, at Oxford, have studied the development of
'peek-a-boo' games in detail, and they point out that a mother
and her baby rapidly develop a set of signals that conventional-
ise the game for them, and that these signals can be built upon
to introduce new ways of hiding and new ways of revealing the
hidden. From seven to fifteen months, the child plays the
revealer more and more often, which indicates not only an
ability to change roles in the game but also a shift in the child's
interest. After nine months or so, a baby who is used to playing
games with his mother will, eagerly and often with great deter-
mination, join in a cooperative task, building up some effect or
structure by adjusting actions to complementary steps from the
partner. In Penny Hubley's study in Edinburgh, of babies
playing with their mothers, it is joint activity centred on toys
that provides the fun. A classic example is 'drop and pick up'.

The slyly grinning child lets his toy fall to the floor and his exasperated mother has to pick it up, again and again and again. In this game facial expressions – surprise, annoyance, refusal – are all involved in communication between mother and child, but so too are gestures like pointing, showing, giving and taking, that draw attention to things.

The one-year-old baby, then, may certainly understand and use a wide variety of emotional and referential gestures or expressions when he communicates and plays games with his mother. Many mothers and their babies have special signs or acts that form a sort of secret code, but in general we can see many similarities in the use of gestures and expressions by all mother–baby pairs. More than that, there is a clear resemblance between the way mothers and babies use gestures and expressions and the way we use them in everyday adult society. Between them, the mother and her baby seem to have re-created, expressed and shared the conventional meanings behind many facial expressions and referential gestures. In some mysterious way, the process of cultural transmission is well under way by the baby's first birthday.

During the second year of life another type of play emerges in subtle relation to the appearance of language. This play is variously termed 'symbolic', 'pretend', 'imaginative', 'socio-dramatic', 'make-believe' or 'fantasy' – it all depends on the investigator's theoretical bias. All these various names refer to children developing the ability to use their own actions to represent objects or experiences that are not actually present, often with the help of toys. In the play of thirteen-month-old children we can see the beginnings of an appreciation of the socio-cultural use of objects as well as the recognition of physical or functional similarities among objects. One-year-olds who cannot use words will, for example, pretend to feed toy animals and dolls, using spoon, cup and saucer, and so on in an appropriate manner. This transfer from real life to play is one of the first easily recognised indications that a child is ready to express some symbolic understanding of objects. Up to this point the child has been interested in investigating and experimenting with facial expressions and gestures, rather than the representational use of objects.

We think that pretence during solitary play should be regarded as a derivative of social play. Imagine a two-year-old putting her doll to bed in a shoe-box. When she plays on her own she is communicating with herself inside her own head; she animates the doll, imagining it has intentions and making it perform meaningful actions to fit in with her current train of thought. She is, in effect, trying out on herself her own ideas about how people behave to each other. To do this she must already know that ideas and intentions exist in other people which can be different from her own, otherwise she could not pretend that a bit of plastic or a corn cob, or whatever, was a person. Similarly, in using the shoe-box as a bed, she is recognising that objects can be used symbolically to represent a meaning which cannot be derived from the object's physical appearance only, but which arises as well from the conventional behaviour of people in her culture. In this sense social play is a necessary precursor of solitary fantasy play. More than this, we suggest that social play is the central activity that allows human imagination, self-consciousness and social awareness to develop and find its occasions for use.

One great paradox of the pretend play of children is that it consists of real action and physical movement, but simultaneously the actions are images of a reality which exists only inside the children's minds. Their actions represent events which happen in a fantasy, so that real circumstances and the use of objects are subjugated to the children's thoughts and intentions, and their creation. In 'real life' children may be doing things obediently to get certain results, without understanding the adult's view of what they do. In contrast, play shows up more clearly what is going on in a child's mind, a fact that play therapists use in an attempt to understand children who have difficulty relating to other people.

Just as younger children are interested in adults' faces, one-year-old children are extremely interested in adults' activities; they want to join in and do similar things themselves. The strength of their motivation to do tasks on their own is reflected in their frequent refusals of adult help even in cases where it is obvious to the adult that the child has no hope of attaining his goal without help. Children of about fifteen months old are notoriously uncooperative in psychological experiments: it has led several investigators to comment on the stubbornness and unwillingness to follow someone else's direct instructions. This is the time of Rene Spitz's famous 'No!', the characteristic response of a fifteen-month-old to almost any request to comply. At the same time, a child of this age typically enjoys playing with adults, but only if the adults follow the child's inclination rather than introducing their own ideas.

Once again, we feel that observation of children of this age at play, both on their own and with others they know well, would reveal more about their intellectual powers than experimental tasks that require the child to comply with the experimenter's wishes or to answer questions. Our belief is borne out by Marianne Lowe, who found that while one-year-olds tended to comb and feed themselves in play, at about twenty-one months they applied these activities to a doll. Lowe sees this as an indication of the child's increased ability to use an object to symbolise a person. Alternatively the child may simply be gaining confidence in applying its imagination to create a playmate. In either case, the increasing abilities of the child may lead to the resolution of the kind of tension expressed in Spitzian refusal to comply.

Observations like these suggest that the make-believe play so common in pre-school children may have its origins in much younger children. It does not seem necessary for the child to be able to verbalise its imaginative thoughts in order to play 'pretend' games. While speech is important to older children when they want to communicate the pretence to other players, one-year-old children manage very well without talking about the game. Nevertheless, the child may wish to refer to the toys in their 'pretend' identity and this might well encourage him to use words referring to such socially derived meanings. Play with others certainly encourages the use of speech, and may even be necessary for the proper development of language. Speaking while playing may help a child to realise that words are used not just to label and describe objects, but to communicate better to someone else the purposes behind actions.

The relationship between play and language is surely more than coincidence, since infant school teachers have noticed that some children who have difficulty in expressing themselves in speech become involved in only little pretend play. Similarly, autistic children, who shy away from contact with other people,

show no representational play; and children on compensatory
education programmes in the United States have been assessed
as lacking make-believe play.

Several studies show that adults have a strong influence on
the way children play. Sara Smilansky, who has found differences in both play and language development between
settled middle-class Israeli school children and underprivileged
immigrant children in Israel, groups these adult influences into
two categories. First, there are the effects relating to the general
emotional, social and intellectual development of the child, and
these have an indirect but important effect on play. Secondly,
parents directly shape the imagination of the child when they
encourage pretend or sociodramatic play. She further suggests
that the differences she found between the immigrant and
non-immigrant children are due largely to differences between
their parents, who tend to see the role of parents in the family
differently.

Until recently, the influence of adults on the development of
children's understanding of culture, at least outside formal
schooling, has been neglected in psychology. Indeed, even
theories that address themselves specifically to the origins of
pretend play fail to recognise that young children develop their
interests through the kind of contact they have with their
parents, and most studies deal with either solitary play, or play
between children of similar age. The Russian psychologists,
following Vygotsky perhaps, do admit the importance of
adults. Fradkina, for example, suggests that adult example is
almost always the spur to the child's substituting one object for
another, or naming objects in a pretend game. Certainly Scottish
children aged between twelve and twenty-four months, who
were observed in mother and toddler playgroups, seek out, and
profit from, their mothers' participation in play; when mother
joins in play the action is less repetitive than when the child
plays alone, and we often see a child with a toy actively seek his
mother's participation in the play.

The important question, we feel, is whether pretend play is
simply a reflection of a child's understanding of reality (the
understanding itself being gained elsewhere), or whether children actually *use* play to develop a greater understanding of
reality. Smilansky thinks that children use play as a tool,

because they often eagerly take up, as themes for play, events that they have been involved in and experienced, but cannot repeat for themselves in reality. Her conclusion is backed up by the difference we see between children in playgroups. First, a toddler displays greater understanding of the conventional symbolic meaning of objects when he plays with his mother, than when he plays alone or with children of the same age. Secondly, a twelve-month-old playing alone will handle and mouth and bang together toys which are miniatures of real things. Only later, by twenty-four months, does he progress to using them appropriately for what they represent. Finally, and perhaps most important, at a younger age we find more mature forms of toy play when a child plays with his mother.

Judy Dunn and Carol Wooding obtained similar results in their study of eighteen- to twenty-four-month-olds in Cambridge. Incidents of symbolic play and representation were closely bound up with the mother's behaviour, especially for the younger children. Of all the types of play, mothers initiated symbolic play most often, and it was in the context of joint symbolic play that mothers went in for the kind of implicit teaching described in other studies. The mother's methods were many and varied, and included extending the child's utterances and commenting on topics to hold or gratify the child's interest. These are the very types of behaviour that psycholinguists stress as being important for speech to develop properly.

Pretend play may be a crucial mode of cultural transmission at this age; the mother uses it to explain, acknowledge and extend the child's comments and actions. As she takes up this kind of play, she responds directly to her child's desires. The majority of such play sessions start with the child approaching the mother with an object or action he wants to show her, and Dunn and Wooding say that it is as if the child seeks confirmation of his play with the new world of symbols.

We expected psychological theories to have something to say about the development of a child's motivation which leads him actively to seek understanding of culture through symbolic play, but few theories actually deal with this aspect of acquiring culture. Learning theories present a child who imitates the activities of adults and develops understanding of his actions only through the success and approval that meet some of his imitative attempts. According to behaviourists, adults guide development, and they determine what the child should do and how he should do it. But behaviourist theories cannot account for the way that the kinds of things children like to imitate change with their age. Nor do they tell us anything about one of the most difficult problems of teaching – how to present children with knowledge in a way that takes advantage of their inclinations and interests. The pupils may be intellectually capable of dealing with the concepts involved in a lesson; they may be familiar with examples embodying these concepts; they may be linguistically capable of describing and discussing the chosen topic, but despite all this the teaching fails, and it fails because the children are uninspired. The children are uninspired because the teacher has failed to identify with the interests of the children. Awareness of this failure is behind attempts to foster 'discovery' learning and, more recently, 'participatory' learning, although, without an adequate psychological theory of the development of children's motives, it is unlikely that such attempts will succeed.

We have looked at the way fantasy play develops over the first couple of years of a child's life, and one conclusion is inescapable. Any theory of the way children learn about the culture they find themselves in must take into account the development of children's motives. It must be based on descriptions of the kinds of experience children are seeking at different ages and how their interests are expressed to other people. From our observations of how very young children share their interests with their mothers during play, it is clear that the elementary meanings of facial expression, gestures and the conventional use of objects are re-created by each child for himself in the seemingly trivial world of fantasy play.

It's Only a Game

JEREMY CHERFAS

OF ALL THE ELEMENTS that go to make up a society, the children are the ones who are most free to engage in inessential activities, for their livelihood is largely assured by their parents. Whereas adults may have much spare time, children seem to have nothing but spare time. And yet children are seldom idle. They engage in all manner of pastimes; they play alone and with each other, help adults and hinder adults, stay hidden and yet get in everybody's way. In much of the world they also go to school, but this they often see as an irrelevant break between play sessions. Surprisingly, anthropologists have not devoted a great deal of attention either to children or their games. There are, of course, notable exceptions, but by and large studies of 'primitive' people were more or less indifferent to the pastimes of those people, adult and child alike, and concerned themselves almost exclusively with the economic, political, and religious life of their subjects.

Fortunately, children's games have not been totally ignored, especially as far as the games of 'civilised' children are concerned. Antiquarians and folklorists were probably the first to take an interest in games, generally to preserve them. These scholars were concerned that the games, dependent as they were on oral tradition, were dying out, and collected them to save them from extinction. (Many of these collections also provide fanciful accounts of the origins of the games, but few reconcile their apparent antiquity and therefore their survival through oral transmission, with the impending extinction that was the impetus to collecting.) There are also passing references to childhood games in many memoirs, and allusions to games are common in literature. More recently, fresh interest in both the collection and scholarship of children's games

Detail from *Kinderspiele* by Pieter Breughel (Kunsthistorische Museum, Vienna)

has been created. Iona and Peter Opie surveyed a vast number of schools throughout Great Britain, collated reports from correspondents around the world, delved into the old works, and published two extensive collections – *The lore and the language of schoolchildren* and *Children's games in street and playground* – that remain the definitive works on childhood pastimes. There are also several good collections from other countries.

The Opies point out that previous writers often assumed that the games they had played as children, and were now remembering, were dying out, and that these authors wrote with an undisguised nostalgia. Nothing could be further from the truth, but it is easy to see how one could form the impression that games were dying out. The best games are those played away from grown-up supervision and interference, so that adults are not likely to be aware of games played by succeeding generations, and might assume that the games they played themselves are no longer current. As with many oral traditions, there is usually no formal transmission of the rules and regulations. Each child absorbs the knowledge for itself, and will in turn pass the information on, but each is unaware of its crucial role in the chain. Children often tell you that they invented a particular game, or that a friend invented it; later, as adults, they forget that they learned it from older children and passed it on to younger ones. If the process has not been interrupted, and there is little reason to think that it has, the children of tomorrow will play together in much the same way as the children of yesterday.

A perfect example of all this is provided by the game depicted by Pieter Breughel in the lower right-hand corner of his painting *Kinderspiele*, which hangs in the Kunsthistorische Museum in Vienna. A boy sits on a low table and acts as both a pillar and pillow, cradling a team-mate's head in his lap. Other members of the team are lined up behind, each bent over and clasping the one ahead, to form a long 'back'. The opposing team leap, one at a time, onto this 'back' and try to stay there despite the 'back's' vigorous attempts to dislodge them by writhing, twisting and tossing. If the leapers succeed they will leap again, but the team will change roles when the 'back' manages to dislodge even one leaper.

Those are the bare bones of the game. There are many

variations that I will discuss later, but they are embellishments rather than major alterations (with one exception), and even though my description fails totally to conjure up the action and excitement of the game I am confident that many readers will recognise it, and remember playing it. But what is it called?

It would give me great pleasure to be able to say that the game Breughel painted is called *Johnny on the Pony* – but I can't. That happens to be its name in most parts of the US, but it also answers to very many others. The Opies called it *Hi Jimmy Knacker*, but they also catalogue the multitude of other names it bears. In the north of England it is *Muntikitty*, a corruption of *Mount a Cuddy*. In Edinburgh, *Cuddy's Weight*, or *Cuddy gie Way* while in South Wales it is *Bumberino*. In Glamorgan they call it *Strong Horses, Weak Donkeys*. *Trust Weight*, or simply *Weights*, are the usual names in the Manchester area, and the Opies report that 'a boy in Liss swore the name was "Squashed Guts" '. Readers of *The Times* seem to favour *Hi Cockalorum*. The list goes on and on.

In some cases it is possible to follow the spread of a word or idea by the form it takes in various localities, but with *Hi Jimmy Knacker* this is almost impossible. For one thing, the game has been around for a very long time. For another, it is a great favourite with scoutmasters, who have probably disrupted any traditional regional differences in terminology with their enthusiasm for the game. That is not to say that there are no regional influences left. The 'trust' in *Trust Weight* refers to a measure of hay or straw used on the Lancashire–Cheshire border, though it may now also be a pun. And 'cuddy' is an old Scots word for donkey. But in East Anglia, where the words 'cuddy' and 'kitty', for a donkey, are unknown, they call the game *Muntikitty*, which is corrupted to *Mad a Giddy*, *Mud a Giddy*, and even *Mother Giddy*.

Different versions are as common as different names. For example, the leapers may not be allowed to creep forward on the backs, so that the first to go has to be a truly prodigious jumper, especially when the teams are large. Or the leapers may be prohibited from talking, laughing, or even opening their mouths. These variants seem to give the backs a better chance to be the leapers next time round. Dangerous play, such as landing on the backs with your knees, is often penalised and may result in the leapers forfeiting their turn. Most of these versions are minor variations, not major differences. There is, however, one fundamental difference, and that concerns the winning team. As I described it the leapers win if they stay on the back, and indeed that is how I myself played. The onus is on the backs to dislodge the leapers, who claim victory and leap again if they stay on. In the other version the leapers attempt to break the back – if they fail and the backs stay upright and connected then the backs claim that they are the 'strong horses', and they jump next time round.

The business of dislodging the leapers, or breaking the back, has to take place within a fixed period of time, usually measured by a ritual chant which again has several variants. About the only constant is that one or more players on one or the other of the teams has to complete the chant before the game is ended. In some places the whole back chants – in Stepney it is 'Hi Jimmy Knacker, one, two three', repeated three times, while in Enfield the chant is 'Onk onk horney, one, two, three'. The girls of Tunstall, who are notable enthusiasts, call the game *Cock Robin*, and they chant 'One, two, three, four, five, six, seven, eight, nine, ten – Cock Robin!' In New York only the pillow chants, three times, 'Johnny on the Pony, one, two, three'. The aim, in all these cases, is to set some time limit to decide the outcome after the last person has jumped. The way in which this is achieved, and the outcome itself, vary from place to place and time to time.

Another method is available for ending the game, and it stresses luck rather than strength. This variant gives a clue to the antiquity of the game. Older versions of *Hi Jimmy Knacker* are inextricably linked with another game known as *Buck Buck* (again there are many different names for what is essentially the same game).

Originally *Buck Buck* seems to have been a game for two, and it is still played this way sometimes. One player leaps upon another's back and, chanting the formula (something like 'Buck buck, how many fingers have I got up?') holds up a number of fingers. The encumbered player has to guess, and if correct the roles are reversed. (A variant is often played by mother and child: one places a hand flat on the other's back or

head and lifts a number of finger-tips. The other has to guess
how many fingers are raised.) *Buck buck* links to *Hi Jimmy Knacker* through the team version.
The two teams first play *Hi Jimmy Knacker* and then, if the
bottom team is still whole, one of the leapers goes through the
Buck Buck routine and the bottom team have to guess correctly if
they want to jump next. (Breughel's game may have just
reached this stage – or the boy with outstretched arm may be
simply losing his balance.) In truth, though, most games of *Hi
Jimmy Knacker* seldom attain this point in the procedure, for
either the back collapses or one of the riders commits a foul.
Nevertheless, many children insist that the trivial guessing
game at the end is the true point of the game. Others, equally
insistent, have never heard of this version. Parenthetically, it is
interesting that in South Africa, where *Hi Jimmy Knacker* is
practically a national sport among adults and children alike,
they actually call the game *Bok Bok*, though few today have the
slightest inkling why.

Immensely popular in eighteenth- and nineteenth-century
England, references to *Buck Buck* can be found scattered
throughout the literature of the time. Nor was it restricted to
England. It was also played throughout Europe, the Middle
East, Russia, India and Japan, and of course in the colonies of
the Empire. In itself this is perhaps not surprising, though the
two-man version sounds a little dull. What is a surprise is that
the sound 'Buck', or something like it, features in many other
languages besides English. Thus in German there is 'Bock
Bock, wieviel Hörner hab ich?' and in Sweden the formula
becomes 'Bulleri bulleri bock, Hur många horn står upp?' The
same sound recurs in many other versions, and crops up in the
earliest known written reference to the game. Petronius
Arbiter's *Satyricon*, written about AD 65, in the time of Nero,
describes an episode at a feast given by Trimalchio, involving
Trimalchio's favoured serving boy:

Trimalchio, not to seem moved by the loss, kissed the boy
and bade him get on his back. Without delay the boy climbed
on horseback on him, and slapped him on the shoulders with
his hand, laughing and calling out 'Bucca bucca, quot sunt
hic?'.

That the same sound should accompany the same game in first-century Rome and twentieth-century Sweden is astonishing testimony to the power of oral tradition. It does not tell us why this particular tradition survived, but the fact that it is bound up in a children's game has, I am sure, more than a little to do with it. *Hi Jimmy Knacker*, in all its many guises, exemplifies several aspects of children's games. It has regional variations that overlie a basic theme, associated rituals that are often incomprehensible but are preserved anyway, and it is old. It is also very, very popular.

Hi Jimmy Knacker is a team game, and the players must be assigned to teams before the game can begin. The same is true for many others games; either players have to be placed in teams or else one player must be singled out to be *it*. Sometimes *it* is a position of considerable power, as in *Mother May I*. Other times *it* is to be avoided at all costs, as in most games of *Tag*. Because of this there are many rituals associated with deciding who is to be *it*, and these are generally referred to as counting out. It seems obvious that counting out provides a fair means of choosing teams or selecting a particular child for a given role; the rhymes are inconsequential and the methods of choosing *it* so arbitrary that the outcome must be random.

It is not only adult collectors who believe that counting out is a fair and democratic process. In a survey, ninety per cent of children said that they used counting out because it gave everyone an equal chance; eighteen per cent said that it minimised friction within the group by preventing fights, and eight per cent said that it allowed for a supernatural decision, because 'God does the choosing'. (The percentages add up to more than a hundred because some children gave more than one answer.)

Kenneth Goldstein (in Avedon and Sutton-Smith 1971) went beyond the easy conclusion and actually looked at the way that counting out was used by groups of children in Philadelphia. He found, to his surprise, that, far from being an affair of chance, counting out is in fact an opportunity to use skill and strategy. The rhymes used, and the ways in which they are used, are manipulated by whoever does the counting to achieve certain goals. Furthermore, there were several ways of doing this. At first the sixty-seven children in Goldstein's study were

reluctant to admit that such was the case, but they finally
agreed with him that counting out was seldom a matter of luck.

One of the simplest techniques involves adding extensions to
the rhyme until the desired person is *it*. In one example a player
used the 'Eenie meenie' rhyme, and ended on player number
four. He wanted someone else to be *it*, so he extended the rhyme
to end on player five, and he could have extended it further to
end on any player of his choosing!

One	*Two*	*Three*	*Four*	*Five*	*Six*
Eenie	meenie	meinie	mo,	Catch	a feller
by the	toe;	If he	hollers	let him	go,
Eenie	meenie	meinie	mo – END 1	(My	mother
says	that	you	are	out) –END 2	(But
I	say	that	you	are	it) – END 3

Extending the rhyme is the most common method of controlling the counting out; Goldstein's study shows that over half the
children used this strategy regularly.

A more common strategy is used when the role of *it* is a good
one, and the counter wants to be *it*. The children all know
several rhymes, and will use a specific one, appropriate to the
number of players involved and ending at the counter. In one
case an eleven-year-old girl used four different rhymes to control
whether she definitely would, or would not, be *it*. Three children, all of them girls, used this strategy. Each had a different
repertoire, and each was fully aware that the other two were
playing the same game.

Yet another strategy for controlling the outcome is to skip
certain counts. The counter avoids becoming *it* by skipping
himself on the second and all successive rounds. The children
who use this strategy have no idea whether a particular rhyme
will in fact end on themselves; if they don't wish to be *it* they will
skip themselves with any and every rhyme. This method is the
second most popular, after extending the rhyme, and one-third
of the children had used it at one time or another. But whereas
other strategies were considered to be 'clever', skipping oneself
was thought of as 'dishonest' and 'against the rules'.

Another strategy, similar to the first, is for the counter to stop

either at the first player designated, or continue counting until
only one remains. Often used with the 'One potato, two potato'
rhyme, this was quite a common strategy, used by just under a
third of the children. It is not as controllable as some of the
other strategies, for the child does not usually know who will be
left; it simply shifts the chance element from first to last.
Goldstein observed that one nine-year-old boy had refined
this strategy considerably.

Samuel, who was considered something of a mathematical
genius at school, had worked out and memorised the 'first out'
position for up to ten players. He would use this information,
changing his own position between each count, if necessary
(which is within the rules), to select teams of any desired
composition and choose *it* completely at will. He had gone
further, and also memorised 'last out' for each group size, and
so could ring the changes in his strategy. Samuel's sophisticated method of manipulation was not undetected by the
group – they knew that something was going on, but they didn't
know what!

Goldstein's small field survey reveals two important things
about children's games. First, if counting out is not a game of
chance but one of skill, are we correct in assuming that our
classification of other games is correct? Second, and more
important, it shows that children – like adults – do not necessarily do and believe what they say they do and believe.

Definition is a notoriously difficult part of any discussion, the
more so when the subject we want to define is familiar to
everyone. It is almost impossible to give a definition of games that
will include everything I want to include but no more, so I will
not attempt it, steering the interested reader instead to the
'Introduction' to Avedon and Sutton-Smith's excellent book.

Games can be distinguished from more general play because
games have rules, while play is generally free-ranging and
unrestricted. Furthermore in every game there is some form of
contrast, either one team against another, one child against
another, or the child against its previous best performance. In
spite of this competitive element it is notable that when children play their own games, as opposed to those organised for
them by adults, they are surprisingly free and easy about the
competitive side of the game. There are rarely umpires or

referees; children are such traditionalists that they all know the rules, and those who do not abide by them are soon made aware of it. Disputes are swiftly settled, and seldom will a child actually keep track of the number of times it has won or lost in a particular session. Honour is of great importance, and cheating hardly considered. In a game of conkers a child may prize a good specimen, one that has conquered several others. He is unlikely to pit it against any challenger, but may risk it against another good conker, for the winner assumes all the previous victories of the loser. All is taken on faith, despite the lack of verification. If a boy claims that his conker is a 'twentyer', or whatever, one does not dispute it – one accepts his word, and perhaps also his challenge.

Many games have this element of trust in them. *Three Stoops* is a very popular chasing game, in which players can gain immunity if they simply stoop to the ground and utter a special word. Ordinarily this would be a very dull game, with the prey sitting out whenever approached by the predator, were it not for the fact that players are only allowed to stoop three times; after that, if you stoop, or are caught, you're *it*. It would be very easy, in the confusion of several players, for the chase to lose track of who has stooped and how many times, but part of the fun of the game for each participant is in saving at least some of his immunity until someone else has been tagged. Then, of course, you start again with a new catcher and three fresh stoops.

Street and playground, as the Opies acknowledge, are the places one is most likely to find children at play, but they are by no means the only places. Wherever children find themselves they will play, and the street is the obvious choice. It is close to home, within earshot, and most children feel it is more their own than the amenities provided by local authorities. It is also not partisan, as someone's garden might be. One of the problems of children living in blocks of flats is that there is sometimes no nearby street to play in, and although large estates often provide playgrounds, those playgrounds are made unattractive by a ban on ball-games and other noisy activities. Large patches of inviting grass are often fenced off and put out of bounds. Who can blame these children for chasing up and

down stairwells and corridors, generally getting in the way?
The street seems to be the natural place for children's games,
even if it is a little dangerous.

The strange thing is that playing in the streets is no new
phenomenon. It seems that children have been in trouble about
where they play for almost as long as they have played. We
should not be surprised that there were complaints about children's games in the nineteenth century because the industrial
revolution had brought many families into the cities, and there
was nowhere for the children to play except on the streets. But
even long before that children were underfoot. In the seventeenth century, according to Richard Steele, the environs of the
Royal Exchange were cluttered with 'uninvited sportsmen', to
the extent that a beadle was employed to whip away the
'unlucky Boys with Toys and Balls'. Further back, in the
Middle Ages, when all houses were close to some open space,
the young still managed to find their diversions at quite
unsuitable places. In 1332, Parliament was so disturbed that it
passed a law that prohibited the playing of games in the pre-
cincts of the Palace of Westminster when Parliament was in
session. Later, in 1385, the Bishop of London spoke out against
the ball-playing that went on near St Paul's. Nor was the
problem restricted to London; the Bishop of Exeter came down
heavily on young people in 1447, complaining that they dirtied
the walls and broke the windows in the cloisters with their
games, with which they persisted even during divine service.

Getting in the way, then, is an honourable tradition, but does
it reveal anything about the world of the child? Most children
love to be away from all adult supervision, hiding out in over-
grown places, empty lots, and the like. But they also, undeniably, like to attract attention and get in the way. Favourite
games in the days before slum clearance involved variations on
the theme of knocking at the door and running away. One gem
from the Opies' collection of door pranks is to select houses on
opposite sides of the street and tie their front-door handles
together with a stout rope.

The art of tying doors together appears to lie in being able to
judge just how much slack rope should be left between the
houses so that if both bells are rung at the same time, and if

both householders come to their doors together, each is able to open his door enough to feel that somebody is trying to prevent him from opening it, but not enough to let him see that nobody is there.

This, and several other pranks and games, are calculated to annoy adults, and more often than not they succeed admirably. The Opies tell of one group of children who knew twenty different games which involved running across the road, and this prompts them to ask whether the children are perhaps trying to make some kind of statement by their behaviour. They suggest that these annoying and dangerous games, like *Last Across* and *Chicken*, are a manifestation of 'protest in the tribe', but it is hard to see exactly what it is that the children are protesting about. Were it not for the motor cars that invade their street they would lack the means to express their protest, but on the other hand there would be no need to protest in the first place. It is true that there have been accidents, even fatal ones, as a result of the admixture of children's games and motor cars, and in some cases these accidents may have been instrumental in getting new playgrounds opened, or routes changed. The problem remains that many children would rather play in the streets than in a playground, even if it does increase the likelihood of a serious accident. I believe that on many occasions children are not fully aware of the possible consequences of their behaviour, so that they simply do not appreciate the danger of what they do. Why else would they play on railway lines? The foolishness, while it is a source of concern to adults, is almost a necessary part of children's play. Children have to dare, for if they do not dare they will never know what they can and cannot accomplish.

Playgrounds also have a mysterious ability to change drastically the quality of the games being played in them. The places that adults decide are good for games are almost never the places children themselves prefer. Adults like open spaces where they can keep an eye on the children. Children prefer to be out of sight. Adults want older children not to interfere with younger children, and girls to be separated from boys. Children often play in groups of widely differing ages, indeed that is often how young children learn the games of a locality, and boys will play quite amicably with girls. Adults provide equipment for play, and then impose strict rules governing its use. Children need little equipment for their games, but are often forbidden to chalk on walls and floors, and prevented from playing ball games. The conflict between adults' ideas of what children's games should be and what the children themselves prefer are many, and it is no surprise that playground behaviour often seems bizarre.

In playgrounds there are more fights, more bullying, more teasing and disrupting other children. 'Tom Brown's Schooldays' may now be behind us, but the cruelty inflicted on younger children by older ones is still appalling, and the system perpetuates itself as each slave climbs the ladder to become a tyrant. Small wonder that, in an off moment, a teacher will describe his charges as animals, and this provides a clue to understanding.playground behaviour.

The notion of a dominance hierarchy, or pecking order, is one that passed rapidly from the science of ethology to the general consciousness. It is a very appealing notion; animals quickly learn who is stronger and who weaker, and one can observe a chain reaction with each animal redirecting received aggression to the next weakest right down to the unfortunate at the lower end of the hierarchy. Ethology, however, has moved on, and it now accepts that some of the earlier manifestations of dominance hierarchies were aberrant artifacts of captivity. Free-ranging animals may have just as firmly entrenched a hierarchy, but are much less likely than caged animals actually to fight in a dispute. The same is very probably true of children. In the school playground they are in captivity. They play the violent games, they go about in gangs, they make a thorough nuisance of themselves. In the street, or park, they play very differently. The aim is the same – to have fun – but the way it is achieved is totally different in the two cases. When they are in a playground, half the fun seems to derive from behaviour that is calculated to challenge the authority responsible for their being there. In a sense the children play *against* the adults. In the street, where the children play *with* one another, such behaviour would never be tolerated, and those who want to play properly soon enforce their will on those who do not. In playgrounds children have no privacy or mastery, and they respond by abusing each other. In the street they are masters of their own fate, at least for the duration of the game, and they respond with understanding and dignity.

I wrote earlier that many adults imagined that the games they had played as children had died out, and I argued that in reality this is seldom the case. But in one respect the games are dying out – children abandon their own traditional games for adults' games earlier and earlier these days. No child's games-playing is static. As it grows up the games a child plays change, as do its attitudes towards those games, and eventually the child either stops playing games entirely or switches over to adult sports exclusively. Preferences change markedly during childhood, and if there is a pattern to be discerned from these changes it is that the youngest children play mostly fanciful games of a loose kind while as they grow older they become first more ritualistic and then more romantic, finally becoming intensely competitive.

Thus five-year-olds play chasing games, but they explain them as pretend games and have not yet formulated them into the classic games of *Tag*. They may clutch at the railings round the playground for safety, but they don't yet know why they are doing so, and unlike the older children do not know that they are playing *Touch Iron*. Slightly older children are increasingly rule-bound, and it is among this group that the whole business of choosing teams and counting-out becomes a game in itself. At about nine years old preferences shift to the more romantic games like *Hide and Seek* and *Cowboys and Indians*. Finally, with the older children who have developed the necessary skills, we see an increasing preference for the very competitive games, like *Ball He*, and other strenuous games.

Nowadays children become self-conscious about playing kids' games at ever earlier ages, aided and abetted by their parents' (and big business's) increasing stress on organised sport, as opposed to games. In the late eighteenth and early nineteenth centuries the favoured games of boys in secondary schools were marbles, tops, leapfrog, hoops, hopscotch and skipping. No boy of eleven would play those games today, and the experts are more likely to be aged eight or nine. Girls, who are probably even greater traditionalists than boys in the matter of games, are not immune to this downward shift in players' ages. The Opies quote two girls describing the same game: One, a ten-year-old, says, 'it is a lovely game ... very enjoyable'. The other, a worldly fourteen-year-old, describes the game as 'very silly and babyish', and goes on to add, 'today I would never dream of standing out in the street chanting "Queenie, ball ball ball" but then I simply wallowed in such fun as I called it.' Two children's perceptions of the same game may differ more than a child's and an adult's.

As they enter their teens children are often overcome with amnesia for the games that used to be their very life a few months before, and usually make very poor informants about games. In fact, nostalgia for the good old games of childhood may start in the teens, and one can hear adolescents bemoaning lost games in much the same way as their elders. This may have something to do with changing schools. At primary school a ten-year-old is near the top, and is simply playing the games learned half a lifetime before, setting an example for all the younger children. In secondary school the eleven-year-old is back at the bottom of the heap, only now the older children no longer play traditional games, they play real games, like soccer and netball. The pastimes of childhood are dropped with frightening rapidity, and a sure way to rile a young adolescent is to suggest that the games he plays are kids' games. The abandonment of the traditional games of childhood has probably been hastened by adults' emphasis on scaled-down versions of sports. This is particularly true of North America, where children of eight or nine play little league baseball or peewee ice hockey before they have ever experienced the thrill of self-organised games that earlier children played. Perhaps this increase in organised sport is just a changing fashion, but there is a real danger that because organised games are formally codified and remembered, and because children are surrounded by them, they will be the only ones left in the end.

Organised sports present another grave problem in that they stress very different aspects of life from the more traditional games, and it may well be that the traditional games have lasted so long because they fulfil some need or needs central to the child's growing up. The sanctimonious mouthings of their proponents notwithstanding, it is abundantly clear that in team games individual performances are what really count.

Woe betide the player who lets the side down. Those who give
the strongest support to organised sports are either those who
excel at them, or adults, whose life is made a lot easier if
children are playing sports rather than their own unfathomable
games. And the traditional benefits of team games – altruism,
cooperation, compassion, character-building and so on – are
probably far better served by a good game of *Relievo* than a bad
game of softball or Rugby.

It would be a great shame were the games of childhood to be
replaced by the children's versions of adult games, for the
former have an earlier place in history than the latter. Admittedly there are reports of games akin to soccer and golf in early
records, but there is far better evidence for the antiquity of
children's games, some of which have hardly changed in
several hundreds of years. I have already shown how aspects of
Hi Jimmy Knacker go back to the first century AD, but this is not
an isolated example. Several other games go equally far back,
and some go further.

Boys in ancient Greece played Epostrakismos (*Ducks and
Drakes*), Schoenophilinda (*Whackem*, a form of tag in which *it* is
slapped on the back to signal the start of the chase), Apodidras-
kinda (*Running-home Hide and Seek*), Ostrakinda (similar to
Crusts and Crumbs, in which two teams do not know who will
chase and who will be chased until the call of crusts or crumbs),
and Chytrinda (*Frog in the Middle*, a catching game where the
catcher is incredibly handicapped by having to stay in a squat-
ting position). They also played at *Blind Man's Buff* and *Tug o'
War*, and used spinning tops; and versions of other popular
games are also known.

Minor variation is as old as the games themselves. Plato
thought about this problem, and urged that boys be forbidden
to make alterations to their games, for if they did so they would
surely have no respect for the laws of the state in later life. He
need not have worried, because tradition-bound children have
seen to it that the games they play have survived more or less
unchanged. That 'more or less' is important, because it is
evidence that children's games are living things, changing
occasionally but staying recognisable through the generations.
The games adapt to the children's needs, and to changes in
circumstances. At one time English schoolboys played several

games that required the use of a cap; few school uniforms now include caps, so these games are dying out. Substitutes take over and may become more successful. Prior to the introduction of the Horse Chestnut into England, boys played with a cobnuts, and held contests to find the strongest nut. Now they play with conkers, and though the materials and conduct have changed somewhat the game is still essentially the same. These kinds of changes have already been discussed for *Hi Jimmy Knacker*, but there is another kind of change that may be all but invisible to even the most diligent investigator. It concerns the games that are actually played.

Games wax and wane in popularity, and as they do so they change in character, but with the exception of fads the changes may be very hard to detect in a single survey. Nevertheless, the character changes can give some idea of the dynamic status of a game. Games that are reaching a peak are easy to recognise, and within their popularity they carry the germ of their own decay. A popular game attracts embellishments, extra rules and formalities, and becomes more and more elaborate. As it does so it requires more finesse, and more time, to finish. Often the very name of the game grows and becomes unwieldy: *Stoop* became *Three Stoops, Three Pokers and Run for your Life* on its way to immense popularity.

Eventually the formalities become too cumbersome and the game goes into a decline. Games on the way down go through the reverse process of games on the way up. They are stripped of inessentials, and the players seem to disdain the trimmings and take an interest only in the actual contest. Sometimes the poetic formulations and rituals of a game that is declining in popularity are saved because they are transferred to another that is in the ascendancy. *Hickety Bickety* is a racing game, in which the different players race over different courses, assigned to them at random. One player has his face to a wall while the others chant:

> North, South, East, West.
> The wind blows the robin's nest.
> Where shall this one go?

Each player is then sent to a different place and when all are in position there is a race to get back to the starter. The game is no longer very popular, but the introductory doggerel has been absorbed into *I Draw a Snake upon your Back*, an ingenious new form of *Hide and Seek*.

There seems to be no clear rhyme or reason to the changing fortunes of particular games. The Opies think that they have spotted a trend, and claim that there has been a decrease in the popularity of games in which one player is repeatedly buffeted by the rest, and an increase, perhaps a corresponding increase, in games in which all the children tackle each other on roughly equal terms. It is hard to be certain whether this is so, for there have been very few studies specifically directed to long-term trends in games.

Granted that games are old, survive, and continue to be enjoyed, can we go beyond joyful participation to discover some sort of relevance to the child who plays them? It seems almost sacrilegious, an invasion of privacy, to attach vast import to a mere child's game, but if we do not at least try to penetrate the strange lure of games we do no more than catalogue.

Collectors and theorists, often anthropologist or psychologists, have come up with several different ideas about the meaning of games. Some take the view that 'ontogeny re-capitulates phylogeny', and propose that in their games children perform activities essential to man's ancestors but not relevant in modern times. Others see games as vital for the physical development of limbs and organs, and to the refining of movement and coordination – the child learns what its body is capable of through games. Alternatively games are a sort of apprenticeship in which the child is acquainted with the duties and responsibilities of adult life. Some see games as a cathartic safety-valve that allows the child to work off surplus energy and work out surplus emotions. Elements of each of these ideas have their place in understanding children and their games, but when carried to their limits such interpretations often go too far to be taken seriously.

From the point of view of the child what matters is not what he makes of the game but what the game makes of him. The child, however, does not enter the game an empty vessel; he brings to the games certain preformed ideas and tendencies which may or may not have some bearing on how he reacts to a given game. For example, some children are cursed with a suspicious, one might almost say paranoid, outlook on life. If, even after all the rituals have been adhered to, they still find themselves being chosen for the unpopular roles their paranoia will hardly be diminished. This does not mean that a game itself is paranoid, any more than a new scientific discovery is irresponsible. It means that a particular child responds badly to a particular game. Other children will suffer the indignities occasionally without feeling that they are being picked upon, and can take comfort in the knowledge that the convoluted choosing rigmaroles ensure that they are not being singled out. Of course the suspicious child may well be correct in his fears, for children are not insensitive to others' weaknesses and are fully capable of engineering things so that the unfortunate is indeed picked upon (see above).

Similar considerations apply to games consisting of tests of strength. For the well-adjusted child they will be no more than that, but for the bully they may provide an additional outlet. Some psychologists have argued that such games set the scene for the later appearance of full-blown sado-masochistic behaviour, and while this is not impossible I confess that I find it a little far-fetched.

One list of the psychological functions of games divides games into initiation rites, competitions, cooperative ventures, and emotional controls. A given game may, of course, fit into more than one category, and in this analysis games are seen primarily as honing the social skills. Initiation rites are vital before the new child can be accepted into the local group, and they often include specific, irksome tasks in addition to simply picking up the rules of the games as they are played in the new neighbourhood. They often seem like thinly disguised bullying, but if he is successful the new kid will soon become used to the games, and will be able to continue his psychological development with a new set of colleagues. If the psychologists are correct he will then be free to compete, and in so doing will develop speed, strength, skill, coordination, daring, courage, and cunning, and will perhaps even sublimate aggressive and murderous feelings. Other games are exercises in getting along with others, learning to give and take orders and to put others before self. Finally, some games help the child to build its tolerance to frustration. And despite the apparent weightiness of these processes, the child can have fun at the same time.

Another analysis of the function of games splits them into the competitive, the aggressive, and the acquisitional. From this sociological perspective games are seen as providing practice for the feelings and values that will be experienced in adult life. The adult society taken as the goal is that of the USA, and as such this view stresses the importance of being the winner, being the tops. Winners gain power and prestige, and are expected to be happy and proud at their achievement. They are also expected to play down the victory and be magnanimous to their opponents. Losers are expected to feel the opposite; they are sad and perhaps ashamed, and provide self-serving excuses for their poor performance. Losers are also allowed, and expected, to display barely concealed anger at the winners. These role expectations apply equally well to the world of the adult and that of the child, and it is held that the child learns through the medium of games not only what is expected but also how to fulfil those expectations.

There are, naturally enough, different types of game within the general class of competitive games. There may be one winner and several losers, as in *King of the Castle* (supposedly Napoleon's favourite game). There may be many winners and one loser, as in *Blind Man's Buff* and several types of *Tag*. Finally, one whole team might win and the other lose, as in *Hi Jimmy Knacker*.

Where there is only one winner the losers seem to have some advantage psychologically. There are many of them and it hurts less to lose simply because one is not alone. There may also be gradations in the loser roles, so that the player who didn't give up can feel superior to the player who did. But even the best loser has in fact lost – nothing can change that – and will feel that in the future it would be more pleasant to win.

This feeling, that winning is better than losing, is magnified several times in games like *Blind Man's Buff*, where the winners gain even more by being in a group while the loser is utterly alone. To be lumbered with the loser of losers role is horrible indeed, which is why the children are so vociferous in their insistence that counting-out rituals ensure a fair selection. Experienced players will do almost anything to avoid being the object of derision, and this can lead to strategies of enlightened self interest. One of the many winners may allow the lone loser to catch him, thereby taking on the burden and hoping that the favour will eventually be repaid. Such games, even more than those with a group of losers, engender an intense dislike of the loser role and increase the participants' striving for success.

Team games would seem to offer the best solution, for both winners and losers gain the psychological and social benefits of being members of a group. But as I have already pointed out, the player who does not make enough of a contribution will have a truly miserable time after the game. This is especially true for the sports games, but it also applies to more traditional games. In many team games there is also an element of specialisation and it is claimed that in playing these games the child comes to terms with the fact of specialisation in life and may learn something about his own unique abilities.

If to win is so wonderful, and to lose so awful, it is equally true that winners win because they are aggressive. The problem here is that although mental and physical aggression are accepted as means to dominate and reach the top they are also frowned upon, at least if expressed too openly. This is reflected in games as in life; there are very few overtly aggressive games. Most aggressive games take the form of a duel between two players, and the central idea is that each has the opportunity to hurt the other, without fear of unexpected retaliation, until one gives up completely. Into this category fall games like *Knuckles* and *Slappies*, where within the rules each tries to hurt the other as much as possible. It is hard to see any real function for this ritual exchange of inflicted and endured pain in our cossetted society. Admittedly each player experiences the dominant and submissive roles in turn, so that each both gives and receives aggression, but why should this be a good thing? One of the players will be the stronger or more aggressive, causing the other more pain and eliciting eventual submission. Perhaps the lure of such games for the losers lies in the possibility of a surprise win, not to mention the threat of less ritualised aggression. In other cultures, and at other times, proving the strength of your friends might reassure you that you could rely on them when it was life, rather than a game, inflicting the pain. But today these hurtful games seem out of place.

Covert aggression is much more common, and may become a feature of almost all games, especially team games. The aggression is covert only in that it is hidden not in that its existence is denied, for all players know that there is a chance of excessive violence and that the skill lies in using the right degree of force and camouflaging it well. In maturing the child has to translate the physical aggression of its games into more acceptable mental aggression, but the games themselves provide all the necessary models; what sort of aggression is possible, who can be aggressive to whom, how to hide the aggression effectively, and, most important, the different feelings associated with aggressor and victim. Sadly, adult sports are increasingly violence-infested, so that children, in their imitations of organised sport, also imitate organised violence and never learn to transmute the physical violence into mental violence.

Being a winner, and using aggression to become a winner, are two of the things for which games prepare children. A few specific games also provide material gains and these are the acquisitional games. Marbles, flipping coins and tossing cards (more prevalent in the US where sports cards are given away with bubble-gum) are examples of this type of game. Again, one can see such games as a rehearsal for later life. In a society that prizes possessions the child quickly learns the joy of gaining, and the distress of losing its possessions, and takes these values with it as it grows. Further, the child may be barred from the fun if it lacks the necessary coins, cards or marbles, and this too is a preparation for later life.

The apprenticeship view of games seems to sit particularly well on the shoulders of games in the US, but is not restricted to that society. It has also been used to explain the organisation of games in more exotic cultures. In many of these, for example among the Tanga, among the tribes of the Liberian hinterland, and in New Guinea, a favourite game is to ape the solemn rituals of the adults, and the form of the children's versions of the rituals has provided valuable insights into the early beginnings of the rituals, for the conservative children change their games much more slowly than the adults change their rituals.

Perhaps it is no surprise that adult interpretations of the

function of children's games are so dull; those doing the interpreting have not been caught up in the thrill of a game for many years and have forgotten that they did not play *Hide and Seek* or any other game to develop skill, strength, or social sense. While the sociological and psychological outcomes provided by games may be important in an overall context they do not provide an immediate reason for children to play games. Children's games, almost without exception, contain an element of danger, and it is this *frisson* of excitement that keeps the children at play. The danger may be real, but it is much more likely to be completely imaginary, part of the mental trimmings that every game has. Will I be caught this time? Will we be discovered? Can I get back to 'home' before I'm spotted? These uncertainties provide the driving force that motivates children to play their games.

Games are not haphazard inventions. They illuminate the preoccupations and problems of growing up, and ease the long journey from infancy to adulthood. They teach the child things it may not think it has to learn and has no recollection of ever learning, and provide it with a diversity of experiences that would be hard to get in any other way. If that sounds like a lot for games to do, it is as well to recall that only adults bother to put this interpretation on games. And grown-ups, being notorious spoilsports, often do something that the children themselves seldom do – they lose sight of the real point of the games of childhood. Above all else, games are fun.

ADULT PLAY

Play and games are not restricted to the
young. Adults too enjoy themselves in pastimes that are limited by rules and rooted in
tradition. Each chapter in this section uses
an activity to hold up a lens to society and
culture. Organised sport and organised
gambling differ – for one the avowed aim is
solely to win, while for the other it is to win
the stake. But both can tell us about the
culture at play. Aggression and violence, an
integral part of many games, are often
channelled and ritualised into less harmful
forms. These also mirror society. Dress is
not normally thought of as a pastime, but
many people spend more time on it than
they strictly need to. Again, mode of dress
reflects mode of social organisation.

Playing with Aggression

WILLIAM ARENS

THERE WAS A TIME when it was possible to pronounce with an understandably grandiose air that the sun never set on the British Empire. Those days may have come to an end, but it still may be said, more modestly, that the sun never sets on a British game. For a people who take such great pride in the notion of fair play, this particular export was inevitable. On the debit side, this sense of achievement in the civilising mission must be tempered by the realisation that the British are often beaten at their own games by a host of outlanders ranging from New Zealand to Jamaica. There is something more to this than a fortuitous correspondence between profound and trivial historical events, since world powers tend to make their presence felt equally in both the diplomatic and athletic arenas.

Americans, on the other hand, have had a different imperial experience. In addition to eschewing the creation of a formal political empire, they have also been less willing or successful at exporting their athletic pastimes. Although cultural innovations such as baseball and basket-ball have filtered through to other parts of the world, they by no means have a universal appeal. More important, American football, which followers like to refer to as 'The Game' – played by professional gladiators during and after their university careers – is a cultural exclusive. The sun rises on the first contest on the east coast at noon on Saturday as hundreds of collegiate clubs take the field before crowds ranging up to a hundred thousand, and eventually sets in the west on the final of fourteen 'pro' games in the Los Angeles Coliseum, with a similar gathering early Sunday evening. Recently, in the attempt to sate this appetite and alleviate withdrawal symptoms, another match has been scheduled for a national television audience on Monday

(Sporting Pictures [UK] Ltd)

evening. Thus, within a two and a half day period, the typical American male, which in this instance includes everyone from the President of the United States to the local postman and errant social anthropologist, spends anywhere from three to fifteen hours in front of the television, entranced by a peculiarly American spectacle.

This drawn-out process, in a season extending from July to January, culminates in a grand finale officially entitled, 'The Super Bowl', which is designated each year by an appropriate Roman numeral. The event also has been aptly characterised as 'the most lucrative annual spectacle in American mass culture' (Real 1975). The subjective experience of these events for the native defies adequate communication to an alien. As with cattle among Sudanese Nilotes, or pigs among New Guinea Highlanders, the game has become a dominant value and cultural idiom. Politicians must have proved themselves on the playing field during their youth and must be able to communicate their visions for the country in football terminology. Thus, national policy becomes a 'game plan'.

A further illustration was provided by the case of a mathematics professor at a major university who refused to leave the jogging track when ordered to do so by the football coach who wanted his team on the infield to prepare for a game in total secrecy. University security personnel were called, but the professor claimed that, as a faculty member, he had the right to exercise on university property. The coach claimed the authority to close the grounds to all personnel in order to prevent spies from the rival institution from observing his team's preparations. Within minutes the professor was led away from the confrontation to be charged with resisting, delaying and obstructing arrest. Then there is the instance of the officials of a small town who, realising that both Hallowe'en (All-Hallows Eve) and a secondary-school football match were to fall on the same day, resolved the dilemma by moving the holiday!

The objective significance of the spectacle is less difficult to appreciate. Consider the following figures for 'Super Bowl VIII' in 1974, staged in Houston, Texas, in the completely-enclosed, air-conditioned, artificially surfaced Astrodome. Attendance was the expected capacity of close to 72,000 fans from all over the country, since the contest is held at a neutral

site for the sake of ideal playing conditions, which in this
instance means 72° F exactly. The television audience for this
Sunday afternoon in mid-January was estimated at somewhere
between seventy and ninety-five million, which at the maximum
meant that forty-five per cent of the entire population of the
United States were involved as electronic spectators. In an-
ticipation of such a response, a commercial television network
paid the National Football League $2,750,000 for exclusive
broadcasting rights, and in turn charged their preferred adver-
tising clients somewhere between $200,000 and $240,000 for the
privilege of presenting a one-minute commercial message,
which was often especially produced to make its debut on this
grand occasion. Not unexpectedly, the network made a hand-
some profit for the afternoon's work, which was reported at
around $4,000,000. (Real 1975).

   In the light of both the economic and the emotional investment Americans were willing to devote to this pastime, it
seemed worthy of some scrutiny from an anthropological perspective. Consequently, a few years ago I set out to provide a
typical anthropological analysis of this cultural phenomenon.
The library research was itself instructive by highlighting
academic orientations towards the study of sport, games, and
other seemingly insignificant pursuits. Sociologists, of course,
by the nature of their subject, had been long interested in these
less profound corners of western industrial societies. Possibly in
the attempt to avoid being stigmatised as trivial themselves,
those interested in such matters often tended to deaden the
material with what they understood to be the heavy hand of
scholarship. Thus it is possible to read in the premier journal of
American sociology a précis of an article which states: 'A model
of failure in sport is considered, with specific references to
failure by those who may fail and their others' (Bell 1976).
There was no correction or apology contained in the subsequent issue, so we can safely assume that, however inelegantly
put, this was exactly what the author meant to say. In a similar
vein, in their commentary on sport and games in other lands,
social anthropologists typically feel the need to rationalise their
interest by suggesting that a cockfight in Bali or a wrestling
match in the Southern Sudan is a key strand in the struggle to
unravel an exotic cultural system. As usual, the sociologists

were taking themselves too seriously, while the anthropologists were doing the same for 'their' people. Nevertheless, more often than not, the essays themselves were informative, and to those such as myself, with a similiar insecure interest in these matters, they served as a source of encouragement. With a desire to avoid the worst excesses and emulate the best features of existing endeavours, I began systematically to order my thoughts on American football. It was not too difficult to convince myself that this was justified by concluding that if a social scientist from a far distant land were to conduct fieldwork in the United States, he or she would undoubtedly be struck by the game and its spectator appeal and suggest that the analysis of this activity would provide the perfect point of entry into the American way of life.

Even at this point, it is worth reiterating that we are dealing with a spectator sport *par excellence*, since the number of Americans actually to have engaged in these contests is probably on a par with the number of Romans who participated in gladiatorial contests. In another historical parallel, almost every team now imports a European or South American to perform the rare kicking function. Playing what is referred to as 'touch' football, minus the specialised bodily equipment and without the bone-crushing physical contact, is light years removed from what transpires on the professional or 'big-time' college field. This means that the game's broad appeal is not based on a middle-aged nostalgia for a youth spent in similar activity. Rather, the game is transmitting meaningful messages in symbolic form to susceptible psyches rooted in dormant bodies. In short, this often brutal pastime appeals to the collective conscience of America rather than to the corporate body. This is significant for a number of reasons, not the least being that as a native and long-standing consumer of these messages, I could examine my own conscience in the quest for cultural meaning. For more esoteric knowledge on the internal organisation and player mentality, I was able to refer to the seemingly endless pile of ghost-written biographies of active and retired combatants. The list of football-hero-authors includes a former anthropology student from Columbia, a couple of PhDs who spent their off-season on the teaching staff of respectable universities, a few part-time physicians and lawyers, and a homosexual who felt compelled to 'come out' to prove that heterosexual virility and football were not synonymous.

The eventual result of digesting this material, as native and anthropologist, was a brief essay, called 'The Great American Football Ritual' (Arens 1975). This appeared by invitation in a glossy magazine intended for the 'educated layman'. Shortly thereafter, a condensed version found its way into the sports section of the *Sunday New York Times*. The result was a notoriety and response surprising and even alienating to someone used to occasional musings in obscure academic journals. However, the response of other natives did provide further relevant data, but first, a summary of the essay which some consumers found so disconcerting.

In the attempt to demonstrate that this game invites a confrontation with a meaningful and peculiar American cultural trait, I detailed the evolution of the sport from its origins in European soccer and British rugby. The transformation over a hundred-year period resulted in an organisational pattern particularly reflective of a contemporary industrialised society. The swaying, haphazard scrum of rugby with the possibility of either side recovering the ball from a heel out was replaced in the American version by a fixed line of scrimmage which required immobility until the ball was set in motion. This is done by a pre-ordained centre snap to the quarter-back of the side in legal possession of the ball. Then, in a flurry of minutely synchronised and even elegantly executed motions, in conjunction with the most basic type of brute force, twenty-two bodies throw themselves at each other in apparent disregard of the potential mortal consequences. All this takes place in a few seconds, and the process is repeated until those in possession of the ball either score a touch-down or fail to gain ten yards in four such attempts. In either event, control over the ball reverts to the opposition, whose offensive specialists then have the opportunity to try the same.

This intermittent activity, resulting in lulls and furies, is a further elementary deviation from the pattern of most other sports where constant and fluid motion is more prevalent. These thirty-second interludes, punctuated by split-second action, only truly appreciated in slow-motion video replays which are now also provided in the newer stadia on monstrous viewing screens, are necessitated by the time it takes to unravel the pile of humanity, allow the injured to be removed, and re-establish the line of scrimmage. During the hiatus, the opposing offensive and defensive squads repair to their respective huddles to decide upon the next move. The particular stratagem selected from the available possibilities is based upon choosing an option in conformity with an overall 'game plan'. This 'plan' is especially designed from written scouting reports, from the endless replaying of films of the opponents' previously-played contests, and from computer print-outs indicating strengths and weaknesses, as well as overall tendencies in the particular situation at hand. The quarter-back who is charged with the decision-making responsibility for the offence communicates his choice in numerical and alphabetical code to his team-mates, who in turn are supposed to recall their peculiar function. This is followed by another clash of forces, which to the uninitiated very often bears a suspicious resemblance to what transpired just a moment earlier. However, to the more perceptive *aficionados* who are steeped in the particular lore, something novel has transpired. Indeed, they are partially entitled to their belief since, although the end result may be all too familiar, the means of achieving it in terms of player tasks are different in almost every instance. Further, every so often, in a dramatic moment of coordinated and specialised perfection, the ideal outcome is achieved in the form of a score, which is enough to restore faith in the system.

This is very often artistically achieved by the forward pass, another radical departure from the ancestral European games. Such incursions into enemy territory through the airlanes, rather than on the ground, usually provide the most exciting and startling moments. In addition to the artistry demanded of a passer who accurately hurls the ball up to fifty or sixty yards downfield to a swift receiver who gathers it in amidst surrounding defenders, this play can immediately alter the complexion of the game. The goal which one team was able to achieve in a wearisome and drawn-out procedure on foot, is elegantly and effortlessly achieved by their opponents in a twinkling. Not surprisingly, this single act, which can so immediately and profoundly alter the fortunes of the contest, is known as 'the bomb'.

It would be foolish to suggest that only this particular sport contains violent and dramatic moments, and that these elements account for its magnetism. In point of fact, the physical component is symbolically a minor one. Any argument for spectator appeal based on this premise of aggression is too facile. There were and are more violent amusements available, such as prizefighting, which have declined in popularity over the latter half of this century. American football's appeal is based on violence acted out in the context of meticulously planned precision, specialised function, coordination and cooperation which is applied in conjunction with a reliance on the most sophisticated technology this society can make available to the combatants. To propose that a game replete with such terminology as the bomb, the blitz and the spike, and involving participants who talk about hitting their opposite numbers hard enough to 'ring their bells', is aggressive, hardly seems worth the effort. On the other hand, considering that this game, as currently played, reflects basic organisational features of a highly industrialised country and permits mayhem in the context of its cultural achievements, seems a bit more reflective. Again, I believe there was more than coincidence in the fact that at the apex of the popularity of the Vietnam War and this sport, the American football player and air-force pilot bore an uncanny resemblance to each other when dressed to carry out their particular function. The decade was an era of Space-Age violence in the name of American values.

As literacy and communication increase, social anthropologists have had to contend with the objections of their living subject matter who claim that either the discipline itself or the particular practitioner is incapable of providing a meaningful interpretation of their culture. For someone who attempted a standard analysis of a prominent activity of the home country, abuse rather than objection was often a more apt characterisation of the indigenes' reaction. In some personal and printed letters my masculinity, patriotism and intelligence were called into question. A busy orthopaedic surgeon, retained for the purpose of reconstructing the joints of injured members of one professional team, was quick to correct me regarding my comments on the alleged incapacitating nature of the game. A former collegiate player challenged me to try a tackle on a rampaging ball carrier without the protective equipment, which I had suggested might actually cause many of the injuries rather than prevent them. Although I pointed out that this is exactly what takes place during a rugby match, it seemed to have escaped his attention. Clearly my minor allusions to violence captured the reader's imagination more than the cross-cultural comparison of this game with rituals in other societies. The liberal critical wing was disquieted by the failure to pounce upon the obvious correlation between the element of violence in football and in American society. The more conservative defenders such as those mentioned above were of the opinion that I had made too much of this factor. In retrospect they were all partially correct in focusing on the essay's too easy dismissal of violence and sport in relation to overall social patterns. However, the relationship between violence on and off the playing field is a complex one.

A social anthropologist who has provided a cross-cultural comparison between sport and sanctioned violence has convincingly demonstrated that peaceful societies tend to engage in non-aggressive games as measured by the permissible levels of bodily contact and territorial incursion (Sipes 1973). American football of course carries these possibilities to their logical extremes. Thus one could draw an obvious correlation between socially-approved athletic aggression and the anti-social but inordinate amount of violence in American life. Yet, if one examines other aspects of the problem, it becomes clear that this does not exhaust the topic. Consider, for example, the behaviour of the enormous crowds which witness these events. Their conduct can only be described as decorous, especially in the light of what transpires on the playing field before them. For the American public attending a football game this is the most civil of occasions, bringing together families or groups who picnic elegantly before the game; dating couples on their best behaviour, and businessmen cementing a more formal relationship in a convivial fashion. A more moderate, content, even angelic collection of American citizens is hardly imaginable. Any disturbances, or the rare physical abuse of players or referees by non-participants is condemned in no uncertain terms as unsportsmanlike conduct not befitting such an urbane occasion. Meanwhile, on the field, in their own words, players 'punish their opponents', 'give up their bodies', and, if this is imaginable, according to the officials, engage in 'unnecessary roughness'. The boundary between the two normative realms was made explicit by a judge who recently ruled in the case of such player conduct which found its way into the civil courts. In response to a suit lodged by one player against another, who in violation of permissible violence flagrantly delivered an unnecessary blow which sent the plaintiff to hospital, the judge dismissed the complaint. He stated that behaviour on the contest field was 'outside of the law'. The barbaric and civilised co-exist in an enclosed physical arena with no apparent unease.

This situation provides some interesting comparisons with soccer and the character of crowd behaviour at matches in Europe and South America. This game permits only minimal expressions of aggressive behaviour, but the combative role seems to shift to spectators. To an American used to the docile behaviour of team supporters in the United States, the comportment of soccer fans is astounding. The 'hooliganism' before, during, and after matches, the riots in the stands and general pugnacious behaviour of the faithful is incomprehensible to Americans who have a greater regard for professional rather than amateurish carnage. The armed guards, barbed-wire fences and escape tunnels which are deemed necessary in some places to protect players and officials from those they have come to entertain reminds those on the other side of the Atlantic of a security system more suitable for a prison. Indeed, it is likely that many of the countries who employ these measures do not find such precautions necessary to protect civilians from the incarcerated anti-social elements.

Finally, the very idea that two Latin-American states seriously considered the result of a match as an acceptable ideological rationale and immediate cause of war must surely indicate that we have far to go in understanding the relationship between sport and social aggression. It may be partially true, as Richard Sipes has suggested, that violent societies tend towards violent sports and thus these pastimes bring people together for the purpose of aggression, rather than provide an outlet for it. However, this sort of hypothesis is not helpful enough for the purpose of interpreting the opposing typical crowd reaction of soccer fans to that of their American counterparts at a similar event. To suggest that Americans somehow have their violent tendencies gratified at a football game, while other people are moved to this state by a different sort of sport is a tempting but unsatisfactory conclusion. The immediate problem is the benign character of crowds at soccer matches in some parts of Europe and America as well, where the sport has been rapidly gaining in popularity. Undoubtedly the correlation between these two phenomena deserves some comment, but the problem is as demanding as many others in social science, where simplistic knowledge has been replaced by a sophisticated ignorance of human behaviour. Part of the problem in this instance stems from the attempt to make too much of the implications of sport for violence as if this were its only or even primary function. In post-industrial societies, where leisure-sport activity consumes such a large part of the average native's attention, it is necessary for the anthropologist to seek other and less obvious cultural implications.

The rise and fall in favour of the many items on the sporting menu in a complex society is one of the other dimensions to be considered, since some meaning must be attached to these fluctuations. The gradual decline in interest in American football in the past few years, and the resurgence of other games at the amateur and professional level, is a case in point. Football's eclipse of baseball, which is America's interpretation of cricket and was once hailed as the national pastime, can be dated for convenience's sake to 1960. This coincided with the inauguration of Kennedy, a former Harvard football player, and continued on through the regimes of Johnson, Nixon, and Ford, each of whom represented his Alma Mater with varying degrees of proficiency on what is referred to as the gridiron. However, it has now become apparent to the sports commentators who keep track of these matters that baseball is enjoying a strong comeback as reflected by viewer interest and newspaper coverage. Furthermore, President Carter never played football as a collegian and was often filmed playing a toned-down version of baseball while on the campaign trail. This might well be the clearest symbol of a change in the tenor of the times in the United States. The decade and a half between the

Kennedy and Carter administrations spanned the country's deepest involvement in the war in Indo-China and the height of football fervour. This is the type of correspondence which leads to the inevitable conclusions about the element of violence. Undoubtedly there is something to this notion, but it does not exhaust the list of potential interpretations.

I would point out that war, in athletic parlance, demands the supreme team effort in all that the phrase implies. As a unique cultural idiom, football came to symbolise this commitment for the phrase-makers and image-makers of various political administrations. In short order the game emerged as American society in its idealised form, not because it sanctioned violence, but because it demanded that the participants work as a specialised unit for the sake of victory. One can still hear the plaintive demands of Johnson and Nixon for the country to get behind their leader in the time of crisis, and their familiar accusations that only dissident elements stood between success and failure. Aggression is merely a single element in both war and football, and is not necessarily the deciding factor today. This thesis is supported by the traditional character of baseball, which demands less in the way of integration and loyalty in a squad. A single offensive player while batting can and often does change the fortune of the game, while his team-mates merely sit and applaud the performance. The individualistic nature of the game was epitomised during the 1977 season by the championship team, the New York Yankees, which was composed of colourful, discontented, recalcitrant and rebellious performers. The owner squabbled with the manager, the manager with the players, and the players with each other, yet they managed to emerge victorious with ease. Indeed, the most vocal rebel and the most highly paid destroyed their opponents almost single-handed. Significantly, it was this club, with its flair for dramatic personal portrayals which dominated the nation's sports pages on a most positive note. There were no demands for harmony, just performance, and the American public revelled in their antics. In 1978 they somehow did it all over again.

To this reversal of what Americans now expect and appreciate in their pastimes, one must also consider the competition at present offered by other sports. European football has exploded into the American sporting scene, especially in the east, where the stadia are now filled to capacity by soccer fans. This has occurred in conjunction with a tennis boom. In addition to being more sedate physical games, capable of being played in short trousers by almost any physical type, both have an obvious international flavour. Americans apparently no longer feel it necessary to concentrate on their own sport in isolation from the rest of the world's interests. Instead, they have taken up sports which are dominated by the World Cup and Wimbledon, not the Sugar and Super Bowl. In effect, Americans have seen fit to join the rest of the world at least as far as recreation is concerned, and compete in a less concretely violent fashion.

Sport clearly has the unique ability to symbolise these shifts in national ethos in a more meaningful and immediate fashion than other forms of communication. It would be self-assuring to think that games assume a greater significance among the world's less sophisticated peoples, but this is not the case. When societies have more time for games, they assume an importance unmatched in comparison to those people who still have to spend most of their waking hours trying to extract a living from the natural environment.

Gambling: Mirror of Society

DAVID RICHES

OVER MUCH of the Canadian arctic the Eskimo economy is still predominantly grounded in hunting, fishing and trapping. But the context of this economy is thoroughly westernised. Before the 1960s most Eskimos followed a nomadic way of life, roaming the tundra in small bands of twenty to thirty people and living in the traditional igloos and tents. Nowadays they live in prefabricated houses in settlements of one hundred or more people; their lives are overseen by Canadian administrators, development officers, teachers and health and welfare personnel. Hunting is no longer a matter of moving from place to place as the seasons change, but of journeying from the settlement to the appropriate hunting grounds and returning home when petrol supplies (for snowmobiles or outboard motors) are exhausted.

My wife and I arrived at Port Burwell, a small isolated settlement on an island just off the northern tip of the coast of Labrador, in January 1970. For the first three months, my anthropological fieldwork was conducted almost entirely within the settlement. It was felt that my inexperience in handling the Eskimo language, operating a snowmobile and generally coping with the rigours of winter would be a liability on hunting expeditions. At this time of the year it is the caribou hunting season, and the hunting grounds are one hundred miles to the south of the settlement in the Labrador mountains, so hunters normally spend at least one week away from home each time they go on an expedition. During this period, then, I spent most of the time visiting people in their houses and receiving visitors in mine. The visitors would huddle round the oil stove; out of politeness they would remove their hats, but otherwise they made no concession to the fact that they were

A Balinese cock-fight (Alan Hutchison Library)

dressed for temperatures of twenty degrees below zero, whilst inside it was at least twenty degrees above. They would stay for hours, drinking tea, making conversation and, most important of all, playing cards. It was apparent that card playing is one of the main recreations in Port Burwell. The Eskimos normally play a kind of rummy. They call it *patik* (clap) because a player should clap when only one card remains in hand. On many an evening one would see clusters of snowmobiles parked outside a house and one would know that there was a card playing session going on inside. Men and women play together in these games, and nearly every adult Eskimo reckons to join a session at least once a week (the few Canadians living in the settlement do not normally participate). Gambling accompanies Eskimo card playing. Before each deal everyone lays a stake: there is a choice between a 'quarter' (a 25 cent piece), a heavy rifle bullet (a bullet for a .222, .303, or .308 calibre rifle), or five light rifle bullets (for a .22 calibre rifle). In a single session no one expects to win or lose more than $25 worth of money or bullets. (To set this in context, the average weekly earnings of an Eskimo household in Port Burwell in 1970 were reckoned to be around $100. But, as we shall see, the Eskimos treat even small winnings as an important economic bonus.) An Eskimo card playing session normally continues for a pre-arranged time or until one player has cleaned out the others of all the money or bullets they have brought along. The others are said to be *kataktuq* (fallen). In other contexts this word describes a person collapsing through thin ice, or a man who drives his snowmobile over a cliff.

When eventually the Eskimos invited me to join a caribou hunting expedition I thought I would try and ingratiate myself by taking along a pack of cards. At the end of the first day's journey, as we sat in a tiny igloo recovering our strength, I produced the cards. 'The people don't like to play cards in camp', I was abruptly told. Feeling rather small I did not ask why and concluded that the Eskimos must consider that it took one's mind off the matter in hand – caribou hunting.

The next time I went on a long expedition with the Eskimos was in early July. At this time of year small groups of two to four families journey together in canoes and set up camps on the

Labrador coast. The Eskimos fish for arctic char (a migratory trout), hunt seals as they bask in the sun on the thin ice that still fills most of the bays and fiords, and visit the islands where the eider ducks are laying, and collect down from the nests. Life can be very agreeable in these camps. Back in the settlement the muck and filth deposited during the spring thaw gets churned up by the summer rains and the settlement's bulldozers, making summer in many ways the least pleasant time of year. So when I was invited to spend three weeks on the Labrador coast I jumped at the chance. I hardly need mention that this time I left my cards at home.

When the weather is good Eskimos in camp work fairly concentratedly at hunting and fishing. But often it is not good; strong winds blow up or pack ice drifts in from the sea so that the canoes cannot be launched. On the first day, when the weather was bad I spent most of the morning in a tent reading a newspaper. The Eskimos were all in another tent, and eventually I went across to join them. The women were sitting around chatting, minding children, and from time to time feeding seal blubber into a stove improvised from an old rusty oil drum. The men were huddled together around this stove gambling.

They were not playing cards, however. They were gambling with a wooden spinning top, which they called *kaitaq*. Mounted on the axis of the top is a cube whose upright sides are each marked in a different fashion. The idea of the game is basically to predict which one of these sides will be exposed when the top falls. Stakes (in camp, bullets only) are laid before each spin and if the player fails to guess correctly they remain in the pool and are added to the stakes laid for the next spin.

How would an anthropologist interpret these gambling games? One way would be to consider the social and economic benefits derived from participating in them – social benefits are clearly important in the card playing sessions in the settlement. The people living in modern arctic settlements today have usually come from a variety of widely scattered traditional nomadic camps. In the past, members of different camps would often not know one another particularly well, and if they were not kinsmen, some hostility might prevail among them. In the modern settlement there are few formal means of promoting friendly relations among such people. To be sure, modern Eskimos are members of a number of social groups of European flavour, such as cooperatives, religious congregations and social clubs. But joining these groups is a matter of personal inclination, and because of a lack of familiarity with European ways, people's participation in them is often rather desultory. In Port Burwell the card playing party compensates for this. A willingness to join a gambling session is the sole qualification for membership in a card playing clique; gambling, therefore, is an important lubricant of social interaction. It was quite clear that the more 'marginal' members of the community – people whose personalities and origins marked them out as socially less desirable than others – manipulated this facility in gambling. These were the people who frequently joined gambling sessions and who were always keen to host them.

The economic benefits deriving from gambling are of course also important. In Port Burwell, they especially relate to the fact that the settlement is often short of important resources. Port Burwell is very isolated. It is not serviced by roads and the next community is three hard-travelling days distant. The shop run by the Eskimo-owned cooperative is the only retail outlet in the settlement. Its main supplies are delivered each August by ship, though planes do bring in small quantities of goods at other times during the year. The main shortages in the settlement are cash, and bullets for heavy rifles.

Eskimo hunters own a variety of heavy rifles of different calibres (the three calibres I mentioned earlier are the most common ones). The cooperative orders the appropriate amount of ammunition each year, but shortages arise because it simply cannot afford to stock each type of ammunition in great bulk. The rarer types of ammunition, particularly, tend mostly to be bought up at the beginning of each year by the better-off hunters. As the winter hunting season approaches more and more people run low on their ammunition supplies, and at the same time bad weather increasingly prevents the twice-monthly planes from landing on the narrow ice air strip.

Cash tends to run short in Port Burwell for rather different reasons. Very little of it circulates in the community. This is because nearly all economic transactions in Port Burwell are made through the medium of credit-debit accounting.

Accordingly, the Canadian development officer, who effectively runs the cooperative, sees little need for the shop to hold large quantities of money; this suits him because the cooperative lacks the security to stock money in bulk. But there are a number of very important transactions for which the Eskimos need money. These are basically transactions with 'outsiders', who of course do not have accounts with the Port Burwell shop, but these outsiders often supply luxury goods not stocked by the cooperative. For example, mail order houses supply fashionable clothing; Canadians visiting the settlement, and the summer ship supply liquor; and shops in other settlements (or in southern Canada) supply goods to Eskimos who are lucky enough to leave Port Burwell to visit relatives elsewhere or to attend a meeting or conference at some administrative centre.

For the Eskimos the main problem with these 'outside' transactions is that they are unpredictable: no one knows exactly when a Canadian will visit the settlement, or when they will be leaving Port Burwell to visit another settlement. So whenever people can get hold of the necessary cash, they tend to hoard it; this, in turn, exacerbates the shortage of cash in the settlement. The way in which cash is snapped up as soon as it is paid into the cooperative shop was once nicely exemplified when I paid in $200 in dollar bills to clear my debts (other Canadians resident in the settlement would probably have written a cheque). Within three days the clerks working in the shop had withdrawn seventy per cent of this cash against their accounts; their relatives had withdrawn the remaining thirty per cent.

The shortages of cash and certain types of bullet mean that the Eskimos in Port Burwell put a very high premium on controlling these resources. This makes them particularly appropriate prizes in gambling sessions. People who have lots of cash, or bullets of scarce types, have an incentive to invest some in gambling stakes; even if they lose in the games, the investment secures prestige for them. In this way small amounts of cash and the scarcer bullets are distributed among the members of the community. People who are anxious to get hold of cash or certain bullets hold on to them if they are lucky enough to win; they hope that the ordinary types of bullet they

have brought to the session will last out the evening and that
they will be able to pocket any cash or 'special bullets' they may
have won. I was once the victim of such a strategy. Unaware
that .303 bullets were running short in the settlement, I happily
staked my supply in spinning-top gambling; horrified, I soon
realised that whenever I won, all I would collect was .22 bullets
– of no use to me since I did not own a light rifle.

Another perspective on gambling games that interests an
anthropologist treats these games as rituals. Then the question
is posed: what is being communicated in these rituals?
Exploring the symbolic significance of gambling games is, I
think, an important issue and I propose to devote the remainder of this article to it.

I want to focus on the similarities between strategies of game
playing and the strategies for bettering oneself in mainstream
economic life. Economists have long recognised these
similarities. The successful businessman takes risks and deals
with uncertainties – and so also does the successful game
player. Games strategies may be studied under laboratory
conditions, and some economists maintain that the sort of
techniques that businessmen employ in the real world may be
exposed in the more simplified and experimental circumstances of the game

An anthropological perspective might be put on the
similarities to which economists have drawn attention. I am
going to propose that playing games – and *gambling* games
particularly – may be treated as a metaphor for mainstream
economic life. In gambling games, the *essentials* of mainstream
economic life are brought together in a condensed sequence of
events and are *repeatedly* (or ritually) exposed each time the
game is played. And through the recreational connotations of
the game, the essentials of economic life which are being
dramatised in this way are given value in much the same
manner as moral ideas are given value in religious ritual
through associating them with the gods. Basically I am arguing
that in gambling games it is being asserted that, whatever the
circumstances, mainstream economic life is worth participating in. It is being asserted that, in competition with one's
fellow men, the right strategies will bring economic rewards.

Supposing my argument to be correct, two simple predictions follow. First, variations in the types of strategy to be followed in mainstream economic life should be reflected in variations in types of gambling game. Second, the people who are eligible to take part in mainstream economic activity should be those entitled to participate in the gambling games. Let us test these predictions with the Eskimo material, and then turn to some other cultures and see if they hold good for them as well.

When I described Eskimo gambling, I indicated that spinning-top gambling was played in hunting camps, while card playing was the appropriate game for the settlement. Certainly, economic life in Eskimo hunting camps is strikingly different from economic life in the settlement. Eskimos treat hunting as a competitive activity – prestige accrues to the man who is a successful hunter. But they recognise that hunting success is to a large extent a matter of good fortune. Of course, they appreciate that skill plays a part in the capture of an animal, but they realise that even the most competent hunter can be unlucky. Hence they stress the interdependence of hunters and the importance of sharing the spoils of the hunt with everyone in the camp, whoever actually catches the animal. In short, Eskimos know that hunting is a chancy business.

Spinning-top gambling nicely dramatises this situation. It is very much a game of pure chance; it is almost impossible to 'fix' a spin and make the top fall in a desired way. Thus, as a ritual, this game asserts that despite the manifest fortuitousness of hunting life, if one invests time and energy rewards are eventually forthcoming. The game also expresses the interdependence of hunters and the necessity for good relations among them in spite of the fact that hunting is a competitive business. The fact that success in spinning-top gambling is a matter of chance means that gambling sessions are normally quiet, harmonious affairs; it would be almost impossible to accuse an opponent of dirty play.

Economic strategy in the Eskimo settlement, by contrast, is much more under the control of the individual. The aim is to maximise particular material assets and the strategy is a purely competitive one: there is no question of sharing money or western goods with other Eskimos. In Port Burwell, economic activity is very largely a matter of manipulating one's cash and credit resources and hiring oneself out to Canadians as paid labour. Now there are many uncertainties in doing these things, but none the less the scope for the exercise of individual judgment is often relatively high. For example, one can anticipate fairly well what the consequences will be if one pays cash into one's cooperative account. Equally, on a particular day, one can normally anticipate whether or not the Canadian administrator is likely to be hiring casual labour, and therefore whether it would be wise to hang around the settlement if one were short of money.

Card gambling fits well with this state of affairs. In rummy, knowing when to play or withhold a card or groups of cards is to a large extent a matter of expertise. The Eskimos play the game with speed and panache. Certain people build reputations for being relatively successful. As a ritual, card gambling asserts that in settlement life anyone can improve his material circumstances, but that those who do will more likely be people who have mastered the necessary skills.

From the point of view of eligibility to participate in gambling games, the symbolic relationship between gambling games and mainstream economic life is again exemplified in the Eskimo material. Among the Eskimos (as among most peoples whose economies incorporate hunting and gathering) hunting is predominantly a male preserve, and in the hunting camp only men engage in spinning-top gambling. But the Eskimo monetary economy, based in the modern settlement, is open to both men and women; thus Eskimo women have accounts in the cooperative shop, and a good deal of wage-earning work is available to women, for example interpreting, handicraft making, clerking and domestic labour. Appropriately, then, women participate with men in card playing sessions.

Let us see if this way of interpreting gambling games works for other cultures. There are two particularly well-known studies of gambling in the anthropological literature. We are fortunate in that one study deals with people whose economy has some affinities with Eskimo camp life, while the other deals with a people whose economy is to some extent akin to Eskimo settlement life. The Hadza of northern Tanzania are the first people, the Balinese are the second.

The Hadza live in a remote and sparsely populated area of Tanzania, around Lake Eyasi; they number only about eight hundred people. Before 1964, when the government introduced them to a settled way of life and encouraged them to take up agriculture, the Hadza lived entirely by nomadic hunting and gathering, moving round the country in small groups (camps), each averaging about twenty people. The anthropologist James Woodburn, who has done extensive research among these people, has presented some fascinating material about Hadza subsistence and ecology. The Hadza live in a fairly benevolent environment: game of many varieties is abundant, and so also are edible fruits, berries, roots and fungi. But the Hadza managed to secure their subsistence through the expenditure of very little work. On average only about two hours per day per person were spent in obtaining food from the wild. Even more remarkable, relatively little food was secured from hunting – as among the Eskimo, hunting was almost entirely a man's pursuit. Indeed some men barely bothered to hunt at all.

It would seem that gambling rather than hunting was a Hadza man's main obsession. Hadza men spent more time gambling than obtaining their food, for in most Hadza camps, a gambling game would be going on more or less continuously all day. As Marshall Sahlins nicely puts it: 'Hadza men seem much more concerned with games of chance than with chances of game.'

As with Eskimo spinning-top gambling, Hadza gambling is almost entirely a game of chance. The rules are quite complicated so I shall give only the essentials. Between two and four men play together. Wooden discs are cut from the bark of a baobab tree, one for each contestant plus a 'master' disc. One player piles the discs and throws them against a tree. The game is won when one contestant's disc lands on the ground the same way up as the master disc. The stakes for the game are various types of 'valuable' articles – poisoned arrows, stone pipes, and items obtained through trade with neighbouring tribes.

Our first impression about the Hadza might be that this is a society where people could quickly satisfy all their material and food requirements; as a result there would be plenty of time for leisure activity. But I am going to suggest that this impression would not be entirely correct. Moreover I think that the leisure activity (gambling) may be intimately connected with people's strategies for obtaining subsistence.

In many ways Hadza hunting was somewhat like Eskimo hunting. The spoils of the hunt would be shared with everyone in the camp and a successful hunter would secure prestige. Indeed, James Woodburn emphasises that the Hadza regard meat as a luxury food and, as a result, in large camps an animal could be divided up so conscientiously that no one would get a decent-sized portion. All this suggests that, contrary to first impressions, Hadza treated meat as a scarce resource: just as we work for about eight hours a day and complain that we are short of money, Hadza men would work for about two hours a day and complain that they didn't have enough meat.

I do not wish to be concerned here with the reasons why a particular society considers a particular number of hours appropriate for a day's work. I simply want to stress that the Hadza were preoccupied with their meat supply and that we may expect them to have emphasised in some way the importance of the hunting enterprise. My supposition is that in Hadza gambling – in games of chance, which are the men's exclusive preserve – the nature of hunting strategy and the importance of the meat that hunting provides are dramatised and given value.

Finally, we turn to rural Bali and consider one of the most well-known and common of gambling games – cock fighting. Balinese rural society is a peasant society. People live in villages of about seven hundred people. The Balinese economy is based very largely on the production of rice using an elaborate irrigation technology. But in most villages many people live as artisans. Indeed, in one village, studied by Clifford Geertz, the majority of people devote the bulk of their productive energies to various local 'cottage' industries, and allow people from elsewhere to work their land under various types of share cropping or tenancy arrangements. Unlike Eskimo and Hadza society, Balinese society is not egalitarian. As befits a basically Hindu culture, inherited rank is an important determinant of social status. This is reflected in the economic sphere. One may certainly raise one's economic standing in the community through sensibly planned economic strategy, but the size of the land holding one inherits obviously has an important effect on the level one may eventually attain.

The Balinese cock fight is quite obviously a game of skill. The gambling that surrounds it reflects people's estimation of the qualities of the birds involved. The game is essentially a man's preserve. Countless hours are spent grooming and preparing the cocks, and among the people who make the most assiduous preparation are the most highly respected members of the village. The cock fighting session attracts a huge audience. Before each fight bets are feverishly laid, but during the fight the onlookers are quiet and tense. When the fight is over all bets are immediately paid, and a new fight quickly takes the stage.

The system of betting surrounding a Balinese cock fight is quite complicated. It seems to be geared towards encouraging people to invest large amounts of money in the game. Two types of bet are laid on each fight. First, there is the bet between the two main protagonists; in terms of the amount of money laid, this is the most important bet, and it is always an even money bet. The second type is among members of the audience; a person will offer odds on a particular bird winning and look around for someone to accept these odds. Because the main bet is an even money one, there is incentive for a fight to take place between evenly matched birds – plainly it makes little sense to accept an even money gamble if one's bird is obviously of an inferior quality. Balinese recognition of this goes as far as interfering with the capacity of a bird to fight; for example, an obviously superior bird may be handicapped by altering the angle of its spurs to a slightly less advantageous position. If the strength of the birds in a fight is well matched, relatively high bets may be agreed. An even money gamble on roughly equivalent birds makes a reasonable investment for both protagonists. Geertz reports that the people who lay the highest bets in this way are invariably the most respected members of the community.

Geertz's description and analysis of the Balinese cock fight is undoubtedly one of the most vivid pieces of writing in the anthropological literature. It also appeals to me because it stresses the metaphoric dimensions in the game. While economic returns from gambling on cocks are obviously important, the game is much more significant to the Balinese in expressing certain values in community life. On one level, Geertz argues that cock fighting is basically an expression of male *machismo*; Balinese men identify with their cocks and the sexual connotation between the cock and the penis is made quite explicit. On another level Geertz notes that in cock fighting people are making a statement about their status in the community. As protagonists in the fight, the pillars of the community declare their standing; in victory their status is affirmed, in defeat it is denied.

It seems to me that we might improve on this second interpretation. On the one hand, the symbolic connection between the cock fight contest and social status is not quite exact: as Geertz acknowledges, no one's status changes as a result of a fight. On the other hand, the importance of the gambling accompanying the cock fight is not clearly exposed.

I believe that cock-fight gambling might be better interpreted as symbolic of economic strategy in mainstream Balinese economic life. It indicates, first of all, that success in mainstream economic life (in the main, a man's preserve) results from estimating the prospects and planning accordingly – there is a parallel here with Eskimo card playing. Second (and here there is a contrast with the Eskimo and Hadza situation) gambling with living objects may well symbolise the fact that success in an important part of mainstream economic life stems from manipulating living, that is, agricultural, resources – indeed, we may add that the sexual connotations of the cock may denote the fact that it is the fertility of resources with which one is concerned in mainstream life. Finally, the gambling arrangements of cock fighting denote the fact that in this culture one's economic advance is made easier if one's status in the first place is high; the 'even money' rule on laying bets means that people with wealth and status are invited to 'invest their privileges' and place large sums of money on a single fight. For Geertz, then, cock-fighting in Bali is a game in which one's status is communicated. For me, it is a game in which the possibilities of investing one's wealth and status in mainstream economic strategy are exposed.

In this article I have considered some of the perspectives on gambling games that might be entertained using an anthropological approach. I recognise that people derive important economic and social benefits from joining a gambling game. But my main concern has been to ask: what makes gambling an acceptable way of securing these benefits in the society concerned? The tentative conclusion is that the legitimacy of a gambling game may lie in its capacity to denote, and give value to, the essentials of mainstream economic life.

Institutions of Violence

SCHUYLER JONES

FIGHTING IN ONE form or another seems to be a universal human characteristic. In some cultures it is accepted, and certain forms of it are permitted at certain times and accommodated in certain places. In other cultures it is denied and suppressed – swept under the carpet. For cultural reasons the form that fighting takes in a given society follows a pattern. This is worth noting, because it means that rules are being followed and that although relationships may seem to have broken down, the participants are still strongly influenced by social considerations.

There is a need to distinguish between an impromptu scrap and institutionalised combat. An example of the former is the street corner fight following an argument; an example of the latter is the duel. The difference is that institutionalised combat has rules and those rules must be followed, otherwise the participants lose, rather than gain, prestige. The ritual of the duel proceeded according to a strict protocol. Fundamentally it was concerned with social control, but it also had other functions. It served as a class indicator, for example. Gentlemen were concerned with honour and fought duels, others merely brawled. This carried over into the first world war when officers (gentlemen) took to the air to engage in a variation of the duel, often exchanging salutes when they ran out of ammunition or when one shot down the other. Captured enemy officers were sometimes wined and dined in the officers' mess before being sent off to prison camp.

Disputes among Kalahari Bushmen rarely involve fighting because it is part of Bushman culture to avoid it if possible, but if all else fails, two men, having exchanged verbal insults, may end up facing each other armed with bows and poisoned

Buzkashi. Kabul, Afghanistan (Alan Hutchison Library)

arrows. Each tries to dodge the arrows and they apparently do not shoot as accurately as when hunting, for misses are common. Both sides know that if a man is hit he will probably die within a few hours.

We at once recognise this as a variation of the European duel with its insult-challenge-combat sequence. In both cases rules are being followed. In the actual confrontation the method of fighting and the weapons also conform to customary usage. These rules are characteristic of institutionalised redress and serve to distinguish this kind of fighting from other forms of violence where there are no rules (murder, assassination, ambush, street brawl, terrorist activities, spectator violence at sports events, etc.).

A duel is a prearranged encounter between two persons, with deadly weapons, in accordance with conventional rules, with the object of voiding a personal quarrel or of deciding a point of honour. In Europe it was the cultural concept of personal honour combined with an absence of other means of seeking satisfaction, that gave rise to the duel as an institution. As a mechanism for righting wrongs the duel became so commonplace in France in the seventeenth century that between 1601 and 1609 some two thousand Frenchmen of noble birth fell in duels. Two hundred and fifty years later Queen Victoria was anxious to discourage what she called 'the barbarous practice of duelling'. Barbarous or not, it had been pointed out earlier that duelling did correct and repress a real social evil. As Bentham observed in 1789, the duel 'entirely effaces a blot which an insult imprints on the honour'.

The concept of honour, bound up with the idea that it is something easily damaged by insult, overlays the fundamental aggressive competition underneath. It is the constant jostling for social, economic, and political positions and the jealousies aroused in the process which come to a focal point in 'honour' and 'insult'. The duel, whatever form it may take, is a symptom of these conditions. The conditions themselves may be altered by changes in society. There seems, for example, to be a clear connection between duelling and law – and it lies not in what the law will allow, but in what the law does not provide for.

Bentham considered that duelling would flourish until such time as the law extended the same legal protection to offences against the honour as to offences against the person. The key was the legal definition of assault. Passing laws to prohibit duelling is not enough. If duels are outlawed without the provision of compensating socio-legal redress, then duelling will either be driven underground or will take on a different form. Competition seems to be an important, if not a fundamental aspect of many cultures. Status, prestige, reputation and honour are the motivating forces behind the contest – the overt form that competition takes. The nature of the actual confrontation varies greatly from one society to another. What does not change, except in degree, is that which gives rise to the contest in the first place: aggression and rivalry. It is in society's own interests to foster these attributes and it does so by setting up competitions and offering prizes.

It might be argued that there is a fundamental difference between a duel and aggressive competition of a social, economic, or political kind because a duel is concerned with a particular point of honour and aggressive competition is general. Not so. The duel is merely a manifestation of the need, forced on participants by society, to maintain, and preferably to enhance their reputations. Thus both the particular duel and the more general aggressive competition found in so many societies have their roots in the same source.

These contests are going on round us every day. In certain parts of Afghanistan one particular form of encounter called *buzkashi* takes place on Fridays from December to March.

Buzkashi is a winter game played in Afghan Turkestan; not in the home or tea-house, but on horseback in an open field. In terms of violence it is roughly comparable with Formula One motor racing. In the last game of *buzkashi* I watched, in 1967, a man was killed by a horse falling on him and the game proceeded without interruption. To play you need from ten to thirty mounted riders, a field at least a hundred by three hundred metres in size, and a dead calf. The body of the calf, minus its head, is thrown down inside a five-metre circle and the horsemen rush in, every man trying to reach down and seize the calf. The successful rider eventually breaks out of the mêlée and gallops off for the opposite end of the field, holding on to the calf. His object is to ride round a post at the far end and come back down the field to dump the calf inside the ring again. The object of all the other players is to prevent him doing this. It's every man for himself. The bravura with which the game is played is due largely to an absence of detailed and strictly enforced rules. Whips are used on opposing horses and riders alike, and collisions are not always accidental. The European spectator, after watching for some time, might paraphrase Bosquet and remark, *'C'est magnifique, mais ce n'est pas le Sport'*.

As Asen Balikci has shown in a recent article, what the spectators are watching is a political event – a contest between rival leaders – taking place in a public arena. The political leaders who are waging the contest are not on the field themselves. They own the horses. They are the wealthy buyers and breeders who make *buzkashi* possible, and they use it as, a political manoeuvre in competition with their rivals. Two or three generations ago such rivalries would have been expressed by raid and counter-raid, with each khan's political activities focused on the building up of ever larger followings by dispensing hospitality, extending protection, and granting favours. The khan who commanded the loyalties of the greatest number of men was the man who counted politically – he had the largest army. Today, as the centralised authority of the Afghan Government has extended to make itself an effective presence in all parts of the country, this has changed. The same political rivalries exist, but they can no longer be expressed in the same way. Now the ritual battle called *buzkashi* provides the occasion, and the khan with the best horses and riders is the one who scores against his rivals. As the earlier pattern of raid and counter-raid could go on for generations without ever producing wholly conclusive results, so *buzkashi*, as the focal point of khan rivalries, goes from one Friday match to another, meeting on the field of honour in a continual jostling for favourable positions in the local political scene.

Many cultures contain elements that have the effect of forcing individual members to compete with each other. This competition is nothing other than controlled conflict. What does society get out of it? In many cases what it gets is a warrior class. It does this by rewarding certain kinds of behaviour and thus instilling certain attitudes. Viewed in this way, a society survives by thrusting on its members an obligation to be competitive and this in turn provides society with the streak of aggression which puts it ahead in the survival stakes. Of course some would argue that the aggression is there as part of man's biological inheritance and that competition is the result. Either way, as a survival technique, aggression has a lot in its favour.

How does the system work? Society sets up a range of 'glittering prizes' which it holds up before everyone with the promise that if they try hard enough they may expect to acquire (a) the prize, and (b) the approval of society. In short, their prestige will be enhanced. An important part of the system is that the range of prizes is never exhausted. No matter how many one has acquired, there are always others waiting to be won. This has the effect of fostering competition, which makes the prizes seem even more desirable. The process begins early in life as is shown by the fact that in our culture there are rewards both at home and at school for outstanding achievement.

When society approves, society confers the honour. This is done with appropriate fanfare, the main purpose of which is not so much to reward the recipient, but to focus public attention on the accomplishment and stimulate others to greater effort so that they too may stand in the limelight. The good example is ever before us. The prizes, and what they do for our prestige, are the bait most of us rise to, and the system that keeps us coming back for more is competition. There is no better way of accomplishing something than either to get the individual members of the group to compete with each other or to divide the group into teams and get the teams competing with each other. Controlled competition is woven into the very fabric of the social, economic, and political institutions of most societies.

What may at first appear to be a very different kind of institution from that of *buzkashi* is found in Melanesia among the Massim of the D'Entrecasteaux Islands. Michael Young, who carried out fieldwork in the area, has aptly named his study *Fighting with Food* and he quotes the islanders as saying 'Before we fought with spears, but today we fight with food'. Fighting with food refers, in this context, to the competitive food exchanges (*abutu*) which are an important aspect of life on Goodenough Island – a place just north of the easternmost tip of New Guinea.

In cases of rivalry or enmity one party may issue a challenge to the other. Two groups promptly form, composed of those who support the contenders, and an *abutu* gets under way – often one village against another. Supporting each contender are groups of individuals who have specific kin-based role responsibilities in the event. These are unconditional supporters, specific supporters, and residual helpers. The principals and their unconditional supporters are committed to supplying the greatest amount of food in proportion to their numbers. The leading contenders are, in fact, expected to exhaust their food resources completely. But beyond this the principals take no other part in the contest that follows. It is the unconditional supporters who face the task of organising the whole contest. Having issued the challenge (or accepted it) on behalf of their man, they then make all subsequent arrangements.

The main purpose of *abutu* 'is to shame the opposing side by giving it more and better food than it is able to pay back simultaneously, thereby demonstrating – within the terms of the culture – greater power, worthiness, and even virtue' (Young 1971, p. 194). The ritual battle is normally fought with yams, though other foods such as taro and bananas may sometimes be used. Domestic pigs are also given in most *abutu* exchanges.

For the inhabitants of Goodenough Island many social values come to a focus in food. In their food exchanges the donors are in effect saying certain things about their relationship to the recipients. Thus 'a certain type of yam, painted and with a pandanus streamer attached, connotes hostility and intent to wound – it wears the dress of warriorhood.'

The actual contest can be divided into phases: the challenge, the first gift of food, the return gift, the second gift, and the final redistribution. Since the person who wishes to initiate the event will need the support of numerous kinsmen, the first step is to invite them over for a meal so that the subject can be broached. If all goes well, plans are laid, resources calculated, and degree of support estimated.

Next day at first light the leader of the unconditional supporters leads the way to the enemy village to issue the challenge This is delivered loudly enough to focus community attention on the event. The specific individual being challenged is soon fully awake to find the group on his doorstep. His name is called, and he is asked if perhaps he has run away, and if not, how about some food? The leader of the visitors thereupon holds out a yam, and if a return gift of the same kind is forthcoming, the contest is on. As they leave the village the challengers are heaped with abuse, which they ignore, and phase one is over.

The challengers return home and spend the rest of the day constructing food display platforms in the centre of their village and bringing food in from the gardens. As the food arrives it is sorted and neatly laid out in categories according to type, size, and donor. Many hours of hard work are put in by the community to make the event a success.

The following dawn, everything being ready, the challengers go back to the opposition village to tell them to come and get their food. This they do under a barrage of insults to which they pay no attention. Several trips are necessary to carry all the food home. Once there, the foodstuffs are sorted according to type and size so that the dimensions of the debt may be determined and arrangements for repayment made. Now it is *their* turn to construct food platforms and ransack gardens for the public display which, they hope, will dismay the challengers. In setting up this reply to the challenge they must take care to match in variety, quality and quantity the foodstuffs they have received. In addition they make every effort to include extra food which they will force on the challengers and which the challengers will have to pay back.

The next day at sunrise the challengers are advised that they can come and get their food. They arrive and sit unconcernedly in the enemy village, awaiting the next move. At this point the hosts may suddenly bring out a pair of extra pigs or produce a few enormous yams with which to further burden the challengers. Whatever their feelings, the challengers put on poker faces. Their leader thanks the hosts for paying back the food so promptly and for adding a small gift as well. He adds that they will now go off and see if they can't find a small return present. Young notes that 'disparagement of the enemy's efforts to shame them . . . is a quite standardised reaction to a highly charged and hostile political situation' (p. 202).

Phase three occurs on the following day when the challengers pay back the extras they have received and try to add extras of their own. If they manage to do this they will have won the contest. Now the results are calculated, each side noting any debts they may have incurred in the contest. The challenger may find that he owes a platform of taro and a dozen yams. His opponents may still owe several bunches of bananas and a pig. The debts must be paid in time, as and when the principals can manage it. Months later, when looking back on the contest, villagers on both sides may consider it a draw, while each of the principals may conclude that they won. 'Only unmatched pigs and a wide discrepancy in the amount of unpaid vegetable food (particularly yams) can add up to victory or loss' (p. 203).

But any debts must be paid, and it may take years before the affair is settled. In the meantime debtors are in a socially insecure position, while creditors have the advantage, both socially and politically. For a debtor the worst social situation is to be publicly reminded by a creditor that 'I'm still waiting for my yams'.

What is the purpose of *abutu*? It is a course of action open to an individual who has suffered an insult. It thus has its basis in rivalry and offers a means of redress to the person whose prestige is being challenged. It also publicises offences and shames offenders. It serves leaders by providing a means of acquiring prestige. But why should the Massim 'reach for their yams instead of their spears' in such situations? Earlier they did fight it out, but as fighting was suppressed by the Australian Government, *abutu* developed and flourished as an alternative – just as the khans of Afghan Turkestan stopped raiding each other and concentrated their energies on *buzkashi*.

Intense rivalries then may be expressed either in ritual fighting or in some bloodless contest which is none the less effective. Fighting – actual combat – seemed to be the preferred form. This works very well in contests between groups, but is socially disruptive in resolving intra-group rivalries. So if the contest is between members of the same group or if a centralised government has extended its authority umbrella-like over diverse and mutually hostile groups, then other devices for redressing wrongs are needed.

A good example is from Nuristan in north-east Afghanistan. Prior to 1900 this area (known then as Kafiristan) occupied some five thousand square miles of the southern watershed of the Hindu Kush mountain range and contained perhaps seventy or eighty politically and economically independent villages. Groups of villages occupying the same valley were loosely linked by language and marriage ties which formed the basis for occasional political alliances. Communities in different valleys were not only separated by mountain ranges, but by language barriers, and relations were often hostile. But against outsiders, that is, Muslims, they were often willing to set aside their differences and unite for the purpose of carrying out a raid.

For the ambitious warrior there was a series of ranks, titles, and symbols which he could aspire to make his own and there was keen competition among warriors to achieve a higher rank than their rivals. The success of one man was invariably seen by his contemporaries as a challenge, and it also served as an example to village youth. Nor was anyone allowed to forget a rival's achievements; the successful warrior could display certain designs on his jacket, have special rank symbols carved on the front of his house, and could carry a spear or an axe, depending upon his accomplishments. At a feast he could sit in a special place reserved for men of rank and receive certain choice portions of food.

The ambitious giver of public feasts could look forward to similar rewards and, like the warrior, he spent much of his time calculating his resources and planning his next exploit.

All this rivalry and competition was controlled by rules and served society well. By encouraging young men to become warriors it kept the surrounding hostile Muslim communities at bay. Because it encouraged feast-giving, much time and effort were expended in increasing food production, and the results were periodically redistributed throughout the entire community.

As a man rose in rank, so his political influence increased – particularly if he was a good public speaker and had a reputation for wisdom. In time he might come to play a major role in the affairs of his village and even extend his influence to other villages in the valley. In Nuristan there are no chiefs, headmen, or other notables occupying clearly defined positions in a political structure. There are no offices to which authority is attached. Instead, men of influence gravitate to *ad hominem* places which are an amalgam of status, role, prestige, and reputation. Such positions are highly desirable, as are the prizes which mark the individual's road to a position of influence. Competition is keen and rivalries run deep.

With regard to Nuristani culture it seems that certain hypotheses deserve consideration. First of all I suggest that the political system is such that it needs aggressive men; it cannot function without them. Second, the culture is orientated to produce the aggressive individuals needed, and the system is maintained by promoting rivalry between individuals and groups. Third, this aggression needs to be controlled and is channelled into organised competitions which contribute to perpetuating the system and ensuring group survival by offering desirable prizes and achieving political ends.

The Nuristani example is interesting because the system provided two entirely separate avenues to success: warrior exploits and feast-giving – always remembering that the really important man was the one who brought to these accomplishments qualities of wisdom and powers of oratory. We might predict that the suppression of warrior raids by an external centralised authority would lead to an increase in feast-giving. If one road to success is closed, then make use of the other. In fact this did not happen. Both warrior raids and feast-giving declined after the Afghan invasion and the conversion of the population to Islam (1896–1900). The warrior raids declined because the Afghan Government found them inconvenient and punished offenders by sending in the troops. Feast-giving declined because the four-year war wiped out Nuristani live-stock herds, destroyed irrigation systems, and upset the entire economic system, which was slow to recover.

And yet the attitudes and values which were the driving force behind both raiding and feast-giving remained; they are still very much a part of the culture today. The traditional political system also remained virtually unchanged. The villages are still economically and, for all practical purposes, politically independent. Raiding still occurs occasionally, and public feasts are sometimes given in a few villages, but the traditional rank system has fallen into disuse. The competitive spirit, however, is very much alive and rivalries are as strong as ever. Competition now takes place in a new political arena which focuses on dispute settlement and involves factional politics.

Rivalries are often expressed in disputes and today's road to political influence is one of ever-increasing involvement in village affairs, especially dispute settlement.

The prestige that an individual has is put at risk either through direct challenge (losing a contest) or in a general way by the status-enhancing activities of other members of the community (getting left behind). A third and closely related risk to status/prestige is failure to fulfil role expectations. In competition there is more than one way to take a rival down a notch or two. In Nuristan one technique is to steal some of his goats. This is a personal affront, regarded in the culture much as we would regard a slap in the face. It is not the loss of the goats that matters, what hurts is the implication that one is weak enough to be taken advantage of. But the most effective and devastating way to assault a man's personality is to seduce his wife. (One way to get ahead is to put others behind.) The husband, if he is to survive socially and maintain his political influence, has two main courses of action open to him: to track down and kill both his wife and her lover, or allow mediators to arrange a settlement in which the lover publicly pays so heavily in valuables that the husband turns defeat into victory. In either case, as in the duel, such action 'entirely effaces a blot which an insult imprints on the honour'.

As the achievement of rank by means of warrior exploits and feast-giving has been replaced by litigation and factional politics in Nuristan, so in Europe the duel as an institution has presumably given way to other ways of expressing rivalry. Ritual war does, however, still exist today, though we have to go to Melanesia to find it.

In the highlands of New Guinea war is not waged for political reasons. The idea is not to end wars, or to subjugate neighbouring peoples, or to acquire more territory. Robert Gardner and Karl Heider have written that 'the Dani engage in "war" to promote the success and well-being of their social order. In a large measure, their health, welfare and happiness depend on the pursuit of aggression against their traditional enemies. Since their enemies share a common culture, the same considerations motivate them' (Gardner & Heider 1968, p. 136).

Battles are caused by the fact that the living have obligations to the dead and if these obligations are not met the ghosts may cause accidents, illness, and crop failure. The risks of going into battle are less than the risks of leaving the ghosts unavenged.

So institutionalised is this warfare that battles are called by individual members of a small group of war leaders. The enemy is appraised of the impending conflict by a group of men who go at dawn to the frontier and shout the news across no man's land. The challenge will almost certainly be accepted and as word spreads from hamlet to hamlet the warriors gather. Only very distant settlements may decline – especially if it looks like rain – as the battle might be nearly over before they could get there.

Usually by 11 a.m. the warriors have converged on the battleground. Early arrivals sit and wait, it being understood that fighting will not start until both sides are ready. Anything from a hundred to more than three hundred warriors may be involved in a battle. Their weapons are spears and bows and arrows. Actual fighting begins with advance rushes from both sides as small groups in the front ranks run out onto the open field to discharge a few arrows. These groups then fall back and the battle is on.

All along the front scattered warriors dodge spears and arrows while groups of men rush forward from the rear ranks to join in. The main focus of the battle takes place in furious bursts of action lasting ten or fifteen minutes at a time, involving perhaps a hundred men at any given moment. Like a game of chess, offensive and defensive moves follow a pattern well known to the participants. Men are frequently wounded; occasionally killed.

'An average day's fighting will consist of ten to twenty clashes between opposing forces. By late afternoon, when the sun is nearing the top of the western valley wall, the men who have come the furthest will already be leaving, since they want to arrive home before night has completely fallen' (p. 141). After a final exchange of insults both sides withdraw into the gathering darkness. The battle is over, calling to mind Tweedledum's suggestion: 'Let's fight till six, and then have dinner.'

Every male Dani is a warrior. From early childhood his interests and aspirations have centred on warriorhood and the skills required of a warrior. The important men of his tribe are all famous warriors. As Heider has noted, 'skill in warfare is a major factor in the prestige of a man.'

We have traced the pursuit of prestige from the European duel through the game of *buzkashi*, on to the compulsory food exchanges of *abutu*, to factional politics in the Hindu Kush, and finally to ritual war in New Guinea. Of course the selection of examples to illustrate a point proves nothing in itself. But the literature of anthropology and sociology is vast and there is a good deal of evidence to indicate that the pursuit of prestige motivates many of our actions. This is why aggression and competition, in various forms, are themes running through most cultures.

Since the duel has been prohibited in Europe it is perhaps worthwhile to pause and wonder what compensating alternatives we have developed. Where is our *abutu*; our *buzkashi*? Is it to be found on the football field, or in the aggressive tactics of the board room? Are academics crossing swords when they write book reviews? Perhaps it is bound up with many of our institutions. I think it was Macaulay who suggested that most dinner parties are given by way of revenge.

The Social Skin

TERENCE S. TURNER

MAN IS BORN NAKED but is everywhere in clothes (or their symbolic equivalents). We cannot tell how this came to be, but we can say something about why it should be so and what it means.

Decorating, covering, uncovering or otherwise altering the human form in accordance with social notions of everyday propriety or sacred dress, beauty or solemnity, status or changes in status, or on occasion of the violation and inversion of such notions, seems to have been a concern of every human society of which we have knowledge. This objectively universal fact is associated with another of a more subjective nature – that the surface of the body seems everywhere to be treated, not only as the boundary of the individual as a biological and psychological entity but as the frontier of the social self as well. As these two entities are quite different, and as cultures differ widely in the ways they define both, the relation between them is highly problematic. The problems involved, however, are ones that all societies must solve in one way or another, because upon the solution must rest a society's ways of 'socialising' individuals, that is, of integrating them into the societies to which they belong, not only as children but throughout their lives. The surface of the body, as the common frontier of society, the social self, and the psycho-biological individual, becomes the symbolic stage upon which the drama of socialisation is enacted, and bodily adornment (in all its culturally multifarious forms, from body-painting to clothing and from feather head-dresses to cosmetics) becomes the language through which it is expressed.

The adornment and public presentation of the body, however inconsequential or even frivolous a business it may appear to individuals, is for cultures a serious matter: *de la vie sérieuse*, as

An Amazonian Kayapo tribesman, wearing a lip-plug of ground and polished rock crystal, attends to the coiffure of another, shaving his hair to a point at the crown. The head-dress will have ceremonial elaborations of feathers and other colourful adornments. (Alan Hutchison Library)

Durkheim said of religion. Wilde observed that the feeling of being in harmony with the fashion gives a man a measure of security he rarely derives from his religion. The seriousness with which we take questions of dress and appearance is betrayed by the way we regard not taking them seriously as an index, either of a 'serious' disposition or of serious psychological problems. As Lord Chesterfield remarked:

> Dress is a very foolish thing; and yet it is a very foolish thing for a man not to be well dressed, according to his rank and way of life; and it is so far from being a disparagement to any man's understanding, that it is rather a proof of it, to be as well dressed as those whom he lives with: the difference in this case, between a man of sense and a fop, is, that the fop values himself upon his dress; and the man of sense laughs at it, at the same time that he knows that he must not neglect it (cited in Bell 1949, p. 13).

The most significant point of this passage is not the explicit assertion that a man of sense should regard dress with a mixture of contempt and attentiveness, but the implicit claim that by doing so, and thus maintaining his appearance in a way compatible with 'those he lives with', he defines himself as a man of sense. The uneasy ambivalence of the man of sense, whose 'sense' consists in conforming to a practice he laughs at, is the consciousness of a truth that seems as scandalous today as it did in the eighteenth century. This is that culture, which we neither understand nor control, is not only the necessary medium through which we communicate our social status, attitudes, desires, beliefs and ideals (in short, our identities) to others, but also to a large extent constitutes these identities, in ways with which we are compelled to conform regardless of our self-consciousness or even our contempt. Dress and bodily adornment constitute one such cultural medium, perhaps the one most specialised in the shaping and communication of personal and social identity.

The Kayapo are a native tribe of the southern borders of the Amazon forest. They live in widely scattered villages which may attain populations of several hundred. The economy is a

mixture of forest horticulture, and hunting and gathering. The
social organisation of the villages is based on a relatively complex system of institutions, which are clearly defined and
uniform for the population as a whole. The basic social unit is
the extended family household, in which residence is based on
the principle that men must leave their maternal households as
boys and go to live in the households of their wives upon
marriage. In between they live as bachelors in a 'men's house',
generally built in the centre of the circular village plaza, round
the edges of which are ranged the 'women's houses' (as the
extended family households are called). Women, on the other
hand, remain from birth to death in the households into which
they are born.

The Kayapo possess a quite elaborate code of what could be
called 'dress', a fact which might escape notice by a casual
Western observer because it does not involve the use of
clothing. A well turned out adult Kayapo male, with his large
lower-lip plug (a saucer-like disc some six centimetres across),
penis sheath (a small cone made of palm leaves covering the
glans penis), large holes pierced through the ear lobes from
which hang small strings of beads, overall body paint in red and
black patterns, plucked eyebrows, eyelashes and facial hair,
and head shaved to a point at the crown with the hair left long
at the sides and back, could on the other hand hardly leave the
most insensitive traveller with the impression that bodily
adornment is a neglected art among the Kayapo. There are,
however, very few Western observers, including anthropologists, who have ever taken the trouble to go beyond the
superficial recording of such exotic paraphernalia to inquire
into the system of meanings and values which it evokes for its
wearers. A closer look at Kayapo bodily adornment discloses
that the apparently naked savage is as fully covered in a fabric
of cultural meaning as the most elaborately draped Victorian
lady or gentleman.

The first point that should be made about Kayapo notions of
propriety in bodily appearance is the importance of cleanliness.
All Kayapo bathe at least once a day. To be dirty, and
especially to allow traces of meat, blood or other animal substances or food to remain on the skin, is considered not merely
slovenly or dirty but actively anti-social. It is, moreover,

dangerous to the health of the unwashed person. 'Health' is conceived as a state of full and proper integration into the social world, while illness is conceived in terms of the encroachment of natural, and particularly animal forces upon the domain of social relations. Cleanliness, as the removal of all 'natural' excrescence from the surface of the body, is thus the essential first step in 'socialising' the interface between self and society, embodied in concrete terms by the skin. The removal of facial and bodily hair carries out this same fundamental principle of transforming the skin from a mere 'natural' envelope of the physical body into a sort of social filter, able to contain within a social form the biological forces and libidinal energies that lie beneath.

The mention of bodily hair leads on to a consideration of the treatment of the hair of the head. The principles that govern coiffure are consistent with the general notions of cleanliness, hygiene, and sociality, but are considerably more developed, and accord with those features of the head-hair which the Kayapo emphasise as setting it apart from bodily hair (it is even called by a different name).

Hair, like skin, is a 'natural' part of the surface of the body, but unlike skin it continually grows outwards, erupting from the body into the social space beyond it. Inside the body, beneath the skin, it is alive and growing; outside, beyond the skin, it is dead and without sensation, although its growth manifests the unsocialised biological forces within. The hair of the head thus focuses the dynamic and unstable quality of the frontier between the 'natural', bio-libidinous forces of the inner body and the external sphere of social relations. In this context, hair offers itself as a symbol of the libidinal energies of the self and of the never-ending struggle to constrain within acceptable forms their eruption into social space.

So important is this symbolic function of hair as a focus of the socialising function, not only among the Kayapo but among Central Brazilian tribes in general, that variations in coiffure have become the principal visible means of distinguishing one tribe from another. Each people has its own distinctive hairstyle, which stands as the emblem of its own culture and social community (and as such, in its own eyes, for the highest level of sociality to have been attained by humanity). The Kayapo tribal coiffure, used by both men and women, consists of shaving the hair above the forehead upwards to a point at the crown, leaving the hair long at the back and sides of the head (unless the individual belongs to one of the special categories of people who wear their hair cut short, as described below). Men may tease up a little widow's peak at the point of the triangular shaved area. The sides of this area are often painted in black with bands of geometrical patterns.

Certain categories of people in Kayapo society are *privileged* to wear their hair long. Others must keep it cut short. Nursing infants, women who have borne children, and men who have received their penis sheaths and have been through initiation (that is, those who have been socially certified as able to carry on sexual relations) wear their hair long. Children and adolescents of both sexes (girls from weaning to childbirth, boys from weaning to initiation) and those mourning the death of a member of their immediate family (for example, a spouse, sibling or child) have their hair cut short.

To understand this social distribution of long and short hair it is necessary to comprehend Kayapo notions about the nature of family relations. Parents are thought to be connected to their children, and siblings to one another, by a tie that goes deeper than a mere social or emotional bond. This tie is imagined as a sort of spiritual continuation of the common physical substance that they share through conception and the womb. This relation of biological participation lasts throughout life but is broken by death. The death of a person's child or sibling thus directly diminishes his or her own biological being and energies. Although spouses lack the intrinsic biological link of blood relations, their sexual relationship constitutes a 'natural' procreative, libidinal community that is its counterpart. In as much as both sorts of biological relationship are cut off by death, cutting off the hair, conceived as the extension of the biological energy of the self into social space, is the symbolically appropriate response to the death of a spouse as well as a child.

The same concrete logic accounts for the treatment of children's hair. While a child is still nursing, it is still, as it were, an extension of the biological being and energies of its parents, and above all, at this stage, the mother. In these terms nursing constitutes a kind of external and attenuated final stage of

118   *Adult Play*

pregnancy. Weaning is the decisive moment of the 'birth' of the
child as a separate biological and social being. Thus nursing
infants' hair is never cut, and is left to grow as long as that of
sexually active adults: infants at this stage *are* still the extensions of the biological and sexual being of their long-haired
parents. Cutting the infant's hair at the onset of weaning aptly
symbolises the severance of this bio-sexual continuity (or, as we
would say, its repression). Henceforth, the child's hair remains
short as a sign of its biological separation from its parents, on
the one hand, and the undeveloped state of its own bio-sexual
powers on the other. When these become strong enough to be
socially extended, through sexual intercourse and procreation,
as the basis of a new family, the hair is once again allowed to
grow to full length. For men this point is considered to arrive at
puberty, and specifically with the bestowal of a penis sheath,
which is ideally soon followed by initiation (a symbolic 'marriage' which signals marriageability, or 'bachelorhood', rather
than being a binding union in and of itself).

The discrepancy in the timing of the return to long hair for
the two sexes reflects a fundamental difference in Kayapo
notions of their respective social roles. 'Society' is epitomised
for the Kayapo by the system of communal societies and age-
sets centred on the men's house. These collective organisations
are primarily a male domain, as their association with the
men's house suggests, although women have certain societies of
their own. The communal societies are defined in terms of the
criteria for recruitment, and this is always defined as a corollary
of some important transformation in family or household structure (such as a boy's moving out of his maternal family household to the men's house, marriage, the birth of children, etc.).
These transformations in family relations are themselves
associated with key points in the process of growth and sexual
development.

The structure of communal groups, then, constitutes a sort of
sociological mechanism for reproducing, not only itself but the
structure of the extended family households that form the lower
level or personal sphere of Kayapo social organisation. This
communal institutional structure, on the other hand, is itself
defined in terms of the various stages of the bio-sexual
development of men (and to a much lesser extent, women). All

this comes down to the proposition that men reproduce society through the transformation of their 'natural' biological and libidinal powers into collective social form. This conception can be found elaborated in Kayapo mythology.

Women, by contrast, reproduce the natural biological individual, and, as a corollary, the elementary family, which the Kayapo conceive as a 'natural' or infra-social set of essentially physical relations. Inasmuch as the whole Kayapo system works on the principle of the cooption of 'natural' forces and their channelling into social form, it follows that women's biological forces of reproduction should be exercised only within the framework of the structure of social relations reproduced by men. The effective social extension of a woman's biological reproductive powers therefore occurs at the moment of the first childbirth within the context of marriage, husband and household. This is, accordingly, the moment at which a woman begins to let her hair grow long again. For men, as we have seen, the decisive social cooption of libidinal energy or reproductive power comes earlier, at the point at which those powers are publicly appropriated for purposes of the reproduction of the collective social order. This is the moment symbolically marked by the bestowal of the penis sheath at puberty.

The penis sheath, then, symbolises the collective appropriation of male powers of sexual reproduction for the purposes of social reproduction. To the Kayapo, the appropriation of 'natural' or biological powers for social purposes implies the suppression of their 'natural' or socially unrestrained forms of expression. The penis sheath works as a symbol of the channelling of male libidinal energies into social form by effectively restraining the spontaneous, 'natural' expression of male sexuality: in a word, erection. The sheath, the small cone of woven palm leaf, is open at both the wide and narrow ends. The wide end fits over the tip of the penis, while the narrow end has an aperture just wide enough to enable the foreskin to be drawn through it. Once pulled through, it bunches up in a way that holds the sheath down on the *glans penis*, and pushes the penis as a whole back into the body. This obviously renders erection impossible. A public erection, or even the publicly visible protrusion of the *glans penis* through the foreskin without erection, is as embarrassing for a Kayapo male as walking naked through one's town or work place would be for a Westerner. It is the action of the sheath in preventing such an eventuality that is the basis of its symbolic meaning.

Just as the cutting or growing of hair becomes a code for defining and expressing a whole system of ideas about the nature of the individual and society and the relations between the two, so other types of bodily adornment are used to express other modalities of the same basic relationships.

Pierced ears, ear-plugs, and lip-plugs comprise a similar distinct complex of social meanings. Here the emphasis is on the socialisation, not of sexual powers, but of the faculties of understanding and active self-expression. The Kayapo distinguish between passive and active modes of knowing. Passive understanding is associated with hearing, active knowledge of how to make and do things with seeing. The most important aspect of the socialisation of the passive faculty of understanding is the development of the ability to 'hear' language. To be able to hear and understand speech is spoken of in terms of 'having a hole in one's ear'; to be deaf is 'to have the hole in one's ear closed off'. The ear lobes of infants of both sexes are pierced, and large cigar-shaped ear-plugs, painted red, are inserted to stretch the holes to a diameter of two or three centimetres (I shall return to the significance of the red colour). At weaning (by which time the child has learned to speak and understand language) the ear-plugs are removed, and little strings of beads like earrings are tied through the holes to keep them open. Kayapo continue to wear these bead earrings, or simply leave their ear-lobe-holes empty throughout adult life. I suggest that the piercing and stretching of these secondary, social 'holes-in-the-ear' through the early use of the ear-plugs for infants is a metaphor for the socialisation of the understanding, the opening of the years to language and all that implies, which takes place during the first years of infancy.

The lip-plug, which reaches such a large size among older men, is incontestably the most striking piece of Kayapo finery. Only males have their lips pierced. This happens soon after birth, but at first only a string of beads with a bit of shell is placed in the hole to keep it open. After initiation, young bachelors begin to put progressively larger wooden pins through the hole to enlarge it. This gradual process continues through the early years of adult manhood, but accelerates when a man graduates to the senior male grade of 'fathers-of-many-children'. These are men of an age to have become heads of their wives' households, with married daughters and thus sons-in-law living under their roofs as quasi-dependents. Such men have considerable social authority, but they wield it, not within the household itself (which is considered a woman's domain) but rather in the public arena of the communal men's house, in the form of political oratory. Public speaking, in an ornate and blustering style, is the most characteristic attribute of senior manhood, and is the essential medium of political power. An even more specialised form of speaking, a kind of metrical chanting known as *ben*, is the distinctive prerogative of chiefs, who are called 'chanters' in reference to the activity that most embodies their authority.

Public speaking, and chanting as its more rarified and potent form, are the supreme expression of the values of Kayapo society considered as a politically ordered hierarchy. Senior men, and, among them, chiefs, are the dominant figures in this hierarchy, and it can therefore be said that oratory and chanting as public activities express this dominance as a value implicit in the Kayapo social order. The lip-plug of the senior male, as a physical expression of the oral assertiveness and pre-eminence of the orator, embodies the social dominance and expressiveness of the senior males of whom it is the distinctive badge.

The senior male lip-plug is in these terms the complement of the pierced ears of both sexes and the infantile ear-plugs from which they derive. The former is associated with the active expression and political construction of the social order, while the latter betoken the receptiveness to such expressions as the attribute of all socialised persons. Speaking and 'hearing' (that is, understanding and conforming) are the complementary and interdependent functions that constitute the Kayapo polity. Through the symbolic medium of bodily adornment, the body of every Kayapo becomes a microcosm of the Kayapo body politic.

As a man grows old he retires from active political life. He speaks in public less often, and on the occasions when he does it is to assume an elder statesman's role of appealing to common values and interests rather than to take sides. The transformation from the politically active role of the senior man to the more honorific if less dynamic role of elder statesman is once again signalled by a change in the style and shape of the lip-plug. The simplest form this can take is a diminution in the size of the familiar wooden disc. It may, however, take the form of the most precious and prestigious object in the entire Kayapo wardrobe – the cylindrical lip-plug of ground and polished rock crystal worn only by elder males. These neolithic valuables, which may reach six inches in length and one inch in diameter, with two small flanges at the upper end to keep them from sliding through the hole in the lip, require immense amounts of time to make and are passed down as heirlooms within families. They are generally clear to milky white in colour. White is associated with old age and with ghosts, and thus in general terms with the transcendence of the social divisions and trans-formations whose qualities are evoked by the two main Kayapo colours, black and red. This quality of transcendence of social conflict, and of direct involvement in the processes of suppres-sion and appropriation of libidinal energies and their transfor-mation into social form which constitute Kayapo public life in its political and ritual aspects, is characteristic of the content of the oratory of old men, and is what lends it its great if relatively innocuous prestige. Once again, then, we find that the symbolic qualities of the lip-plug match the social qualities of the speech of its wearer.

Before the advent of Western clothes, Kayapo of both sexes and all ages constantly went about with their bodies painted (many still do, especially in the more remote villages). The Kayapo have raised body painting to an art, and the variety and elaborateness of the designs is apt to seem overwhelming upon first acquaintance. Analysis, however, reveals that a few simple principles run through the variation of forms and styles and lend coherence to the whole. These principles, in turn, can be seen to add a further dimension to the total system of meanings conveyed by Kayapo bodily adornment.

There are two main aspects to the Kayapo art of body painting, one concerning the association of the two main col-ours used (red and black) on distinct zones of the body, the other concerning the two basic styles employed in painting that part of the body for which black is used.

To begin with the first aspect, the use of the two colours, black and red, and their association with different regions of the body reveal yet another dimension of Kayapo ideas about the make-up of the person as biological being and social actor. Black is applied to the trunk of the body, the upper arms and thighs. Black designs or stripes are also painted on the cheeks, forehead, and occasionally across the eyes or mouth. Red is applied to the calves and feet, forearms and hands, and face, especially around the eyes. Sometimes it is smeared over black designs already painted on the face, to render the whole face red.

Black is associated with the idea of transformation between society and unsocialised nature. The word for black is applied to the zone just outside the village that one passes through to enter the 'wild' forest (the domain of nature). It is also the word for death (that is, the first phase of death, while the body is still decomposing and the soul has not yet forsaken its social ties to become a ghost: ghosts are white). In both of these usages, the term for black applies to a spatial or temporal zone of transition between the social world and the world of natural or infra-social forces that is closed off from society proper and lies beyond its borders. It is therefore appropriate that black is applied to the surface of those parts of the body conceived to be the seat of its 'natural' powers and energies (the trunk, internal and reproductive organs, major muscles, etc.) that are in them-selves beyond the reach of socialisation (an analogy might be drawn here to the Freudian notion of the id). The black skin becomes the repressive boundary between the natural powers of the individual and the external domain of social relations.

Red, by contrast, is associated with notions of vitality, energy and intensification. It is applied to the peripheral points of the body that come directly into contact with the outside world (the hands and feet, and the face with its sensory organs, especially the eyes). The principle here seems to be the intensification of the individual's powers of relating to the external (that is, primarily, the social) world. Notice that the opposition be-tween *red* (intensification, vitalisation) and *black* (repression) coincides with that between the *peripheral* and *central* parts of the body, which is itself treated as a form of the relationship between the *surface* and *inside* of the body respectively. The contrasting use of the two colours thus establishes a binary classification of the human body and its powers and relates that classification back to the conceptual oppositions, *inside: surface: outside*, that underlies the system of bodily adornment as a whole.

Turning now to the second major aspect of the system of body painting, that is, the two main styles of painting in black, the best place to begin is with the observation that one style is used primarily for children and one primarily for adults. The children's style is by far the more elaborate. It consists of intricate geometrical designs traced in black with a narrow stylus made from the central rib of a leaf. A child's entire body from the neck to below the knees, and down the arms to below the elbows, is covered. To do the job properly requires a couple of hours. Mothers (occasionally doting aunts or grandmothers) spend much time in this way keeping their children 'well dressed'.

The style involves building up a coherent overall pattern out of many individually insignificant lines, dots, etc. The final result is unique, as a snowflake is unique. The idiosyncratic nature of the design reflects the relationship between the painter and the child being decorated. Only one child is painted at a time, in his or her own house, by his or her own mother or another relation. All of this reflects the social position of the young child and the nature of the process of socialisation it is undergoing. The child is the object of a prolonged and intensive process of creating a socially acceptable form out of a myriad of individually unordered elements. It must lie still and submit to this process, which requires a certain amount of discipline. The finished product is the unique expression of the child's relationship to its own mother and household. It is not a collectively stereotyped pattern establishing a common identity with children from other families. This again conforms with the social situation of the child, which is not integrated into communal society above the level of its particular family.

Boys cease to be painted in this style, except for rare ceremonial occasions, when they leave home to live in the men's house. Older girls and women, however, continue to paint one another in this way as an occasional pastime. This use of the infantile style by women reflects the extent to which they remain identified with their individual families and households, in contrast to men's identification with collective groups at the communal level.

The second style, which can be used for children when a mother lacks the time or inclination for a full-scale job in the first style, is primarily associated with adults. It consists of standardised designs, many of which have names (generally names of the animals they are supposed to resemble). These designs are simple, consisting of broad strokes that can be applied quickly with the hand, rather than by the time-consuming stylus method. Their social context of application is typically collective: men's age sets gathered in the men's house, or women's societies, which meet fortnightly in the village plaza for the purpose of painting one another. On such occasions, a uniform style is generally used for the whole group (different styles may be used to distinguish structurally distinct groups, such as bachelors and mature men).

The second style is thus typically used by fully socialised adults, acting in a collective capacity (that is, at a level defined by common participation in the structure of the community as a whole rather than at the individual family level). Collective action (typically, though not necessarily, of a ritual character) is 'socialising' in the higher sense of directly constituting and reproducing the structure of society as a whole: those painted in the adult style are thus acting, not in the capacity of *objects* of socialisation, but as its *agents*. The 'animal' quality of the designs is evocative of this role; the Kayapo conceive of collective society-constituting activities, like their communal ceremonies, as the transformation of 'natural' or animal qualities into social form by means of collective social replication. The adult style, with its 'animal' designs applied collectively to social groups as an accompaniment to collective activity, epitomises these meanings and ideas. The contrasts between the children's and adults' styles of body painting thus model key contrasts in the social attributes of children and adults, specifically, their relative levels of social integration or, which comes to the same thing, their degree of 'socialisation'.

The greater part of Kayapo communal activity consists of the celebration of long and complex ceremonies, which generally take the form of collective dances by all the men and boys or all the women and girls of the village, and occasionally of both. These sacred events are always distinguished by collective body-painting and renewed coiffures in the tribal pattern, as well as by numerous special items of ritual regalia, such as feather head-dresses, elaborate bracelets, ear- and lip-plugs of special design, belts and leg bands hung with noise-making objects like tapir or peccary hooves etc. The more important ceremonies are rites either of 'baptism', that is, the bestowal of ceremonially prestigious names, or initiation. Certain items of regalia distinguish those actually receiving names or being initiated from the mass of celebrants. In a more fundamental sense, the entire repertoire of ceremonial costume marks ceremonial activity in contrast to everyday activities and relations. In the ceremonial context itself, the contrast is preserved between the celebrants of the ceremony and the non-participating spectators, who wear no special costume. An important group in the latter category are the parents of the children being named or initiated in the ceremony, who may not take a direct part in the dancing but must work hard to supply the many dancers with food. In this role they are treated with great rudeness and disrespect by the actual celebrants, who shout at them to bring food and then complain loudly about its quantity and quality.

Kayapo bodily adornment in its secular and sacred forms constitutes an integral system of differentiated categories of social status, together with the roles, or modes of activity and relationship characteristic of each status. This comprehensive social classification is represented in Table 1A. The various forms of bodily adornment that distinguish each category, together with the roles or modes of activity they symbolise, are summarised in Table 1B. Note that the distinctions among the various forms of sacred and secular 'dress' in Table 1B generate the full structure of Table 1A.

The names bestowed in the great naming ceremonies belong to a special class of 'beautiful' names which are passed down from certain categories of kinsmen (mother's brother, and both maternal and paternal grandfathers for boys, father's sister and both grandmothers for girls). In keeping with the ritual prestige of the names being transmitted to them, the children being honoured in the ceremony are adorned with special regalia, notably elaborate bracelets with bead and feather pendants. Initiands are similarly distinguished by bracelets, although they are so huge as to cover the whole forearm, and are exceptionally heavy and bulky in construction. The initiation ceremony itself is named after these bracelets; it is known as 'the black bracelets', or literally 'black bone marrow'. The name at first strikes one as odd, since the bracelets are painted bright red. It may be suggested that the symbolic appropriateness of bracelets as the badges of initiands and baptisands derives from the same set of ideas about the connotations of different parts of the body and the associated colour symbolism. If the extremities of the body represent the extension of the psycho-biological level of the self into social space, and if the hands are in a sense the prototypical extremities in this regard, elaborate bracelets are an apt symbol for the imposition of social form upon this extension. This is, of course, what is happening in the ceremonies in question. In the case of initiation into manhood, which involves a first, symbolic marriage, both the repression of childish, merely individualistic libido and the accentuation of sexuality and procreativity in the service of social reproduction are involved. Black and red, as we have seen, are the symbols of repression and sensory accentuation, respectively, and the accentuation of sexuality and procreativity in the service of social reproduction are involved. That what is 'blackened' or repressed is the inner substance of the bones aptly conveys the idea of the suppression of the presocial, biological basis of social relatedness, while the actual redness of the so-called 'black' bracelets through which this is achieved simultaneously expresses the activation of this basis in the social form represented by the bracelets themselves. The initiation bracelets thus condense within themselves a number of the fundamental principles of the whole system of bodily adornment and the social concepts it expresses.

Among the ordinary ritual celebrants, there is considerable variation within the standard categories of ritual wear, such as feather head-dresses, ear-plugs, necklaces, bracelets and belts or leg bands already described. Many of these variations (for example, the use of feathers from a particular sort of bird for a head-dress, or distinctive materials such as wound cotton

		SACRED (more prestigious)	SECULAR (less prestigious)
SOCIAL	(relatively socialised)	initiands, baptisands	senior men / junior men
		ritual celebrants	women — ADULTS
NATURAL	(relatively unsocialised)	spectators	CHILDREN / older children
		parents of initiands	infants

TABLE 1A: *Kayapo social classification: status*

	SACRED	SECULAR				
SOCIAL	*Undergoing initiation,* *Receiving names* special bracelets	*Expressiveness* lip-plug small/large	*Socialised* *procreativity* penis sheath	*Physical* *extension: children* long hair	*Agent of socialisation* adult painting style	*Socialised understanding* ear holes
	Dancer in ceremony ritual ornaments					
NATURAL	*Spectator or* *parent-'worker'* no ornaments			*No physical* *extension* short hair	*Object of socialisation* children's painting style	
				Physical *extension* *of parents* long hair		*No* *understanding* ear-plugs

TABLE 1B: *Kayapo classification of roles (qualities and modes of social activity) with 'dress' indicators* string or perhaps fresh-water mussel shells for ear-plugs, or the breast plumage of the red macaw for bracelets, etc.) are passed down like names themselves from uncle or grandfather to nephew or grandson (or the corresponding female categories). They thus denote an aspect of the social identity of the wearer that he or she owes to his or her relationship with a particular kinsman. These distinctive items of ritual dress make up the 'paraphernalia' mentioned above that is bestowed, in parallel to, but separately from, names, in the ritual setting. The Kayapo call such accessories by their general (and only) term for 'valuables', 'wealth', or 'riches'.

Ask a Kayapo why he is wearing a certain sort of head-dress for a ceremonial dance, and he will be likely to answer, 'It is my wealth.' Ask him why he dances, or indeed why the ceremony is being performed, and he will almost certainly answer, 'To be beautiful' ('For the sake of beauty' would be an equally accurate Englishing of the usual Kayapo expression). Wealth and beauty are closely connected notions among the Kayapo, and both refer to aspects of the person coded by items of prestigious ritual dress. Certain 'beautiful' names are, in fact, associated with specific forms of adornment (that is, with certain types of 'wealth') such as ear-plugs. 'Beautiful people' (those who have received 'beautiful' names in ceremonies) generally possess more 'wealth' than 'common people' who have not gone through a ritual baptism, and thus possess only 'common' names.

The connection of 'beauty' with 'wealth' in the form of bodily adornment is strikingly expressed in the lyrics of the choral hymns sung by the massed ritual celebrants as they dance, with uniform steps which vary with each song, the successive rites that constitute a 'great' or 'beautiful' naming ceremony. These songs are almost invariably those of animals, especially birds, the muses of Kayapo lyric and dance, who have communicated them to humans in various ways. Two verses from the vast Kayapo repertoire may serve as examples. A bird proudly boasts to his human listener,

Can we [birds] not reach up to the sky?
Why, we can snatch the very clouds,
Wind them round our legs as bracelets,
And sit thus, regaled by their thunder.

Another calls out a stirring summons to earthbound humanity:

> I fly among the branches [rays] of the sun;
> I fly among the branches of the sun.
> I perch on its branches and
> Sit gazing over the whole world.
>
> Throw yourselves into the sky beside me!
> Throw yourselves into the sky beside me!
> Cover yourselves with the blood and feathers of birds
> And follow after me!

The admonition about blood and feathers refers to the technique of covering the body of a dancer with his or her own blood, which is then used as an adhesive to which the breast plumage or down of macaws, vultures or eagles is fixed. This is perhaps the most prestigious ('beautiful') form of sacred costume. These verses may help one to grasp the connotations of the fact that dancing (and by extension, the celebration of any ritual) is called 'flying' in Kayapo, and of the term for the most common item of ceremonial adornment, the feather head-dress, which is the ritual form of the word for 'bird'.

Birds fly, and 'can scan' the *whole* world. They are not confined by its divisions, but transcend them in a way that to a Kayapo seems the supreme natural metaphor for the direct experience of totality, the integration of the self through the perception of the wholeness of the world. This principle of wholeness, the transcendental integration of what ordinary human (that is, social) life separates and puts at odds, is the essence of the Kayapo notion of 'beauty'.

Two aspects of this notion, as embodied in items of ritual costume and the sacred activities in which they are worn, seem incongruous and even contradictory in the context of what has already been said about everyday Kayapo 'dress' and its underlying assumptions. First, whereas everyday bodily adornment stresses the imposition of social form upon the 'natural' energies and powers of the individual, ritual costume (such as feather head-dresses, body painting with 'animal' designs or the covering of the body with blood and feathers) seems to represent the opposite idea: that is, the imposition of natural form upon social actors engaged in what are the most important social activities of all, the great sacred performances that periodically reconstitute the fabric of society itself. Secondly, sacred costume, together with the notion that the ritual songs and dances themselves originate among wild animals and birds, seems to reverse the meaning of everyday bodily adornment. The latter is implicitly based upon a relation between a 'natural' core (the human body, or on the sociological level, the elementary family) and a 'social' periphery (the space outside the body in which social interaction takes place, or in the structure of kinship, the more distant blood relations outside the immediate family who bestow names and ritual paraphernalia upon the child). Ritual space, in contrast, seems based on the relationship between a 'natural' periphery (the jungle beyond the village boundary, as the abode of the birds and animals that are the sources both of ritual costume and of the rituals themselves) and a 'social' centre (the central plaza of the village, where the sacred dances are actually performed).

This inversion of space and the fundamental relationship of nature to society encoded in sacred costume turns out upon closer examination to parallel two other inversions in the organisation of everyday social relations which form the very basis of the sacred ceremonial system. The first of these involves the types of kinship relations involved in the key ritual relations of name giving and the bestowing of ritual 'wealth' (such as special paraphernalia), as contrasted with those involved in the transformations of family relations marked by the everyday complex of bodily adornment (penis sheath, ear- and lip-plugs, etc.). The latter typically involve immediate family relations like parent–child, husband–wife, or the key extended-family relationship of son-in-law to father-in-law. These relations have in common that they directly link status within the family, or two families by marriage; they may therefore be thought of as *direct* relations. Ritual relations, on the other hand, connect grandparents and grandchildren, uncles and nephews, aunts and nieces: they skip over the connecting relatives (the parents of the children receiving the ritual names or paraphernalia, who are themselves the children or siblings of the name-bestowing relatives) and may thus be described as *indirect* relations.

The structure of *direct* relations functions as a sort of ladder or series of steps up which the developing individual moves from status to status within the structure of the families, extended families and households to which he or she belongs in the course of his or her life. The first step in this process is the 'natural' domain of immediate family relations, within which the individual is at first defined as merely an extension of his or her parents' 'natural' powers of reproduction. The course of the life cycle from there on is a series of steps by which the individual is detached from this primal 'natural' unity and integrated into the social life of the community. As a corollary of this process, his or her own 'natural' powers develop until they can in turn become the basis of a new family. The highest step in the socialisation process, however, comes when this second 'natural' family unit is dispersed, and the individual becomes a parent-in-law, thus moving into the prestigious role of extended family household head at home and, in the case of men, political leader in the community at large. Each major step in this process is marked, as we have seen, by modifications of bodily adornment of the 'everyday' sort. The overall form of the process is that of a progressive evacuation of 'natural' energy and powers from the 'central' sources of body and elementary family and its extrapolation into social forms and powers standing in a 'peripheral' relation to these sources in physical and social space. The result is that 'social' structure is created at the expense of the evacuation and dispersal of the 'natural' powers and relational units (elementary families) that comprise its foundation. The 'natural' at any given moment is the socially *un*integrated: embodied at the beginning of the process by the newborn infant or new family, as yet not completely absorbed into the wider community of social relations, by the end of the process it is represented by the scattered members of dispersed families, whose younger members have gone on to form new families. The integration of society made possible by this transformation is achieved at the cost of the dis-integration of the primal natural community of the immediate family and the externalisation and social appropriation of the 'natural' powers of the individual.

Seen in this perspective the ritual system represents a balancing of accounts. The dispersed *direct*, 'natural' relations of the parents (their parents and siblings from the family they have left behind) now become the key *indirect* relations whose identification with the children of these same parents becomes the point of the ritual. I use the term 'identification' deliberately, for this is what is implied by the sharing of personal names and idiosyncratic items of ritual costume. The point of this identification is, of course, that it reasserts a connection between, or in other words reintegrates, the dispersed, disintegrated or 'natural' relations of the parents' previous families with the not-yet-socially-integrated relations of the parents' present family (their children). This integration, however, is achieved, not on the basis of *direct* relations as is characteristic of 'natural' groups like the elementary family, but on a new, *indirect* footing with no natural basis; in short, on a purely 'social' basis. The new integrated 'whole' that is established through ritual action is thus defined simultaneously as reintegrating and transcending the 'natural' basis of social relations. It therefore becomes the quintessential prototype of 'social' relationship, and as such, the appropriate vehicle of the basic components of individual social identity, personal names, distinctive ritual dress and other personal 'wealth'.

In terms of social space, what has happened from the point of view of the central name-receiving individual and her or his family is that 'socialisation' has been achieved through the transference of attributes of the identity of 'natural' relations located on the *periphery* of the family to the actor located at its *centre*. In terms of the equilibrium of 'natural' and 'social' forces and qualities, the prospective evacuation of natural powers from the individual and family has been offset (in advance) by an infusion of social attributes, which are themselves the products of the reintegration, through the social mechanism of ritual action, of elements of the 'natural' infrastructure dispersed as the price of social integration.

The symbolic integration of 'natural' attributes from the periphery of social space as aspects of the social identity of actors located at its centre, can now be understood as a metaphorical embodiment of the integrative ('beautiful') structural properties of the social relations evoked by the rituals. The regalia, of course, does more than simply encode this process. It is the concrete medium (along with names) through which the identity of the ritual celebrants is simultaneously redefined, 'socialised', and infused with 'beauty'.

The foregoing analysis should help to clarify the full meaning of the Kayapo notion of beauty as wholeness, integration or completion. In its primary context, that of sacred ritual, it is the value associated with the creation of a *social* whole based on *indirect* (mediate) relations, capable of reintegrating the dismembered elements of simpler *natural* wholes (elementary families) constituted by *direct* (immediate) relations. 'Beauty' is an ideal expression of society itself in its holistic capacity. It is, as such, one of the primary values of Kayapo social life.

Just as the value of beauty is associated with the complex of social relations and cultural notions involved in ritual action, so the complex of relations and categories that constitutes the social structure of everyday life is focused upon another general social value. This value is in a sense the opposite of beauty, since it pertains to relations of separation, opposition, and inequality. We may call it 'dominance', meaning by that the combination of prestige, authority, individual autonomy and ability to control others that accrues in increasing measure to individuals as they move through the stages of social development, passing from lower to higher status in the structure of the extended family and community. It is doubtless significant that the Kayapo themselves do not name this intrinsically divisive value with any term in their own language, whereas they continually employ the adjective 'beautiful' in connection with the most varied activities, including those of a divisive (and thus 'ugly') character which they wish to put in a better light.

The lack of a term notwithstanding, there can be no doubt of the existence of the value in question and its importance as the organising focus of Kayapo social and political life outside the ritual sphere. It reaches its highest and most concentrated expression in the public activities of senior men, for example their characteristic activity of aggressively flamboyant oratory. The lip-plug, and particularly the senior man's lip-plug as the largest and most spectacularly obtrusive in the entire age-graded lip-plug series, is directly associated with this value as a quality of male, and particularly senior male, social identity. 'Dominance' is, however, to be understood as a symbolic attribute, a culturally imputed quality expressing a person's place in the hierarchy of extended family and community structure, rather than as a relation of naked power or forcible oppression. It is, as such, an expression of the whole edifice of age, sex, family and communal status-categories marked by the whole system of everyday bodily accoutrements described earlier. Younger men and women can acquire this quality in some measure within their own proper spheres, making due allowance for the fact that in the context of community-wide relations they are subordinate to the dominant senior males.

These two values, 'dominance' and 'beauty', inform the social activities and goals of every Kayapo, and constitute the most general purposes of social action and the most important qualities of personal identity. The identity of social actors is constituted as much by the goals towards which they direct their activities, as by their classification according to status, sex, age, degree of socialisation, etc. I have tried to show that bodily adornment encodes these values as well as the other sorts of categories; it may thus be said to define the total social identity of the individual, meaning his or her subjective identity as a social actor, as well as objective identity conceived in terms of a set of social categories. It does this by mediating between individuals, considered both in their objective and subjective capacities, and society, also considered both in its objective capacity as a structure of relations and its subjective capacity as a system of values. I have attempted to demonstrate that the symbolic mediation effected by the code of bodily adornment in both these respects is, in the terms of Kayapo culture, systematically and finely attuned to the nuances of Kayapo social relations. The structure of Kayapo society, including its highest values and its most fundamental conceptual presuppositions (such as the nature–culture relationship, the modes of expression and understanding, the character of 'socialisation', etc.) could be read from the paint and ornaments of a representative collection of Kayapo of all ages, sexes, and secular and ritual roles.

Bodily adornment, considered as a symbolic medium, is not unique in these respects: every society has a number of such media or languages, the most important among which is of course language itself. The distinctive place of the adornment of the body among these is that it is the medium most directly and concretely concerned with the construction of the individual as social actor or cultural 'subject'. This is a fundamental concern of all societies and social groups, and this is why the imposition of a standardised symbolic form upon the body, as a symbol or 'objective correlative' of the social self, invariably becomes a serious business for all societies, regardless of whether their members as individuals consciously take the matter seriously or not.

It may be suggested that the 'construction of the subject', is a process which is broadly similar in all human societies, and the study of systems of bodily adornment is one of the best ways of comprehending what it involves. As the Kayapo example serves to illustrate, it is essentially a question of the conflation of certain basic types of social notions and categories, among which can be listed categories of time and space, modes of activity (for example, individual or collective, secular or sacred), types of social status (sex, age, family roles, political positions, etc.), personal qualities (degree of 'socialisation', relative passivity or activity as a social actor, etc.) and modes of social value, for example, 'dominance' or 'beauty'. In any given society, of course, these basic categories will be combined in culturally idiosyncratic ways to constitute the symbolic medium of bodily adornment, and these synthetic patterns reveal much about the basic notions of value, social action, and person- or self-hood of the culture in question.

In the case of the Kayapo, three broad synthetic clusters of meanings and values of this type emerge from analysis. One is concerned with the Kayapo notion of socialisation, conceived as the transformation of 'natural' powers and attributes into social forms. The basic symbolic vehicle for this notion, after the general concern for cleanliness, is the form of body painting by which the trunk is contrasted with the extremities as black and red zones, respectively. This fundamental mapping of the body's 'natural' and 'social' areas is inflected, at a higher level of articulation, by hair style. The contrast between long and short hair is used to mark the successive phases of the development and social extension of the individual's libidinous and reproductive powers. Finally, the penis sheath (correlated with the shift to long hair for men) serves to mark the decisive point in the social appropriation of male reproductive powers and, perhaps more important, the collective nature of this appropriation. A second major complex concerns the distinction and relationship between the passive and active qualities of social agency. The basic indicator here is again body painting, in this case the distinction between the infantile and adult styles. This basic distinction is once again inflected by the set composed of pierced ears and ear-plugs, on the one hand, and pierced lips and lip-plugs on the other. This set adds the specific meanings associated with the notions of hearing and speaking as passive knowledge and the active expression of decisions and programmes of action, respectively. Finally, both these clusters are cross-cut by a broad distinction between modes of activity. The most strongly marked distinction here is between secular and sacred (ritual) action, with the latter distinguished from the former by a rich variety of regalia. This distinction, however, may be considered a heightened inflection of the more basic distinction between individual or family-level activities and communal activities, not all of which are of a sacred character. Secular men's house gatherings or meetings of women's societies, for example, may be accompanied by collective painting and perhaps the wearing of simple head-dresses of palm leaves, even though there is no ceremony.

An important structural principle emerges from this analysis of the Kayapo system – the hierarchical or iterative structure of the symbolic code. Each major cluster of symbolic meanings is seen to be arranged in a series of increasingly specific modulations or inflections of the general notions expressed by the most basic symbol in the cluster. A second structural principle is the multiplicative character of the system as a whole. By this I mean that the three basic clusters are necessarily simultaneously present or conflated in the 'dress' of any individual Kayapo at any time. One cannot paint an infant or adult in the appropriate style without at the same time observing the concentric distinction between trunk and extremities common to both styles.

The conflation first of the levels of meaning within each cluster, secondly of each cluster with the others, and finally of the more basic categories of meaning and value listed above that are combined in different ways to form each cluster, is what I mean by 'the construction of the cultural subject' or actor. (It is sometimes necessary to speak in terms of *collective* subjects, such as the class of young men, or of workers, but for the sake of simplicity I shall leave this issue aside here.) It is, by the same token, the construction of the social universe within which he or she acts (that is, an aspect of that construction). As the Kayapo example suggests, this is a dynamic process that proceeds as it were in opposite directions at the same time, towards equilibrium or equilibrated growth at both the individual and social levels (it goes without saying that in speaking of equilibrium I am referring to cultural ideals rather than concrete realities, either social or individual).

In the Kayapo case, the externalisation of the internal biological and libidinous ('natural') powers of individuals as the basis of social reproduction, and the socialisation of 'external' natural powers as the basis of social structure and the social identity of actors otherwise defined only as biological extensions of their parents, are clearly metaphorical inversions of one another. Each complements the other, just as the social values respectively associated with the two aspects of the process, 'dominance' and 'beauty', complement each other; a balance between the two processes and their associated values is the ideal state of Kayapo society as a dynamic equilibrium. It is also, and equally, the basis of the unity and balance of the personality of the socialised individual, likewise conceived as a dynamic equilibrium.

The point I have sought to demonstrate is that this balance between opposing yet complementary forces, which is the most fundamental structural principle of Kayapo society, is systematically articulated and, as it were, played out on the bodies of every member of Kayapo society through the medium of bodily adornment. This finding supports the general hypothesis with which we began, namely that the surface of the body becomes, in any human society, a boundary of a peculiarly complex kind, which simultaneously separates domains lying on either side of it and conflates different levels of social, individual and intra-psychic meaning. The skin (and hair) are the concrete boundary between the self and the other, the individual and society. It is, however, a truism to which our investigation has also attested, that the 'self' is a composite product of social and 'natural' (libidinous) components.

At one level, the 'social skin' models the social boundary between the individual actor and other actors; but at a deeper level it models the internal, psychic diaphragm between the pre-social, libidinous energies of the individual and the 'internalised others', or social meanings and values that make up what Freud called the 'ego' and 'super-ego'. At yet a third, macro-social level, the conventionalised modifications of skin and hair that comprise the 'social skin' define, not individuals, but categories or classes of individuals, (for example, infants, senior males, women of child-bearing age, etc.). The system of bodily adornment as a whole (all the transformations of the 'social skin' considered as a set) defines each class in terms of its relations with all the others. The 'social skin' thus becomes, at this third level of interpretation, the boundary between social classes.

That the physical surface of the human body is systematically modified in all human societies so as to conflate these three levels of relations (which most modern social science devotes itself to separating and treating in mutual isolation), should give us cause for reflection. Are we dealing here with a mere exotic phenomenon, a primitive expression of human society at a relatively undifferentiated level of development, or is our own code of dress and grooming a cultural device of the same type?

WORD PLAY

It seems natural that the study of man should focus on his unique attribute – language – which, more than anything else, is not essential for survival but vital for culture. All other species manage to survive without it, but those that come closest to culture also come closest to language. We use language to joke, and to fight. We use it for dramatic effect, formally and informally. And we use words to shock our sensibilities.

What's So Funny?

HOWARD R. POLLIO

'How could there possibly be a scientific study of humour?' he asked.

'Why not?' I replied. 'We've studied all kinds of things scientifically. Whoever thought we would have plotted the number of orgasms per week as a function of age, socio-economic status, and place of birth – but we have. If science can go into the bedroom, why can't it study humour?'

'Ah,' he said, 'sex is important biological business. But humour; there's nothing really worth serious study there.'

'Surely,' I said, 'you're not going to tell me that science isn't up to the job?'

'Come now,' he said somewhat firmly, 'do be serious. Science is an objective enterprise and humour is so thoroughly subjective that it seems likely that the whole project must fall apart from the very beginning. There's no way to study humour and retain any vestige of credibility, not to mention rigour. Why don't you leave the whole business to literary critics and magazine writers – not only are they better able to deal with subjective experience, they also write a good bit better than you. Anyway, it's not a very important topic to bother about.'

THIS CONVERSATION, or one very much like it, is one that I have heard many, many times since I began to study humour. And the answer (or answers) to my friend's objections seems straightforward enough:

1 While it has its subjective aspects, humour can be studied objectively: after all, laughs and smiles do get seen by other people.

2 Humour is an important topic: there is no existing society in

Popov, the Russian clown (Keystone Press Agency)

which people don't laugh and smile and many societies have elaborate ceremonies set up to evoke laughter. Then too, can we consider someone truly healthy if they never laugh or smile?

3 Some pretty good philosophers and literary critics have tried to deal rigorously with humour for over two thousand years. Unfortunately, everybody seems to see in humour just exactly what they want to see in it; no one has ever tried to understand it on its own ground.

Take the question of theory first. Here, every first-rate and some not-so-first-rate philosophers have all had their say. Thomas Hobbes saw hostility and self-aggrandisement as the essence of humour, thereby making the 'put-down' or humorous insult a basic comic form. Immanuel Kant, on the other hand, saw 'strained expectations dissipating into nothing' as of prime importance thereby implying incongruity and unpredictability as primary factors. Freud, as usual, saw technique wedded to impulse, thus suggesting that certain topics were more likely than others to evoke laughter.

In a very general sort of way, theories of humour can be divided up on the basis of three factors: it is the behaviour mostly helpful or disruptive, is it primarily emotional or intellectual, and is it an individual or social-interpersonal matter? For this reason, almost all theories of humour can be included within the following 2 × 2 × 2 classification scheme:

FIGURE 1: *The humour box and some well-known entries*

Effect	SOURCE			
	INDIVIDUAL		SOCIAL	
	Emotional	Intellectual	Emotional	Intellectual
Disruptive	Thomas Hobbes ◄——— Anthony Ludovici	Immanuel Kant ———►		
Facilitative	Some therapists (sometimes)	Arthur Koestler	Konrad Lorenz	

Koestler's theory of humour, presented in his book *The Act of Creation*, basically takes an individual, intellectual, facilitative view. Thomas Hobbes, on the other hand, takes an individual, emotional, disruptive view. Even though most theories, from Kant to Lorenz, can be placed in one of the eight boxes produced by this scheme, most fall on the *individual* rather than the *social* side of the ledger. More often than not, humour is seen as an aspect of or response from the person rather than as an aspect or consequence of the social setting in which it occurs. Such theories mimic common sense where people are said 'to have' a sense of humour which they may or may not use in certain situations.

Despite this view, research has been singularly unsuccessful in trying to discover what it might mean to be someone who has a sense of humour. Although a few personality tests have been developed on the basis of which jokes people like and dislike, such tests have not been a great success nor have they enjoyed widespread clinical or experimental use.

The major problem with any approach to humour that focuses on the individual, is that it is so thoroughly a social phenomenon. Here some anthropological data are important. In 1945 a folklorist, L. H. Charles, went through the Yale Area Files dealing with various cultures. Of 136 cultures listed in 1940, Charles found that 56 contained some information about an institutionalised comic role or a specific comic-like ceremony. This was true even though no anthropologist was specifically asked to describe such phenomena. Comic events just seemed to be so apparent in these cultures that not reporting them would have been a serious oversight.

One of the most revealing of these ceremonies concerns the Koyemci clowns of the Zuni Indian tribe found in the southwestern part of the United States. Koyemci clowns are allowed extreme licence in their behaviour, as the following description indicates:

Each [Koyemci clown] endeavours to excel his fellows in buffoonery and eating repulsive things, such as bits of old blanket or splinters of wood. They bite off the heads of living mice and chew them, tear dogs limb from limb, eat the intestines and fight over the liver like hungry wolves. The one who swallows the largest amount of filth with the greatest gusto is most commended. A large bowl of urine is handed . . . to a man of the fraternity, who, after drinking a portion, pours the remainder over himself by turning the bowl over his head.

Aggressive impulses are not the only ones allowed to run riot. Among other American Indian tribes observers have reported the following ceremony:

> Two clowns come in on the west side of the court and, seeing the woman, drop on their hands and knees and crawl towards her, each loosening his breechcloth and displaying a false penis made of a gourd neck. When the old woman finishes washing an old fringe of rags, she washes her legs, displaying a great false vulva so that all the spectators can see it and laugh at her. The . . . clowns – all whitened with clay – finally converge around her, and as she sits on the sacred shrine they propose copulation with her. She points to the presence of her boy as an obstacle. The clowns send the boy to get a jar of water and then proceed upon the shrine either to copulate or to imitate copulation with the utmost grossness. The boy returning, rushes among them, thrashes his immoral mother, and a general brawl ensues amid loud plaudits.

All of this is strong enough medicine on its own. There is one more thing, however, that is important to know: Koyemci clowns are not only clowns, they are also members of the priestly class. To be a Koyemci clown is not to be lowly or demeaned; rather, to be a Koyemci is to be an important and significant member of the Zuni tribe.

There is a powerful dynamic that runs from priest to clown and back again, and this concerns a close relationship between the sacred and profane aspects of communal life. Both clown and priest deal with what is important in a society and, therefore, often taboo, and both priest and clown exhibit control over these matters in different ways: one by mocking it, the other by sanctifying its rules of restraint. While the priest emphasises a need to submit himself (and the rest of the tribe) to sacred rules, the clown emphasises such rules by playing with them in an exaggerated, profane way. In his play, however, the clown lets everyone know that although he behaves licentiously, he knows, and his audience knows, and each is aware that the other knows, that he is *not* licentious except under special conditions. Once make-believe passes into everyday reality, the clown stops being funny – only ineffective and pathetic.

The joint status of Koyemci as clowns and priests should dispel one of the major myths surrounding humour: that it deals with unimportant matters and that it always involves frivolous and/or demeaning actions. One particularly articulate presentation of this myth was made by an old English Kantian named Anthony Ludovici. In his major book *The Secret of Laughter*, published in 1932, Ludovici saw little in humour that was worthy of the human spirit. Despite a reasoned, and reasonable, analysis of laughter, Ludovici ended by convincing himself that such behaviour was an enemy to progress, frittering away man's creative fire in the trivia of laughter. As he put it a bit heavily: 'Had Napoleon recognised the overpowering disproportion between his absurdly inadequate personality and the stupendous task he was undertaking . . . he would have had to crack some paralysing joke about it.' Or again: 'who could ever imagine Christ laughing?'

Well, someone – G. K. Chesterton to be exact – could, and for this reason has earned Mr Ludovici's everlasting scorn. The view that laughter and humour must be considered as more than trivial aspects of culture is perhaps best expressed by Konrad Lorenz in his book, *On Aggression*. Citing the Gospel according to Nature and Chesterton in equal measure, Lorenz sees in humour and laughter an appropriate vehicle whereby seemingly rational and serious schemes of control and domination can be exploded by the pin-prick of a Will Rogers, a Charlie Chaplin or a Grock. It is *tierischer Ernst* that produces the paralytic effects of militarism, and it is laughter which periodically explodes these profane myths. For Lorenz, behind the comedian or the clown's mask there is a moralist ready to restore balance to that which is upset, repressed or distorted in society.

A final blow to the idea that humour and laughter are unimportant can be found at almost any intake interview conducted at a psychiatric hospital. There seems to be a level of laughter that is expected: anything more merges into hebephrenic silliness; anything less, stuporous depression. Laughter and smiling are constants in human life and excesses in either direction betoken misery and woe.

Humour is important; and more, it *should* be easy to study. Laughing and smiling have a good deal of face validity to them as indicators of humour. But the matter cannot be closed quite so easily: often laughing and smiling turn out on closer examination to be something other than expressions of humour. Several specific types of laughter, for example, seem clearly unrelated to humour in any usual sense of the term:

1 Laughter brought about by nitrous acid; laughing gas;
2 'nervous' laughter;
3 the laugh (complete with upraised arms) that follows victory in a contest;
4 laughter that results from a wide range of brain conditions such as cerebral arteriosclerosis or frontal lobotomy.

If these were not problems enough, there is also the case where a person says something funny but his or her peers fail to laugh or smile at it. Sometimes, for example, when a person is made the butt of a quite telling remark, social skills demand that neither the person aimed at, nor other members of a group laugh. There is also the opposite case: when the boss tells a bad joke, social skills now demand a laugh or at least an amused smile.

What all this suggests is not that the would-be researcher throw up his hands and say 'I quit', but that great tact and understanding are needed to interpret the meaning of a laugh or smile. Laughing and smiling are not unfailing indicators of what is funny; they serve only to mark out a territory in need of further exploration. Laughing can only be understood in context, where such context must include not only the person and the situation, but that person's understanding of the situation. A tricky business at best.

Because it is impossible to know how to do all this at once, audience-laughter seems a good place at which to begin the study of humour; especially if we keep these caveats in mind. In this context, it seems reasonable to assume that laughter indicates that something funny has happened. If the audience is attending a movie, we can also assure ourselves that comic

FIGURE 2: *Sample oscillographic tracing of audience laughter–movie performance*

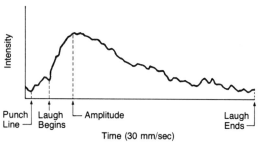

material will be presented in the same way for a second, third, or even fourth, run-through.

When the response of an audience is put on audiotape and then fed into a sound-level recorder, a record very much like that presented in Figure 2 is the result. At least three measurements can be derived from a record of this sort:

1 How long it took before the audience laughed, given the punch line;
2 how long the laugh lasted;
3 how loud or intense the laugh was.

This trio of measures can be recognised as equivalent to Pavlov's latency, duration and amplitude. As such, they are no less precise than those derived from salivary conditioning; not to mention a good deal drier.

When a procedure such as this was used with an audience attending a performance of the film *Bob and Carol and Ted and Alice* in 1970, results showed positive correlations between amplitude and duration, but not between either of these measures and latency. A second set of data, gathered at a later showing of the film, essentially verified these conclusions. The second, or 10.00 p.m. audience, however, laughed only twenty-two times during the performance while the earlier, 8.00 p.m., audience had laughed twenty-six times. Twenty-one of these laughs did occur in response to the same punch lines across both performances.

Results like these would seem to indicate only small differences between the two audiences. When, however, cross-performance correlations were computed between latency,

duration and amplitude, values were found to range from .20 to
.60 indicating jokes that produced guffaws at 8.00 p.m. sometimes fell flat at 10.00 p.m., and vice-versa. Since the film was
obviously the same on both occasions, it seemed clear that what
was funny for one group of people was not as funny for another
group of people.

Comic movies, like all humorous events, take place within a
social context, and a person's tendency to laugh (perhaps even
their tendency to find something funny) depends not only on
the material but also on the context. In order to disentangle
these effects experimentally, it is not possible to use naturally
occurring audience groups. After all, it is not easy to approach a
person leaving a film and say 'Excuse me, sir, could you please
tell me why you laughed fourteen times for a total of 12.64
seconds?'

This suggests a move to the laboratory. There the psychologist can live up to the definition which sees him as a person
who watches the audience rather than the performers at a
showing of *Oh! Calcutta!* To study humour in the laboratory it is
first necessary to find appropriate comic material. Here we did
what experimenters have done from time immemorial: we tried
out our experimental material on available laboratory personnel. Unfortunately, this had an unexpected side effect: records
of comic performances which people in our laboratory found
hilarious, often produced little or no response when played to
an audience composed of randomly selected individuals.

Fortunately, why this happened was made clear one very
rainy day, when a group of people assembled for the purpose of
taking part in the experiment spent half an hour or so talking
to one another as they waited for the experiment to begin.
Although no previous group ever laughed at one particularly
nasty routine done by the American comedian Don Rickles, the
'rainy-day' group laughed often and loudly. This observation
suggested that a collection of strangers brought into a laboratory will probably not laugh at nasty comic material until they
have had the opportunity to coalesce into a group.

To test this notion more systematically, we solicited the aid
of groups of friends and strangers and played comic routines to
them performed by two different comedians: the acid-tongued
Don Rickles and the more benign Bill Cosby. Rickles works by

insulting his audience; Cosby works by creating the world of the nice guy ruminating on the misadventures of childhood. In our experiment, audience participants were videotaped (with their consent) and careful records taken of what each one did. These records included their general activity level as well as specific attempts at talking to, or looking at, someone else in the group. Laughing and smiling were also recorded.

When all these records were evaluated, friends and stranger-groups showed only slight differences when listening to Cosby, and vast differences when listening to Rickles. In the case of Rickles, friends moved and laughed a great deal, while strangers moved very little and scarcely at all after the first minute or so of the routine. Most seemed rather embarrassed by the whole business. Parenthetically, strangers laughed slightly more than friends at the various Cosby routines.

Perhaps the most important implication to be drawn from these results *vis-à-vis* comedians is that Cosby and Rickles seem to define two different comic styles. One of them, Rickles, focuses the individual audience member on the here-and-now of his or her experiences, while the other, Cosby, invites the audience member to transcend the present situation and roam about in a sensibly-nonsensical world. The terms usually applied to these differences are those that distinguish the comic from the humorist. The comic (and some of his kin – the nasty clown, the sarcastic wit, etc.) all focus the person on his immediate situation thereby making group structure and group solidarity a key issue. The humorist (and his kin – the story-teller and the fabulist) all focus the person on experiences outside the present context, thereby making the present situation much less critical.

It is perhaps for this latter reason that there was slightly more laughing and smiling to Cosby under the 'strangers' conditions than under the 'friends' condition. For Cosby, a situation or context other than the present one is crucial, and for this reason, audience composition had little effect. On the contrary, because Rickles does focus the individual audience member on the here and now of his or her experience, great differences were found in the responsiveness of 'friends' and 'strangers' groups, and this too is to be expected.

Although more could be said about the social nature of the

audience situation (about the whys and hows of humour claques, etc.), the major point seems to be that what's funny is not simply a consequence of comic material. Rather, the nature of the audience and the comedian's personal style all combine with one another to produce a given comic effect. Although it is possible to measure the behavioural aspects of these artfully created comic worlds, such measures are useful only to the degree that they tell us something about the highly personal nature of *my* reaction to *that* comedian in Situation *A*, *B*, or *C*. Laughing and smiling are only indicators of what is funny; indicators which must be used with tact and delicacy if their implications are to be read unequivocally.

If tact and delicacy are required in understanding the meaning of an adult's laugh or smile, so too are they indeed in deciphering the laugh or smile of a child or infant. In the case of an infant's smile, at least three different theories have been proposed: the cognitive, the ethological and the social conditioning theory. From the cognitive point of view, smiling results when the infant is able to match an internal schema with an external stimulus (that is, the infant recognises something); from the ethological point of view, smiling results when an innately programmed response is released on the basis of rather specific external stimuli; while from the social conditioning point of view, smiling results only when the behaviour has been strongly encouraged by social rewards.

A similar range of theories exists in regard to laughing. Here, however, additional notions of arousal, ambivalence and tension-release are usually invoked. For all theories, laughter is always seen as a more intense and demanding event than smiling.

Given such different theories, the need for data is obvious. But what kind of data? Although many different investigators, from Darwin to Gesell, have looked at laughing and smiling in early infancy, two major research strategies have usually been tried. In one of these, the baby is tickled, dropped, whistled at, hugged, threatened, played peek-a-boo with, and so on. Almost all these procedures have been perpetrated on unsuspecting infants within the safe confines of the developmental laboratory. A second strategy is more benign and involves careful

observation of mother–child interactions as these occur spontaneously in the home or laboratory environments.

Characteristic of the tickle-kiss-peek-a-boo studies, is one by
Sroufe and Wunsche in 1972. Building on earlier more classic
studies done in the United States by Washburn (1929) and by
Amrose (1961) in England, Sroufe and Wunsche used twenty-
four test items grouped into the categories of auditory, touch,
social and visual. They hypothesised that since social and
visual items were cognitively more demanding than either
auditory or touch items they ought to elicit laughter later in
infant development than the less complex tactile and auditory
items. Results involving the study of seventy infants did, in fact,
show that the oldest group of infants (ten–twelve months)
laughed most often in response to visual and social items while
seven- to nine-month-old infants laughed most often in
response to auditory and tactile items. As expected, there were
substantial increases with age in the total amount of laughter
produced.

All these data led Sroufe and Wunsche to conclude that
laughter in infants serves many different functions. For one, it
has a positive bonding effect on infant and caretaker. For
another, it signals that the infant is unsure of whether to carry
on in a situation or to end it by crying. Under conditions of
ambivalence (such as might be created in peek-a-boo), the
infant will pay close attention to the situation thereby leading
to the building-up of tension. If the infant interprets the situation as aversive or threatening, he or she will cry and/or try to
avoid the situation. If, however, the infant interprets the situation as one of play (and if the tension is high enough) he or she
will laugh and approach the 'exciting' event. To laugh thus
signals an infant's intention of going ahead in a situation that is
unclear but not without strong attraction. To laugh is to risk,
and in the context of development, to risk is to grow.

Similar studies dealing with smiling as the response of interest have also produced some interesting results. Here, the most
important finding concerns the very strong role of a human face
in bringing about a smile. This is particularly true for the first
six to seven months of life where any configuration having the
overall qualities of a facial Gestalt were found to induce smiling. Many of the tickle-kiss-peek-a-boo stimuli were also found

to produce smiling; always, however, a number of weeks earlier than they evoked laughter.

While a few studies have observed smiling and laughing in infants in more naturally occurring environments, a recent study by Douglas Nowicki provides the most systematic data yet collected. For this work, specially trained observers recorded twelve infants for a twenty-minute period once a week for the first twenty-six weeks of life. All observers made a running verbal account of each infant's behaviour (including bodily positions and emotional mood). In addition, a complete record was made of the various events going on in the infant's immediate environment.

From the great mass of data collected, 'smiling' curves such as those shown in Figure 3 turned out to be quite revealing. Three different categories of smiling were noted: spontaneous smiling (where there was no obvious social or non-social event in the infant's immediate environment), non-social smiling (where there was an object such as a rattle or a toy, but no person) and social smiling (where the stimulus was clearly another person or group of persons). The data presented in Figure 3 are quite clear in showing that spontaneous smiles, which equal the number of social smiles during the first six weeks of life, almost completely drop out by week twelve and that non-social smiles, which do not make their first appearance until the thirteenth week, become progressively more frequent as the infant grows older. The majority of all smiles, almost from the second week on, are clearly social in nature.

When Nowicki looked at laughing, he found that it did not occur in any of his infants until at least the third or fourth month of life. He also noted that laughing often occurred in continuing bursts and then only in active, awake infants who had been intensely stimulated. The overall occurrence of laughing was much less than that of smiling and reached its peak during weeks seventeen to twenty.

A comparison of the patterns by which laughing and smiling develop suggests a clear ground plan for what these events might mean for the growing infant. If we start with the fact that spontaneous and social smiling occurred in most infants during the first few weeks of life, but that social smiling did not reach its peak until the third month, we can see that laughing only

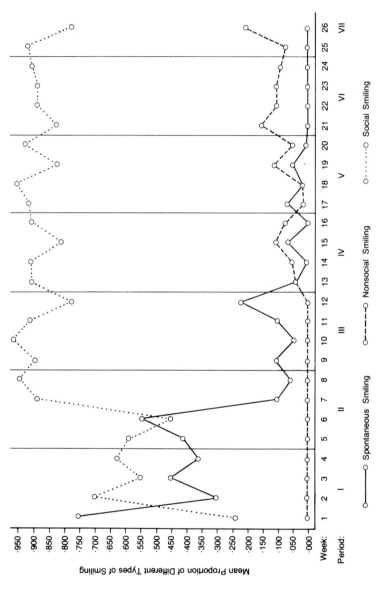

FIGURE 3: *Mean Proportion of different types of smiling per week for all infants*

came on the scene once social smiling had already reached a stable level. Non-social smiling also began about the fourth month, this leads us to suspect that smiling is not only instrumental to social behaviour but also serves as an indicator of cognitive activity at this time; that is, when the infant is able to recognise a known object or person.

While both smiling and laughing occur primarily in social settings, it is clear that laughing is the more demanding and intrusive behaviour. One conclusion seems to be that once smiling (at about three or four months of age) is no longer sufficiently powerful or reinforcing to the mother or caretaker to maintain behaviours essential for the infant's survival (feeding, changing and so on) a much more intense form of social behaviour – laughing – appears on the interpersonal scene. Laughing thus comes to parallel crying in terms of its ability to demand and get the attention of others.

This reconstruction suggests that each of the various theories used to explain laughing and smiling has some validity; none, by itself, is adequate for the job. Nowicki's results suggest that smiling shifts initially from a behaviour associated with physiological conditions to one more closely related to social activities. At about the fourth month another shift occurs when smiling begins to appear in contexts not involving another person. This second shift reflects the gradual emergence of cognitive-recognition factors as important to smiling.

Laughing, on the other hand, first emerges as an important behaviour at about the fourth month; that is, at about the same time as smiling comes partially to serve as an expression of cognitive activity. The nature of the conditions associated with laughing (at the fourth month and beyond) further suggest that it is evoked by, and evokes, more intense forms of stimulation than smiling. Anyone who has ever seen a laughing infant or child knows that he or she is pretty hard to disregard, and this would seem to be how mother is captured once smiling ceases to work its own powerful summoning magic.

Whether we look at laughing and smiling in the crib, night club or public ceremony, social and interpersonal factors are undeniably important. For this reason, it seems a good idea to see what we can learn about humour as it occurs in ongoing groups. Here, as before, there are almost as many theories as observers, and the wise theorist begins by looking at where and when laughing and smiling occur and what possible effects these events might have on what happens next in the group.

An early study by Rose Coser sets the tone. In this work, Coser (1960) studied humorous remarks as they occurred at mental hospital staff meetings over a three-month period. All staff meetings were formally structured and were attended by eighteen members of the hospital administration. In this supposedly benign setting, Coser reports that 97 of 103 humorous remarks were directed at some target or other. These targets included a patient, the patient's relatives, another member of the staff, or the speaker himself (or herself). Ninety of these remarks were made by permanent staff members and formed the basis of a further analysis. In this more fine-grained analysis Coser found that twenty per cent of the remarks were self-directed, twenty-seven per cent were directed at another member of the group, and thirty-two per cent were directed at people, events or things not present in the group. Only eighteen per cent were without specifiable targets.

Coser also looked at 'targetting' in terms of social status. Here she found that humorous remarks provided a good guide as to who was, and was not, important in the group. Of the ninety humorous remarks considered, fifty-nine per cent were produced by senior staff members, thirty-seven per cent by junior staff, and only four per cent by paramedical staff. Such percentages obviously parallel the status of participants. In terms of targetting, senior staff people were found to aim at junior staff or patients fifty-seven per cent of the time. Other staff members of equal or higher status, however, were aimed at only six per cent of the time. Junior staff members aimed at those lower in status thirty-nine per cent of the time, and those superior only six per cent of the time. Not once did a junior staff member aim at a senior staff member. Clearly humour is directed downwards and it is safe to say that it is the prerogative of those in charge.

The idea of humour being used to aim at other people in a group is an interesting one. In order to pursue this idea more rigorously a number of people in my laboratory (Allen Childs, Pat Peterson, and Forrest Scogin) investigated the role and nature of targetting in group process. As a start, reports of naturally occurring groups were secured from the existing experimental literature and combined with our own observations.

Table 1 presents results for six groups providing usable data. The first two groups involve research done in other contexts (both are field reports of staff conferences) while the pool-playing group is based on direct observation by one of our own participating researchers. The remaining three sets of results were all derived from extensive video-tape recordings. One of these involved five group therapy sessions (each roughly seventy minutes long) conducted at a local mental health centre; another involved five growth group sessions (each sixty minutes long) conducted at a college counselling centre, while a third involved twenty-eight problem-solving sessions, each of twenty minutes, held in the laboratory. With the exception of problem-solving groups, all data concerned the same set of individuals observed over all meetings of the group.

TABLE 1: *Nature of attempts at humour in six different group settings*

| Setting | Number of incidents | REMARK OR ACTION DIRECTED AT: | | | Non-directed | Un-classified |
		Self	Other in group	Generalised other		
Psychiatric staff conferences	174	6%		49%*	47%	0%
Mental hospital staff conferences	90	20%	27%	32%	18%	0%
Pool-playing elderly men	246	13%	56%	1%	16%	12%
Growth group	318	21%	26%	9%	24%	20%
Therapy group	301	28%	26%	16%	22%	6%
Problem-solving groups	183	12%	10%	14%	61%	2%

*Values cannot be separated from published report

The first rather obvious aspect of these data is that humorous remarks are not always nice. Although individual values vary, only one situation produced more non-targetted than targetted humour. In the remaining five settings well over fifty per cent of the incidents were directed at someone: either oneself, another member of the group, or some person or institution outside the group. Since the twenty-eight problem-solving groups were of reasonably short duration, fifty per cent seems the more reasonable estimate of group targetting.

A close look at the results produced in each of the settings provides some obvious differences. For example, the highest number of self-directed remarks occurred in the therapy group, while the smallest number of self-directed remarks occurred in the first set of psychiatric staff-meetings. This makes sense in that people undergoing therapy talk about themselves, which is what they are there for, while people at staff conferences talk about patients which is why *they* are there! In this latter regard, the second set of staff conferences seems more typical than the first, with about eighty per cent of these remarks seeking out, and finding, a target. The pool-playing group had a great many remarks directed at other people in the group and almost none directed at events or people remote from the present situation. The technical term for such remarks (whether at billiards or bridge) is *kibbitzing*, with everybody giving it to the person missing (or making) a particular shot (or trick).

Using the word *target* to describe humorous remarks suggests that most, if not all, humour in a group involves a *put-down* of one sort of another. Actually, some targetted remarks note the person appreciatively, and if we divide humorous remarks into positive (appreciative) and negative (put-downs), the overall ratio for all groups turns out to be about 3:1 in favour of negative – a little better, but still not remarkable. For the three categories, self, other, and generalised other, the ratio of negative to positive is 2:1, 3:1, and 4:1, respectively. As the topic gets further away from the person, the number of put-downs increases. Saying it another way, 'if I'm not kind to me who will be?' or alternatively, 'If I'm not nasty to *them*, who will be?'

These data also suggest that most humorous remarks have to do with people who are in the group. Self and other-directed remarks are always more frequent than remarks directed at people or events not in the present situation. This means that humour deals as much with ongoing group process as it does with the topics of discussion. If we look just at self-directed and other-directed remarks an egalitarian sort of parity is apparent: 'them that gives a lot are them that gets a lot'. Although there are occasional bullies and victims, the usual finding is that of a strong correlation between the 'giving' and 'getting' of humorous remarks. While it is no more blessed to give than to receive, it is also no more blessed to receive than to give.

All these results might suggest that each humorous remark occurred as a single put-down or pat on the back. The truth of the matter is that within these groups, most humorous remarks occurred in what can only be described as a humorous episode. For all groups the number of remarks that occurred alone (not as part of an episode) was less than forty-four per cent with the general average about thirty-five per cent. Although most episodes contained only two or three continuous remarks, some episodes (particularly for therapy groups) contained fifteen or sixteen items.

Are such episodes largely positive or negative? The overwhelming impression given by looking at the percentage of positive, negative and untargetted remarks in each of these episodes was that the longer the episode, the greater was the number of remarks with a negative twinge to them. For isolated remarks forty-nine per cent were negative, thirty-five per cent neutral, and sixteen per cent positive; comparable values for episodes of sizes two and three were sixty-five per cent negative, twenty per cent neutral and fifteen per cent positive. The longer the episode, the greater the number of negative remarks and the smaller the number of neutral or non-targetted remarks. When things get going, they can get a bit nasty and this nastiness seems to be the power needed to keep the episode going.

If humour does provoke action, it is reasonable to wonder what effect humorous remarks have on groups that are doing something other than talking about themselves. For this reason we tried to determine whether a group of funny people were (or were not) good problem-solvers. Folk wisdom on this topic is best expressed by the maxim: 'Okay, we've had our fun; now let's get down to business.' Both our parents and Martin Luther usually talk about things this way.

The data, unfortunately, are a little less certain on this issue (theologians are, after all, a lot more certain than psychologists). When groups of students were asked to solve problems in our laboratory and we looked at the amount of joking and laughter that went along with their work we found that certain problems were eased under conditions of laughing and joking while other problems were disrupted. One type of problem that was particularly facilitated by 'not getting down to business' was an anagram task in which subjects were given ten scrambled letters and were asked to produce as many different four-letter words as they could. In the ten-minute period, subjects in high joking groups produced an average of seventy-five different words; subjects in medium joking groups produced an average of fifty-six words, while subjects in serious groups produced an average of forty-five words.

One type of problem disrupted by joking concerned a group's ability to decide which, in a set of items needed for survival on the moon, were more important than others. This task was so designed as to have a logically correct order and, for this reason, group-problem-solving skill could be evaluated against this standard. For our groups, there was a strong tendency for high-laughter groups to do worse than either medium or low-laughter groups. Business-like groups did the best.

The effect of laughing (and other humour-related antics) on problem-solving seems to depend on the job a group is asked to do. Where the task is one requiring sustained attention, joking and fooling around disrupt the process; where the task is one having a great many individually solvable parts (such as words), joking facilitates the process. In the disruptive case, laughter serves to focus group members on the here-and-now of the problem. In the facilitative case, laughter serves to keep group-members involved in the situation and thereby to keep them at a task which otherwise would easily have lost their interest.

The person who is funny in a small group is but a natural counterpart to his or her more professional cousin: the stand-up comedian. There have always been people who know how to make other people laugh and it seems reasonable to wonder how they do it.

If there is one thing that emerges over and over again in naturally occurring humour it must be that the social situation is crucial. In the case of the comedian, the social situation always involves at least the following three components: the comedian, the audience, and the target. Taken *in toto*, it seems proper to call this complex interacting structure, the comedian's world.

In trying to find some way of talking about these worlds, we first asked different groups of people to describe the comic *personae* created by a number of different comedians. The major result of this work was that the vast majority of adjectives used to describe comedians were negative. Of thirty-two adjectives produced twenty or more times by fifty different people, seventeen were negatively toned: *fat, sarcastic, stupid*, and so on. Of the remaining fifteen adjectives, eleven were somewhat pleasant, while four were clearly ethnic in nature – like *Black, Jewish*.

This last bit of data is of some interest, especially since all the neutral adjectives concerned minority groups. No comedian was ever hit with the adjective Protestant, Episcopalian or Church of England. Does this mean that there are no Protestant comedians or, alternatively, that there is nothing funny about being a Protestant? Heaven forbid: what this means is that minority group comedians often incorporate ethnic background into their comic *personae*, while non-minority comedians do not. Comedy and humour meet so many diverse needs for minority group members that it seems inevitable that a professional comedian would make use of this in his or her own act. From a larger sociological perspective, it also seems clear that where you can't scream, you can joke.

Although strategic humour has been at work since antiquity, it was most extensively documented in recent times by the sociologist A. J. Obrdlik during the Nazi occupation of Czechoslovakia. Consider the following riddle made by the Czechs at the expense of the Nazis:

Do you know why daylight-saving time has been exceptionally prolonged this year? Because Hitler promised that before the summer is over, he and his army will be in England.

It is clear that such humour serves both to draw a line against the oppressor and to re-establish a bond among the oppressed, and the oppressed of every nation have always known this.

The comic *persona*, with its attendant sociological *shtick*, is only one aspect of the world a comedian creates for his or her audience. In approaching this world, it is not enough to study its elements; what is needed is some way of describing the interactions between *persona*, world and audience. The difficulties involved in such an analysis can perhaps be glimpsed in terms of the following fragment of a routine by the American comedian, Woody Allen:

> I was so depressed that I even contemplated committing suicide. . . . I finally decided against it because I was in analysis at the time . . . and I would have had to pay for the sessions I missed.

The first thing that is obvious here is that Allen (the performer) is letting his audience in on a secret: he's depressed and under treatment. This is a very clear aspect of Allen's approach to an audience: they and he are intimate to the point that he can talk about all his taboo topics – sex, depression, being Jewish and hating (loving) it, and so on. Being buddies with Woody has its price: you never know whether he's doing a routine or whether he's telling you something true, something serious. In addition to violating his audience's right to privacy, Allen also defines himself as an incompetent tactless person: what technically is called a *nebish*. Finally, however, most Allen routines end with him getting the job, the girl, the raise, the applause, and so on. Thus, Allen violates our expectations of him in still another sense: he is not *really* a *nebish*.

Woody Allen only does what skilful comedians have been doing for years: he tells us what we don't want to know about his way of doing the things we *do* want to know about (such as power, sex and money). In Allen, as in most stand-up comics, we find that the comedian always deals with at least two different realities: the reality created by his or her comic art and the reality of the audience situation. The skilful comedian continually and abruptly moves his audience through these realities, leaving them breathless and exhausted from the trip.

Although this work on comedians might make some sort of

impressionistic sense it seems fair to wonder how we might go about making such impressions a bit more objective. One preliminary way of doing this has already been described in terms of the American comedians Don Rickles and Bill Cosby. There, a sympathetic cross-reading of a great many different audience behaviours led us to the conclusion that Rickles and Cosby create vastly different comic worlds. This conclusion was only reached on the basis of being able to make sense of all that had been carefully observed.

Direct and continuing observation (reading behaviour backwards, if you will) is the key by which it is possible to enter the comic world created by a skilful comedian. In this, the study of comic worlds need be no less objective than a study of the herring gull's or a duckling's world so carefully mapped by ethologists such as Tinbergen and Lorenz. Any attempt to read the 'self-world' of an organism is always fraught with difficulty, and only if we approach this task on the basis of sympathetic, rigorous and continuing observation will it be possible to understand what these worlds are like and how they work. This is no less true for the created world of the comedian than for the more naturally occurring world of the herring gull.

A Short Epilogue

'Well, my friend,' I said, 'what do you think now that you've read all this?'

'I'll tell you one thing,' he said, 'you psychologists do have a way of making interesting things dull. People who write about humour ought, at a minimum, be funny; alas, that, I fear, is too much to hope for. After all, we all know that people do research on a particular topic because they know nothing about it – hence the number of certifiable analysts, ill-mannered behaviourists and inarticulate linguists. Now I know for sure the humour-researcher is no exception.'

With that, he turned and laughed derisively, looking for all the world like some latter-day Thomas Hobbes. Ah, what a fine mess you've got us into, Stanley.

Fighting Words

DONALD BRENNEIS

John L. : 'I'll take you to the last man.'
Junior : 'I'll take your mother.'
Rel : 'I took your mother.'

WORDS ARE DEEDS. They delight, persuade, instruct and offend.
Just as the rhymes and riddles of children help to shape their
experience as much as do their lessons, so adults also live in a
world where small words have large effects. Thus, the exchange
cited above should not be taken as inconsequential banter but
as a significant event in itself. It is an example of 'sounding', a
type of verbal contest common among lower-class black
American adolescent boys, quoted from a study by William
Labov. Sounding involves the exchange of usually obscene
insults and invective which might well, in other circumstances,
lead to violence; in sounding, however, one fights with words
rather than with fists. Such verbal duels are not limited to
young black Americans, but have been found in a wide range of
societies throughout the world. Although varying in their
specific features, all include allegations or abuse which would
most often be socially censured or personally dangerous.
Rather than leading to disapproval or revenge, successful duelling frequently forestalls conflict and enhances one's stature.
The widespread incidence of verbal duelling therefore raises a
number of questions for anthropologists. In what kinds of
societies, for example, is such duelling found? Who duels, and
why? What kinds of insults are taken most seriously? Most
significantly, since their performances play upon crucial moral
concerns, how do duellists get away with it?
   I will examine these questions from a sociolinguistic perspective, an approach which focuses upon patterns of language-use

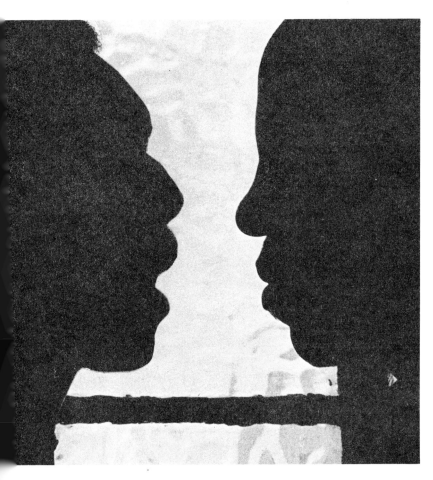

Iron is iron, and steel don't rust,
But your momma got a pussy like a Greyhound bus.

(Photo: Nick Hunter)

in a community and the social and cultural features of those contexts in which speakers perform. Text and context are closely linked and require equal attention. The types, or genres, of performance recognised by community members constitute an important aspect of context. Each genre implies a specific set of constraints and opportunities for the individual; would you, for example, tell a dirty joke to your grandmother? Finally, speakers' pragmatic intentions must be considered, as speaking is a social performance serving a variety of ends not necessarily evident in the text itself.

A definition of verbal duelling is necessary before discussing specific instances. I use 'verbal duelling' to refer to the competitive exchange of invective and insult between at least two parties, whether individuals or groups. Performers are expected not to show the anger or embarrassment usually caused by such attacks. The element of overt abuse is important as it distinguishes duelling from other contests, such as competitive riddling and guessing games. In each society where they occur duels are considered to be representative of a distinct genre and are constrained stylistically and in content by generic conventions.

Anthropologists, folklorists and literary scholars have noted the practice of verbal duelling in a wide variety of societies. In early Europe, examples range from the *aischrologia*, or abusive songs associated with various Greek fertility rituals, to the invective verses of Irish and Scandinavian bards, whose words were considered to be supernaturally powerful. In Britain, the best-known instances are the highly obscene flytings of medieval Scotland. Duels were common in the western Mediterranean as well and found literary expression in the *tenzone* of early Italian and Provençal poetry; the duelling tradition remains strong in Sardinia and Malta.

Turkish boys duel, and several Turkic groups in central Asia have adult competitions. Duels have also been reported from a number of west African tribes, including the Tiv, Yoruba and Efik. African slaves very likely brought the tradition with them to the new world – abusive verbal contests are important in many black American groups, both in the Caribbean and in the United States. Spanish colonists similarly brought their own variety of duelling to Mexico. There are also several indigenous

American instances of verbal duelling, particularly among the Eskimo and the highland Mayan peoples of southern Mexico. In the south Pacific, the descendants of east Indian immigrants to Fiji duel with offensive songs; although invective was an important art during the Vedic period, there are no accounts of such contests in contemporary Indian society.

Many descriptions of verbal duelling are unfortunately brief and lack either sample texts or adequate contextual data. In this article I will therefore draw my illustrations from those societies for which relatively full accounts are available; my interpretations are similarly based upon this somewhat restricted sample.

A first important feature of verbal duelling is that participation is essentially limited to males. Girls and women may be in the audience, and duels may occasionally be intended to embarrass passing females. Women rarely perform, however, and there is as yet no evidence that they have analogous performances among themselves. This sets verbal duelling apart from such mixed-sex banter as the suggestive songs exchanged by groups of young men and women in Nepali hill tribes.

A basic distinction can be drawn between those varieties of duelling in which only juveniles or adolescents take part, and those which are adult performances. In making this distinction, I am concerned not with chronological age but with the 'social age' of the performers, that is, the extent to which they are considered responsible, mature and consequential members of the community.

The Turkish duelling rhymes analysed by Allan Dundes, Jerry Leach and Bora Özkök are clearly confined to young boys. The highland Mayan Chamula duellists whom Gary Gossen studied were adolescents and young men who had not yet reached 'full ritual masculinity'. Similarly, the *albures* or duels described by John Ingham in his account of a Mexican town are performed by boys and men who consider themselves to be *machos* in contrast with the *miserables* who are burdened with family and practical concerns. It is more difficult to generalise about black American duelling, but interest in, and opportunity for, extended duelling apparently decline as individuals become more involved with work and family and less active in all-male peer groups. In his study of verbal art in the West

Indies, Roger Abrahams found a particularly complex situation, as a variety of duelling genres was available. Younger duellists usually participated in 'rhyming', an exchange of obscene claims about each other's mothers similar to sounding, while adults competed through more difficult forms such as songs or speeches; adults occasionally included 'rhymes' in their performances.

Other instances of verbal duelling involve only adult performers. Adult males are individuals whose relationships with each other matter to the larger group. They have dependents and responsibilities, and their cooperation or conflict with other adults can affect community stability and well-being. Performers have different characteristics in different societies, however. Groups of co-religionists compete in Fiji Indian challenge singing, while individual Tiv performers are supported by kinsmen and friends. Among the Eskimo, performers usually sing their invective verses alone, although they may be accompanied by family members. In some Eskimo groups, a man composes songs to be sung by his wife; in others only men perform. Eskimo men may form amicable partnerships in which abusive songs are regularly exchanged, but Eskimo duels are often caused by conflicts, as they are among the Tiv and the Fiji Indians. Abrahams has noted that such public events as wakes and carnivals offer opportunities for both individual and group duels among West Indian men; he does not suggest, however, that they are politically motivated as in the other three societies.

Maltese and Sardinian duels are usually performed by semi-professional singers, although amateurs may compete. These contests serve as a means of intra-guild competition rather than as a way of expressing community conflict. In this they are like the bardic duels of the Kazakh and Kirghiz, where the display of individual artistry is more important than political goals. Pointed political commentary is, however, a common theme in all of these genres.

Disputes among adolescents and young, relatively independent adults may have serious consequences for the individuals involved, but they are less likely to threaten the community than are conflicts among adults. Adult contests which might lead to overt fights, therefore, are of considerable interest and concern to others.

Anthropologists and folklorists have long argued that one major function of traditional performances is the expression they allow to sensitive or otherwise prohibited thoughts and concerns. Telling a fable, for example, might enable a parent to discipline a child without engendering the resentment likely to result from a more direct comment. The conventional nature of such performances helps the audience to anticipate their course and provides clues to guide their interpretation.

The scurrilous attacks made in verbal duels often lay bare the most sensitive moral tissue of a community; in other contexts they might lead to physical violence; or, among Fiji Indians at least, to suicide. A duel, however, is not a free-for-all with no holds barred but a rule-governed event. The standards for style, content and context characteristic of duels in each society force duellists to shape their performances in accordance with the aesthetic expectations of their listeners. These constraints also assure the audience of the traditional, predictable and, hence, safe nature of the contest. Duels are only possible because they are, despite their often outrageous content, conventional performances; adherence to generic rules shields both performers and audience from the dangers usually linked with such topics. Adult duels, which often result from mutual enmity and might have serious consequences, are stylistically more rigorous than those limited to adolescents, among whom duelling is usually spontaneous and friendly. Adult performers must master quite complex and demanding standards before they can duel, but adolescents face less forbidding requirements.

All the adolescent varieties of duelling I have studied consist of spoken insults, challenges and retorts. In each society, duels have a specific stylistic shape; failure to respond in proper style counts against the duellist. The shape of Turkish duels is constrained by the requirement that the response must rhyme with the opponent's comment, as in this example from Dundes, Leach and Özkök:

> Speaker A : *Hiyar.*
> Cucumber.
> Speaker B : *Götüne uyar.*
> It fits your ass.

The Mexican *albures* studied by Ingham consist of rhymed couplets including sexual *double entendres*:

> *Te saludo buen anciano,*
> *Con el sombrero en la mano.*
> I salute you, good old man,
> (*anciano* = *ano* = anus)
> with my hat in my hand.
> (*sombrero* = penis)

In Chamula, the adolescent duellists whom Gossen studied must respond with a 'minimal sound shift', as in this sequence, an excerpt from a considerably longer duel:

poko   Wash it
              That is, 'Wash your scrotum'. Also a play on the
              Spanish *poco*, 'small amount', thus insulting the size
              of the other's scrotum.

pok'ok'   Toad
              The scrotum, when swollen, is thought to look like a
              swollen toad.

pok' sat   Swollen face
              An insult, for this is a species of fish.

at ot   Your father
              That is, your father has a fish face.

atol   Semen
              A play on the Spanish *atole*, 'sweet corn gruel', which
              the Chamula say resembles sexual fluid.

Each pair of insults is linked by the subtly modified repetition of a syllable recast to create a new affront.

The stylistic rules for adolescent black duels in the United States are more variable. The older genre of the 'rhyming dozens' consist of rhymed couplets, as in this example from Labov's study:

> Iron is iron, and steel don't rust,
> But your momma got a pussy like a Greyhound bus.

The insults used in sounding need not rhyme, but they usually
fit one of a number of structural patterns, such as 'Your mother
is (like) . . . ' and 'Your mother got . . . ' Some of Labov's
transcripts suggest that duellists try to imitate their opponents'
syntax while modifying the content:

> Your mother got on sneakers!
> Your mother wear high-heeled sneakers to church!
> Your mother wear a jock-strap!
> Your mother got polka-dot drawers!
> Your mother wear the seat of her drawers on the top of her
> head!

The example given at the beginning of the chapter shows that
relatively minor changes may be quite effective.

The West Indian 'rhymes' analysed by Abrahams are strikingly similar to the 'dozens':

> Ten crapaud (inedible frogs) was in a pan;
> The bigger one was your mother, man.

In all of the adolescent genres, duelling ability depends
heavily upon mastery of a traditional repertoire of statements
and responses and to a smaller degree upon individual creativity. An agile, extensive memory and a dirty mind are one's chief
assets.

Adult contests are stylistically more demanding in several
ways. Individual turns are usually longer and more complex.
Fiji Indian songs, for example, are from six to twenty lines long
and are composed of couplets in blank verse. The Maltese and
Sardinian songs are especially complex, consisting of a lengthy
series of rhymed stanzas and concluding, in the Maltese case,
with a long and improvised *gadenza*. The audience is quick to
notice errors in rhythm, rhyme or grammar and to laugh at
inadequate performers.

Some adult duels are spoken; these speech contests are more
complicated than their adolescent counterparts. In the 'Speech
Bands' which Abrahams studied in Tobago, members of competing bands exchange boasts and insulting speeches, some
composed beforehand and some spontaneous.

Most adult genres, however, require that insults be sung rather than spoken. One must pay attention not only to text but to rhythm and tune as well. Performers often play an instrument while singing, which makes things even more difficult. Eskimo song duellists in Greenland must meet especially demanding standards, as they butt each other on the head while singing; a performer who lets up on either the head-butting or the singing is jeered at by the audience. Adult duellists in all groups must observe a wider range of conventions than younger men; breaking any of a number of rules may detract from an otherwise effective song. Furthermore, while adolescent duels depend largely upon memory, the spontaneous performance of new pieces is particularly important among adults.

Interesting contrasts are also evident in comparing the contents of duels. Adolescent duellists are markedly concerned with forcing their opponents into passive roles; this is especially clear in the Turkish boys' emphatic accusations of homosexuality. This theme is less common in adult texts, which focus upon accusations that opponents are socially impotent and have betrayed their community obligations.

Other family members figure strongly in duels, but they are treated differently by adults and younger performers. Adolescents usually attack each other by making insulting remarks about their opponents' parents. In sounding and rhyming, for example, mothers bear most of the abuse; Turkish boys also attack each others' mothers, while fathers are more likely targets among the Chamula. In adult duels, insults more frequently focus upon wives and sisters, and men are accused of failing to behave properly towards them. In this song from my study of Fiji Indian duelling, the most telling insult is the accusation that the victim's sister is misbehaving while he, the victim, is still alive:

You're going to come and beat me? You and who else?
Who will dare to boast in front of me?
We will beat you and break off your head; streams of blood will flow. Who will come to your aid?
Your mother and sisters will mourn after your death; your wife will become a widow, and who will care for her?

Your sister has become a prostitute, and she roams from
village to village.
She has become a prostitute, and who will pay the price?

The theme of failed family duties is also evident in this Eskimo
duelling song, translated by Hoebel from Rasmussen's text:

Insolence that takes the breath away,
Such laughable arrogance and effrontery.
What a satirical song! Supposed to put blame on me.
You would drive fear into my heart!
I who care not about death.
Hi! You sing about my woman who was your wench.
You weren't so loving then – she was much alone.
You forgot to prize her in song, in stout contest songs.
Now she is mine.
And never shall she visit singing, false lovers.
Betrayer of women in strange households.

In their study of white American boys' adaptations of the
'dozens', Ayoub and Barnett suggest that insults against
mothers enable adolescents to show their loyalty to friends
rather than to familial values; such abuse is a means of breaking
free from the parental household into a wider social world.
Adult duels, on the other hand, reflect the importance of
upholding kinship obligations; being a man means honouring
and protecting one's female relatives, especially those of the
same generation. The idiom of kin and family organises the
world of invective much as it does the social world. Younger
men, however, support each other in demeaning their kin,
while adults emphasise their responsibilities. In this regard, it
is interesting that, just as 'mother-fucker' is a salient obscenity
among many young black Americans, *bahanchot* ('sister-fucker')
is singularly offensive to Fiji Indians.
   Boasting of one's own sexual prowess and bad behaviour is
common in adolescent duels, while adult duellists usually lam-
baste opponents for their alleged misconduct. Fiji Indian and
Eskimo song duellists often draw upon specific misdeeds in the
past of competitors. In at least two genres, however, sounding
and Tiv 'drumming the scandal', insults and allegations must

be impossible or highly unlikely, or they may lead to denials
and reprisal rather than appropriate responses. A successful
Tiv song reported by Paul Bohannan, for example, told how a
philandering opponent 'changed himself into a pig at night and
made it unsafe for every sow in the countryside'; the song struck
home even though its premise was incredible.

In professional duels, a single topic is often set for the contest,
either by the first singer or by the organiser of the duel. The
Sardinian singers studied by Elizabeth Mathias might argue,
for example, about the relative virtues of honour and money.
Professional singers prefer artfully allusive comments to out-
right abuse; insults must be woven into more topical verses.
Blatant attacks can be turned against the singer, as in this
Maltese song collected by Marcia Herndon, in which the performer responds to an opponent who called him an ass:

The plow presses down for me
Because in the fields, that's what you need.
And when you say, 'Gee-haw, let's go',
With my hind legs I crush your face.

Adolescent duels are only informally marked off from ordinary speech; they slip easily into and out of conversation.
Performances in all the adolescent genres may begin with an
obscene response to an apparently innocent phrase, as in this
Turkish example:

Speaker A: *Hayrola?*
            What's going on?
Speaker B: *Götüne girsin karyola.*
            Stick a bedstead up your ass.

Adolescent duels may also start with any of a limited range of
traditional opening gambits; the phrase 'Your mother' is often
enough to catalyse a sounding session. Boys can either accept
or reject the challenge. Such duels take place within groups of
friends rather than with strangers.

Adult duels are much more sharply set apart from ordinary
discourse. Although Eskimo and Fiji Indian song duels may
start spontaneously at social gatherings, adult duels are usually

initiated by a challenge. A special setting is used, whether a neutral homestead as in Fiji, or the stages where Sardinian song wars are held. Adult West Indian duels almost always occur in a festival context, as during carnival.

The role of the audience is another important contextual difference between the two types of duel. It is not clear that an audience is necessary for adolescents. When it is present, however, it is important in evaluating performances; onlookers cheer skilful insults and mock at boys whose retorts are clumsy or faltering. Such comments in turn influence the duellists. In the sounding sessions observed by Labov, duels ended when one boy was unable to produce any further sounds; derision and catcalls hastened such failure. Despite these effects of audience participation, adolescent duels are basically dyadic interactions. The audience is rarely neutral; it may be recruited as an ally through clever performance. The responsibility for controlling the contest, that is, for ensuring that tempers do not flare and fights result, lies with the duellists themselves and not with the audience. Perhaps most important, adolescent duels end with clear winners and losers. Verbal contests provide an opportunity for informal social ranking, both in one's own eyes and in those of the audience. Patterns of dominance and leadership can be shaped and maintained through duelling.

The audience is much more important in adult duels; indeed, without an audience the duels could not take place. Onlookers not only evaluate songs but provide the most effective restraint on tempers as well. In offering and accepting a challenge, Eskimos and Fiji Indians agree to the rule that getting angry during a duel means defeat. The audience is an authoritative witness to performers' conduct and self-control; it can also stop the contest if a fight seems imminent. Both Eskimo and Fiji Indian societies are basically egalitarian and lack internal legal officials; conflicts are most frequently resolved by those immediately concerned alone. The voluntary submission to third-party control in duels allows them to serve as courts of a sort.

Duelling among the Tiv is similarly triadic, but it differs in some important details. 'Drumming the scandal' begins with performances at separate households, first by the parties themselves and then by the professional songmakers they employ; such independent singing may continue for weeks. When the local leader charged with keeping the peace feels that the two parties are nearing the end of their patience with each other, he invites both parties to his compound to perform and promises to judge both their songs and the original conflict which brought on the duelling. Both parties sing at the same time, and he names the winner.

Accounts of professional duels suggest that artistry and entertainment are more important concerns than personal conflict. They take place before an audience, but its major role is evaluation rather than control. The Maltese contests studied by Herndon often reflect factional disputes within the ranks of professional singers, and successful duelling is an important means of achieving leadership in this group. Such contests, however, have political implications for a relatively small and specialised guild of fellow professionals rather than for the audience as a whole.

The actual outcomes of duels are particularly significant. Adolescent duels end with clear victors, as do the Maltese and Sardinian competitions. Other adult contests present a different picture. Fiji Indian challenges end when one group is made so uncomfortable that it sends for other villagers to stop the contest. These men reprimand both parties equally, insisting that the duel cease and that the singers swear off such performances in the future, as they are divisive. In the Tiv case cited by Bohannan, the local leader declared one party to be the better singers and the others to have won the case which started the duels. Descriptions of Eskimo duels are less specific, but various ethnographers have suggested that the opportunity to vent one's anger restores a balance between disputants. In the 'Speech Band' contests on Tobago studied by Abrahams, no winner is declared; instead, in the words of one band member, 'When everyone is finished [their speeches], they shake hands and go and part.' The absence of a clear victor in these four societies is important; each party can feel they have proved themselves to be the others' equals. Rather than providing the chance for social ranking which duelling affords adolescents and professionals, these adult performances result in the public rebalancing of the interests and reputations of individuals and help to ensure their good relations in the future. Such ensurance is not foolproof, but duelling usually leads to amity.

To sum up, adolescent duels, where the consequences of overt conflict are minimal, are informally demarcated and stylistically less demanding than other varieties; insults attack passivity and familial values. Professional contests are the most demanding and formally staged; their social effects, however, are limited. Both adolescent and professional duels help to define hierarchical relations within small groups sharing both common interests and common definition *vis-à-vis* the larger social world. Adult duels are potentially threatening to many more people. They are marked as safe and conventional performances by rigorous stylistic demands; social obligation is a central theme. Such contests are particularly salient in egalitarian societies lacking internal third-parties for conflict management. Duelling makes it possible to meet one's opponent as an equal and to enlist the audience as judge.

Verbal duelling clearly has social implications for its participants and allows them considerable scope for personal politicising. Equally important, however, is its playful and artistic character. Verbal skill is highly prized in all societies where duelling occurs; audiences come not to referee but to enjoy the wit and creativity of their fellows. Duels delight as well as decide.

Sherzer and Kirshenblatt-Gimblett have suggested a distinction between instrumental discourse, in which one is concerned with outcome, and speech play, where speakers focus on the process and textures of their talk. Verbal duelling combines these interests. Stylistic conventions, for example, limit performers but also offer the chance for creative variation within their bounds. On the other hand, duels necessarily affect future relationships between participants. In considering the varieties of duelling I have discussed, the distinction between intent and effect is important. While a sounding session may realign leadership patterns, this is unlikely to be the intent of the duellists; sounding is enjoyable in itself. By contrast, Eskimo performers consciously aim at humiliating their opponents and gaining the support of the audience; artistry is necessary to accomplish these ends.

Play and purpose are inextricably linked in verbal duelling. Only the gamelike and playful definition of the duel makes it possible; insult unrestrained by traditional practice could be deadly serious. Blending abuse with artistry allows one, in Owen Wister's famous phrase, to 'Smile when you say that'.

Drama: Aristotle in Indonesia

LAURENCE G. AVERY and
JAMES L. PEACOCK

LIKE EVERY symbolic form, drama distils a view of existence. Fundamentally, the conditions of drama such as stage and audience imply a dualistic world-view; stage and action, representing fiction, are opposed to life and audience representing reality. Western theories of drama, reflecting a wider dualism in Western thought, have conformed faithfully to such dualism. Do the same premises underlie drama in other cultures? Especially relevant to the question is drama in Asian culture, where Buddhist and other philosophies have claimed as illusion what the West is accustomed to call reality; what view of existence is distilled in Asian drama?

Perhaps the major contribution which social anthropology has made to knowledge is to confront theory with example. Centuries of refined thought in an intellectual tradition encounter an intensive, systematic, ethnographic effort at uncovering a concrete experience. Here the theory is that developed for drama in the West over the past 2,500 years. The case is a particular dramatic form studied by an anthropological investigation during one year in an industrial city in Indonesia.

Theories of the drama in the Western tradition deal with plays in terms of four basic relationships: the relationship between a play and (1) its author, where the concern is with the work as an expression of its creator; (2) its audience, where the concern is with the effect of the work on those who witness it; (3) its object of imitation, where the concern is with the work as a projector of some aspect of the outside world; and (4) itself, where the concern is with the formal characteristic of the work (its structure and unity). Reasonably adequate theories deal

A Javanese ludruk transvestite dancer-singer poses as an aristocrat.
(Laurence G. Avery)

with matters in all or most of these areas; but even comprehensive theories tend to emphasise one of the areas, to find within
one relationship the questions that seem most in need of exploration, the major categories for analysing the work, and the
chief grounds for evaluating it. At the beginning of the Western
tradition of speculation about the arts the Greeks emphasised
the relationship between a play and some aspect of the world
outside it. Imitation, the concept designating that relationship,
was central in the theories of art of both Plato and Aristotle.
Beyond that similarity, however, the two founders of the
Western tradition had little in common. The differences
between them are so wide that together they contain by
implication all the theories of the drama developed during
the twenty-five hundred years since their times.

For Plato imitation meant copying. A truth or virtue could be
copied, as in Aesop's fables (or the *Republic*). But usually the
object copied in plays was emotional behaviour – for example,
unpremeditated murder or crying. Plays tended to copy emotive actions because more people are moved by emotion and its
displays than by reasoned restraint. Furthermore, noting that
playwrights speak altogether through their characters, Plato
described the drama as pure imitation in contrast with mixed
modes such as the epic, in which the author speaks sometimes
in his own voice. Plato related the effect of a work to its degree of
imitativeness. Thus the drama, being the only pure imitation,
was the most moving of the arts. Finally, his theory of effect
made Plato think of the drama as the most dangerous of the
arts. Artistic effect was stimulation. Behaviour in a literary work
encouraged, or stimulated, the same kind of behaviour in its
audience, who after the experience of the work were apt to feel
and act in the ways imitated in it. Since he distrusted the
emotions, and assumed that a play's effect was to stimulate like
behaviour in its audience, Plato was more hostile to the drama
than to any other art.

For Aristotle, on the other hand, the drama, tragedy in
particular, was the most admirable of the arts. This divergence
from Plato stems from the fact that in Aristotle the notion of
imitation involves nothing like actual copying. For Aristotle the
playwright is not the creative artist supported by nineteenth-
century theories of the imagination, or the philosopher artist

encouraged by twentieth-century cultural fragmentation, but neither is he a mere copyist. He makes something quite different from anything else in existence – a play, with its own purpose, materials, and criteria for evaluation. 'Imitation' is the term Aristotle uses to designate the process involved in making a play. Nowhere did Plato consider the drama, or any other art, in terms of its characteristics as art. Aristotle limits his consideration precisely to those characteristics.

The most important characteristic, and logically the first, is indicated by Aristotle's statement in the *Poetics* that a play imitates a human action. The key term is 'action'. Aristotle's theory of imitation leads to an emphasis not on character or verisimilitude, but on plot. From the multiplicity of actions performed by a person (usually one whose life is recorded in history or mythology), the playwright selects a single action that he can make intelligible and meaningful by the elaboration of its beginning, middle, and end. This elaboration is the basis of the plot, which Aristotle called the soul of a play because it dictates the other elements of the work. The action must be carried out by agents, and the agents must do the things made necessary or probable by the action. So the playwright provides the needed characters and episodes. And to manifest fully the action and its meaning the characters must externalise their thoughts, so the playwright gives them language. Thus dialogue, episode, and character are functions of the plot, and the plot imitates a human action.

In contrast with Plato, whose consideration of a play was always in terms of its moral or social function, Aristotle considered a play in terms of its structure. Tragedy imitated a noble action and in its structure moved from stability to catastrophe, while comedy imitated a base action and moved from adversity to harmony. And he judged a play not by its correctness of belief but by its ability to produce the effect appropriate to its kind. The effect appropriate to tragedy Aristotle described as catharsis. Exactly what he meant by the word is not certain, and historically 'catharsis' has been interpreted along three main lines: to mean (1) a working off of audience emotions, or purgation; (2) a balancing of audience emotions and reason, or purification of personality; and more recently (3) an enhancement of audience understanding. Whatever Aristotle intended, however, it is clear that he understood the effect of the drama in a different way from Plato. Catharsis carries no suggestion of stimulation. Its varying interpretations have in common an emphasis on the opposite, on a final release from the grip of emotion.

In antiquity after Aristotelian rhetoric replaced aesthetics as the concern of literate minds, the drama was treated mainly by church fathers such as Tertullian and Augustine, who denounced it. The Aristotelian idea of the drama as a formal structure survived, however, and Dante could justify himself in calling his long poem a comedy by saying that it followed the direction of a comic plot in moving from adversity to happiness. The Renaissance saw a renewed interest in the drama, spurred on in part by the discovery of classical texts; and the rise of modern drama in Western Europe and England is accompanied by an impressive body of speculation on the subject. In terms of the conception of the drama reflected in the discussions, the years from the late sixteenth through to the eighteenth century make an integrated period. Writers on the drama invoked Aristotle frequently, and, as Ben Jonson put it in *Timber* in the early 1620s, everybody was 'busy about imitation'. But in truth the structural considerations that had dominated Aristotle's concern did not have a similar prominence in seventeeth- and eighteenth-century studies. And the relationship that controlled people's conception of the drama was not the relationship between a play and the object it imitated but the one between a play and its audience. The first classic of English criticism, written in the early 1580s, Sir Philip Sidney's *Defence of Poesie*, presages the next two hundred years with its appeal to Aristotle on behalf of a definition that is decidedly non-Aristotelian in its emphasis on the drama's effect:

> Poesy therefore is an arte of imitation, for so Aristotle termeth it in the word *mimesis*, that is to say, a representing, counterfetting, or figuring foorth – to speake metaphorically, a speaking picture: with this end, to teach and delight.

In the *Defence* Sidney generates all aspects of the drama out of that understanding of its purpose. The playwright is a teacher, and in moving men to virtue he is more effective than philosopher or historian because, by combining the abstract ideas of the one and the concrete examples of the other, he makes his lessons as delicious as cherries. Again, in order to guarantee the moral purpose of his play the playwright imitates not what has been or is but what should be. And the playwright who understands the limitations of the audience in imagination and feeling will observe the unities of action, time, and place and will not mix comic and tragic events. During the two hundred years following the *Defence* not everyone arrived at conclusions identical with Sidney's on these and related questions. But during that time everyone reasoned identically about them. A play was made to produce an effect in its audience. Hence the norms of art and the canons of critical judgment were grounded in the needs, wishes, and capabilities of the audience.

Unity of time, a concept treated in terms of audience imagination, is an example. Sidney and his educated contemporaries thought that the time covered by the plot of a play should approximate to the time needed for its performance. If the events of the plot spanned no more than a day, they reasoned, an audience could be caught up imaginatively in the experience of the play and its attention held throughout. But if the plot spanned a longer time, a time measured in weeks or months or years, it seemed a different matter. Most of that time would of necessity be omitted in a two and a half hour performance, and an audience could not fail to notice the gaps. Its attention called to the artificiality of the play, the audience would no longer suspend its disbelief and participate imaginatively in the performance. The playwright, as Jonson put it in the prologue to one of his own plays in 1600, would have 'outrun the apprehension of [his] auditory'. Jonson and a few of his contemporaries observed the unity of time in their plays, but most Elizabethan and Jacobean playwrights did not, among them Marlowe and Shakespeare. And it could not be observed that their plays, after gaining the imaginative participation of an audience, lost it by leaps in fictive time. As a result, with the Restoration, speculation about the drama changed and began to deny the need for unity of time. 'Spectators never confuse the play with reality', Samuel Johnson said in his *Preface to the Plays of William*

Shakespeare, published in 1765, and he went on from there to explain that only the unity of action is essential to a play. Since spectators are aware from the first that the play before them is only an imitation of successive 'events, not the events themselves, 'why,' he asked, 'may not the second imitation represent an action that happened years after the first, if it be so connected with it, that nothing but time can be supposed to intervene? Time is, of all modes of existence, most obsequious to the imagination; a lapse of years is as easily conceived as a passage of hours.' And on the unities of time and place he summed up the verdict of the age by announcing that a concern with them had 'given more trouble to the poet, than pleasure to the auditor'.

Unity of time and place and action were aspects of a larger concern, unity of effect. During the two hundred years from Sidney to Dr Johnson experience showed that the imagination of audiences was more flexible than originally supposed and that a unified effect did not require unity of time and place. Important structural questions were thus decided by recourse to the capabilities of the audience. Speculation about other questions relating to the drama moved to the same source for reasons and answers, to the audience. And during the hundred years following Johnson the critical orientation did not change. New kinds of plays became prevalent by the late nineteenth century. Melodramas replaced tragedies, and sentimental plays and farces replaced comedies as staples of the theatre. But these developments came in the wake of the changing conceptions of the audience, that is, human nature. The eighteenth century saw the beginnings of a new valuation of feeling that rose to its crest in the Romantic era and then spilled over through the nineteenth century and later. The passions, which had been the distrusted element in the human personality, constantly in need of control by the understanding and judgment lest they lead to ill-health, sin, and treason, became the emotions, the fundamental and reliable part of the personality emanating from the heart, and the source of goodness and health in individuals and communities. This new valuation was a conceptual revolution of gigantic proportions, and in the drama it gave rise to the kinds of plays that provide pure and uncritical experiences of emotion, that is, to melodrama,

sentimental drama, and farce. But it was still the audience that
provided the reference point for the drama. So the more things
changed, the more they stayed the same. From the late sixteenth century until most of the nineteenth, it was to the needs,
desires, and capabilities of the audience, however differently
these were perceived, that people looked as a matter of course
for guidance in constructing and evaluating plays.

What we call modern drama began when some people in the late
nineteenth century turned from the audience to the world as the
primary reference for plays. The imitative, or mimetic, conception characteristic of modern drama differed in detail from
Aristotle's. Where he saw the playwright as a builder of plots
whose chief need was craftsman-like skill, modernists saw the
playwright as a philosopher whose chief obligation was,
through his plays, to make truthful statements about life. And
such was the influence of naturalistic determinism in the mod-
ernist era that the statements were usually gloomy. Two kinds
of plays, differentiated by their techniques, emerged as vehicles
for these statements. First to appear was the realistic play,
brought to attention by Ibsen in the 1870s and perfected by
Chekhov in such a play as *The Cherry Orchard*. The technical aim
of realistic plays is to create an illusion of reality. Typically,
therefore, plot is implicit rather than emphatic, dialogue is
prose rather than verse, characters and their problems are
ordinary rather than extraordinary, and setting is contemporary rather than historical. Skilful use of the techniques can
produce the verisimilitude suggested by Ibsen when he said
that with his plays he wanted to create the impression of real life
transpiring in a real room with only the fourth wall removed. In
order not to disturb the impression of life-likeness, the realistic
playwright conveys his interpretation indirectly, through his
selection and organisation of material.

Expressionistic plays, the other kind of mimetic drama in the
modern era, are not indirect in that way. Strindberg brought
out the possibilities of the expressionistic play in his work
between *Crimes and Crimes* (1899) and *The Ghost Sonata* (1907),
and this kind flourished into the 1920s in such plays as
O'Neill's *The Hairy Ape* and Rice's *The Adding Machine*. The
technical aim of expressionistic plays is to objectify the playwright's meaning. Hence any of the play's elements – plot,

character, dialogue, setting, stage movement, lighting, and properties – may become artificial, non-life-like, symbols. Examples are the dialogue in *The Adding Machine* which consists of newspaper headlines and the adding machine itself, which grows to the size of the stage.

The closer we come to the present, the harder it is to see the forest for the trees. On the one hand the modern mimetic conception still has adherents. The absurdist drama, with its depiction of an existentialist world-view, is an example; and its chief kind of play has been expressionistic, as with Ionesco. On the other hand, since the 1930s it seems that the more prevalent way of thinking about plays has involved a return to an emphasis on their relationship with the audience. Beyond basic orientation, however, the contemporary effective, or pragmatic, era has little in common with earlier pragmatic eras, and the most obvious difference is the fragmentation of the contemporary, its division into groups and individuals each with a different design on the audience. The variety of aims has been great. The social drama associated with Brecht and Odets and the 1930s sought to educate audiences about the nature of social reality. The theatre of cruelty, based on the ideas of Artaud and exemplified in the work of Albee, Pinter, and Weiss, takes its name from its aim of disturbing its audience. And black ritual drama, a phenomenon peculiar to the United States, strives to enhance the racial consciousness of its audience. Individuals too have had their own programmes. Maxwell Anderson revived poetic drama in order to increase the emotional impact of his plays; Thornton Wilder experimented with the stage to stimulate audience sensitivity, and T. S. Eliot turned to the theatre to carry his Christian message – the list of groups and individuals could be expanded. And the pragmatic orientation of the present can be seen in other ways as well. For instance, there is now a revival of farce, the kind of drama designed purely as theatrical experience, as in the recent work of Tom Stoppard.

Four relationships make up the context of a play, the relationship with its author, its audience, the world it imitates, and its own structured requirements. Despite the great variety among theorists in the Western tradition, only two of those relationships have been the centre of focus. For most of the

2,500 years since Plato and Aristotle, theories of the drama have been orientated towards the audience, but at the outset of the Western tradition, and again in the late nineteenth and early twentieth centuries, the orientation was towards the subject of imitation. Thus the main concern has been either the relation between dramatic action and reality (the question of imitation) or the relation between dramatic action and audience (the question of effect).

During 1962–3, one of us spent a year in and about the industrial Indonesian city of Surabayà studying plays known as *ludruk*, and the life surrounding them. Created, performed and viewed by the working class, the ludruk combined comedy, melodrama, songs, and dances into performances that lasted from several hours to all night. Drawing on traditions ranging from the classical puppet plays to contemporary Marxist propaganda, the ludruk troupes improvised action and dialogue without benefit of script, and during the year their audiences totalled hundreds of thousands. Since the 1966 massacre that accompanied the shift of government from Sukarno to Suharto, the ludruk has come under the control of the army. Despite losing some of its political pungency, it remains popular.

In order to grasp as least some of the meaning of ludruk, a method was followed which drew as much from ethnography as from drama theory. For a year, the investigator, an anthropologist, lived among the working class Surabayans while attending more than eighty performances of the ludruk – in commercial theatres, at political meetings, in village and shanty-town celebrations. He travelled with the troupes, interviewed actors and directors, and analysed music and audience responses as well as on-stage action. Reconstructing the ludruk performance as a total communicative event, he endeavoured to relate it to the wider social and cultural context of the participants. (For details, see Peacock 1968.)

What do ludruk and Western dramatic theory say to each other? Western drama theory has been portrayed as revolving round two relationships: first, the relation between dramatic action and reality (the question of imitation), and, second, the relation between dramatic action and audience (the question of effect). Before discussing the substance of the theories, it is

necessary to inquire whether even these general relationships
have meaning for our example (ludruk).

Imitation implies a distinction between on-stage and off,
fantasy and reality. Indonesia partakes of an Asian tradition
perhaps best epitomised in Buddhism where the 'really' real is
the unseen, and it is the 'apparently' real that may be fantasy.
Does this epistemology underlie the Indonesian drama?
Perhaps, but it still permits a distinction between fantasy and
reality and thus some notion of imitation. More immediately
relevant is the rhetoric of contemporary Indonesian society
which draws on an incredibly active and revered dramatic
tradition (especially that centred on the *wajang kulit* or shadow
play) to couch existence in the metaphors of drama. President
Sukarno styled himself a *dalang*, the shadow-play narrator,
implying that society was his puppet. He once wrote a newspaper column under the pen name of the *wajang kulit* hero,
Bima, and he bestowed the name of the *wajang kulit* heroine,
Srikandi, on female paratroopers who landed in West New
Guinea. Quite appropriately, experts on Indonesian politics
have written major treatises on that interplay between drama
and event. It seems that here, indeed, all the world's a stage.

In the face of such an epistemology, it is well to begin with
simple questions. Is there a stage? Does the Javanese drama
even recognise physically a separation between dramatic
action and off-stage existence? There is, it does. Ludruk is
performed on a raised platform, separation from life. The
extent of separation increases as one moves from village and
neighbourhood to commercial performances. In commercial
theatres, walls separate the communicative event from its contexts, and within that theatre an orchestra pit (occupied by the
percussion orchestra) separates stage from audience. In villages and neighbourhood performances, there is no pit between
stage and audience, and children crowd onto the edges as the
action unfolds in the centre. Occasionally sudden violations
occur. Once at the close of a Communist performance a mob of
children stormed the stage to grab all the decorations, and once
in a village a man, regarded as strange and retarded, jumped on
the stage to rescue the heroine – an action reminiscent of the
spectators at American football games who run onto the field to
tackle the opponent as he races for a touch-down. That such

violations of stage-space are regarded as inappropriate and are
made by children and the child-like confirms the conclusion
that boundaries are there. The stage is both physically and
conceptually a separate place. That the on-stage world is separate is illustrated by a single
dialogue. Two ludruk clowns were enacting a scene in which
they stole someone's chest. Suddenly one clown said to the
other, 'Someone's watching!' 'Who?' asked the other, startled.
'They are', replied the first, pointing to the audience. He suddenly widened the perceptual frame to include more than the
on-stage world. The laughter proved that this world is normally kept distinct.

Within the ludruk performance itself, different degrees of
removal from the world are signalled by various symbolic
devices. The greatest removal is signalled by transvestite
singer-dancers; the least, by melodramatic plots, and in between are the clowns who shuttle back and forth between
abstraction and involvement. The melodramas do not imitate
life obsessively, but they are fairly realistic; characters speak a
daily language, wear street clothes; scenes are set in familiar
locales, and plots depict contemporary problems – albeit in
schematic and stereotyped ways. Positioned between scenes of
the melodrama is the transvestite dancer-singer. He dresses in
an aristocratic Javanese sarong and blouse rather than street
clothes and wears an aristocratic hair style. He sings his quasi-
classical chants in a refined language instead of street Javanese.
He is set against a backdrop depicting mythical palaces and
gardens instead of domestic and street scenes, and his songs are
of mythical loves and exalted political sentiments. The shift
from the more worldly melodrama to the less worldly singer-
dancer is marked by lowering and raising a curtain.

The clown is both in and out of the world or, as was said of St
Paul, in it but not of it. On one side, he is the reality factor in the
ludruk. While the transvestites posture as aristocrats, and the
melodramatic actors change roles with plots, the clown always
represents the status of the working-class audience. He is the
servant, peasant, worker, or reprobate. In his opening song and
monologue, positioned as complementary to the idealistic
chant of the transvestite, he groans about the real problems of
daily life in a corrupt society – low wages, high prices, standing

in line for government rice. His language is low Javanese, his clothes humble, his posture unpretentious. In the melodrama he plays servant to the wealthy families, moving like Falstaff with Prince Hal round the fringes of the action on which he shrewdly comments. His humour is of a type the Surabayans term *nglètèk* – deflating. He reduces the high to low, the romantic to real, representing the unblinking vision of the sturdy working man.

Yet the clown is not a carbon copy of the Javanese worker. He is a symbol. His status is signalled by his stylised clothing, usually a white servant's coat and a sarong; by his name, which remains the same even as the plot varies (whereas melodramatic characters take on different names for different plots); and by the sacral Hindu-Javanese tradition, to which he is an heir, that selects as the wisest and most powerful of the gods Semar, a clown. As a symbol, the clown is complementary to the transvestite. It is these two who transcend the naturalism of the melodrama, the transvestite by his between-scene song and dance and the clown by his prologue and within-scene jokes that mock the action. Where the transvestite stands for mythical romance and idealistic ideology, the clown veers in an equally stylised manner towards hard-knocks realism. (The regular patterning of this as well as other oppositions in the ludruk form is indicated by the fact that although political propaganda had been doled out to the troupes collectively, in fact in all troupes and all performances the transvestite sings the idealistic slogans while the clown rasps out criticism.)

In sum, imitation is a viable category within the world view of ludruk. Ludruk awareness of that notion is revealed in the existence of a stage, in distinctions between on-stage and off-stage, and in implicit but quite systematic classification of characters (transvestite singer, clown, and melodramatic actor) according to the extent and way each imitates daily life.

The second major relationship assumed by Western dramatic theory is that of action to audience (effect). Again, it is well to start with a basic question: does ludruk have an audience? Yes, a category of people can be recognised who buy tickets, sit in special places, and do not normally clamber on-stage (that children and the retarded sometimes do is the exception which proves the rule). Beyond that, a brief comparison can show that *audience* is a category which ludruk takes carefully into account. Consider three plays. *Bitter Sugar Cane* is a Marxist play which begins with oppressed masses and ends with revolution. *Wave of Trikora* is a nationalist play which ends by a young girl sacrificing marriage and family to dedicate herself to Indonesia's capture of West New Guinea. *Revenge in the Night* depicts the domestic trials of two couples, one upper class and the other lower class, and it ends with the bad spouse from each couple suffering while the good spouses marry happily. The Marxist play was presented by a troupe which included actors hired by that most formidable anti-Communist outfit, the army. The second play, which subordinated class-struggle to nationalism, was performed by a troupe with the strongest Communist ties. The bourgeois, domestic play was done by a troupe under contract to the army. Everything seems mixed up; the plays do not express the apparent political loyalties of troupes or actors and, in fact, just the opposite. The explanation lies with the audiences. The Marxist play was presented to workers at a Communist labour union meeting. The nationalist play was given at a benefit performance for government dignitaries. The domestic play was staged in a commercial theatre whose audience was largely married couples. In each case, audience determines action.

But what does action do for audience? Here we come back to the Western theories of effect which are essentially the Platonic and the Aristotelian. Dramatic action is viewed either as stimulating the audience to imitate that action in life, or as providing catharsis so that it is relieved of the desire to do that action in life. Millions of dollars worth of research on the effect of television on children have come up with these same alternative notions; they have remained pervasive through two millennia of Western thought regarding drama.

Within the ludruk, the clown is more Aristotelian and the transvestite Platonic. Complaining outrageously and enacting the forbidden, the clown obviously provides catharsis. Audience responses are continuous and loud, as they express their agreement with him and laugh. The transvestite, too, permits the expression of taboo impulses, but he is distinct from the clown in adopting the posture of the instructor, the singer of propaganda songs which seemingly aim to stimulate action:

Organise! Vote! The flood of responses to the clown contrasts
with the trickle for the transvestite's message. The figure himself elicits reactions (either obscene insults or infatuated admir-
ation) but not a single instance was recorded of an overt
response to his message during a performance. The only
response was after the performance, around midnight, when
beggar women bedding down for the night in the street were
heard to sing some of the transvestite's songs. But these ver-
bally activistic chants (Organise! Vote!) were sung for their
soothing melodies – as lullabies to put their children to sleep!
Platonically, at least in the specific sense of stimulating action,
the transvestite appears to fail.

What about the melodrama? It is useful to distinguish two
types of melodramatic plots, which I shall term 'T' (for traditional) and 'M' (for modern). T-plots are set in colonial,
pre-independence society. They are cyclical, always beginning
and ending with a scene of family harmony. In between there
occurs a 'Tom Jones' type of story which moves by coincidences
and far-fetched kinship entanglements towards discovery of a
lost child and its final reinstatement into the family of origin.
This process takes many years, is out of the control of any
individual hero or heroine, and does not culminate in the
destruction of any villain or scapegoat. The clown is prominent
throughout, and the final group scene of family rejoicing is
rather like classic comic endings as we know them.

M-plots are set in post-independence society. They are
linear, always ending with a circumstance different from that
with which the play began. The moving force is an individual
rather than coincidence; the process takes only ten days or
months, and successful culmination always follows the 'tragic'
destruction of some villain or scapegoat. The percentage of
scenes dominated by the clown decreases, as does the number
of persons in the final scene. One can thus speak of M as being
more 'tragic' in that sacrifice of individuals is necessary to bring
about the final result which is enjoyed by only a few, and
comedy is less prominent. The trend is towards M. During the
year of study, the M-plots circulated among the various
troupes, whereas no T-plot circulated beyond the troupe that
originally performed it, so each T-plot would eventually die out
as its troupe disbanded.

The success achieved by M-plots is that a lower-class female manages to marry an upper-class male, an achievement which occurs only after the destruction of some relative or friend of the female. One may return to the question of effect by wondering what this means to the lower-class audience. They do not respond overtly to the final marriage itself, though they do scream with vehemence their satisfaction at the destruction of the selected victim just before that. There are certain interesting social discontinuities between the typical audience of these plays and the final scene. The couple on-stage is young, newly married, and as yet childless (which in traditional Javanese conception means not yet fully married at all), while the couple off-stage is typically older, longer married, and with several children. The couple on-stage is of mixed class and is played by actors of the same sex (men); off-stage the couples in the audience are heterosexual and of the same class. These facts suggest that the M-plot is not designed to stimulate imitation of its action, for it carefully defines its action as that which the audience could not, or would not, normally imitate. Does it, then, provide the other alternative, catharsis, by permitting a somewhat oblique, fantasy achievement of at least certain desires of the working class? Doubtless the M-plot does do this, but consider also an audience/actor relationship which is different from either the stimulation or the catharsis alternatives.

In their most vulgar form, as they are represented in some of the latest Western notions of drama and media, the Platonic and Aristotelian concepts of effect are quite mechanistic. Drama stimulates like an electric shock or releases like a toilet-flush, and the causal chain between action and audience is tracked as simply as that. In Javanese theatre, a different relationship is envisioned. The point of drama is not so much to mount a climactic action unified in time and place that culminates in an effect; rather it is to vitalise a classificatory scheme, a cosmology, that is shared by actors and audience. Such a scheme orders a wide range of elements – values, regions, substances, statuses, orders of spirituality – and these include such components of the drama as genres, musical themes, and character types. The patterns in terms of which these elements are ordered are complex, but one dominant structure is built up of opposites: high is contrasted to low, male to female, spiritual to material. Overriding the oppositions, however, is a fundamental unity, and this is demonstrated in the plays by myriad mixtures, reversals, and other relationships. Thus, the clown shows that low is really high; the transvestite, that male can be female. Extending the system off-stage, the audience and actors are both opposed and united: one pays and the other is paid, one expresses and the other responds, and, to take the last scene of the melodrama as an example, an on-stage couple reverses the heterosexual, same-class feature of the audience by being homosexual, and of mixed class. One function of the ludruk, then, is to vitalise for actors and audience a shared system of categories, a cosmology, in which they jointly partici-pate and which bestows meaning on existence by joining oppo-sites in unity. Such a function can be claimed even more strongly for the traditional dramas, rites, and etiquette which are the *grundlage* of the Javanese civilisation.

This said, it must be quickly admitted that in other respects the ludruk does act to stimulate and release in the way envisioned by the Western theory. Indeed, this is claimed by the ludruk people themselves, especially the Marxists among them, who speak of the plays as weapons, torches, and the like. The trend from the T-plot to the M would seem to move ludruk away from the cosmological towards the effecting pattern envisioned by the West. That direction has not been gained without conflict. Sjamsudin, the Marxist, versus Bawa, the clown, fought over whether plot or comedy (and, thus, cosmol-ogy) would dominate – until Bawa was mysteriously run over by the troupe bus.

Certainly Javanese culture and drama express phenom-enological features rather outside the Western mould. In the background lies a philosophy that subtly reverses dis-tinctions between fantasy and reality customary in the West, and in the foreground is a rhetoric that permits drama to spill into life. The bestowing of unity and meaning on experience by interplay of opposites is perhaps more strongly a component in the Javanese plays than those envisioned in Western theory, which has concentrated on the creation of climax and effect.

Yet considering the difference in cultural and philosophical foundations, the Western dramatic theory and the Javanese ludruk plays share fundamentals quite remarkably. Both turn

on the basic relationships of stage to life (imitation) and action
to audience (effect). In part, this convergence can be explained
by pragmatics; for drama to operate, it would seem to require
an audience, and need to depict an existence which in some
sense both imitates and contrasts with daily life; to achieve
these objectives it would seem to need stage, plots, characters,
and the like. Then one must ask, why drama? Why not some
other form? The answer would seem to lie in phenomenology
and sociology. Humans distinguish between fiction and life,
and at certain levels of social complexity they express this
distinction by building stages that are separate from their
surroundings, by hiring actors separate from audiences, and by
creating that system of dialectical relation between staged or
enacted fiction and responding audiences that we know as
drama.

Tell us a Story

VENETIA NEWALL

STORYTELLING is an ancient, universal phenomenon. Often people tell each other stories when they are thrown together casually in groups formed by circumstances beyond their control. An army barracks after dusk, an old people's home, a spell in hospital – all these are occasions when people feel the urge to pass their time in this way.

Travel also lends itself to storytelling and it is a custom with long antecedents. This was how Chaucer's pilgrims on their way to the shrine at Canterbury whiled away the hours. Sailors on board ship are famous for their yarns, and Linda Dégh, author of the classic *Folktales and Society*, describes peasants in her native Hungary telling stories on the long road home from market. She gives a graphic account of miners from Nógrád Couty rising while it was still dark and walking twelve miles to work. Stories made the cold trek seem less disagreeable.

In many cultures storytelling was usual during long and monotonous manual tasks. In Europe it lightened the evening work for women sitting by the fire in winter and spinning, or preparing a variety of home-grown products – but of course household chores continue throughout the year. Susie Hoogasian-Villa, an Armenian scholar, remembers the women of her homeland lightening the dreary task of preparing dough for noodles by telling stories. Jobs such as this were often collective, with neighbours lending a helping hand, or they might be confined to the immediate family circle. Storytelling under these circumstances also went on out-of-doors. Men swopped tales while guarding their herds, or perhaps protecting a valuable crop of grapes against marauders – quiet agricultural work that was not too demanding provided an ideal opportunity.

A Sicilian storyteller outside a factory in Palermo (Axel Poignant)

But it is the evening, when the day's work is done, that we think of as the classic occasion for telling stories. It is the proper time to relax, and storytelling induces sleep by relieving tension and anxiety. It is said that, unless he listened to his three blind storytellers before retiring, Ivan the Terrible was unable to rest. Many storytelling sessions ended with the listeners falling asleep, and indeed these sessions served the same function as sleeping-tablets and were probably much better for the health! All over the African continent storytelling is an evening activity. True it can also occur sometimes during simple undemanding day-time tasks, but there is a widespread belief that it is unlucky to tell tales at any time other than dusk. Those who violate this custom will grow horns, according to the Zulu; the Kamba say their cattle will perish.

More than anything else, storytelling is a cheerful activity. It gives pleasure at social gatherings and informal happy occasions, whether at the local pub, or in the rural coffee houses of Moslem Yugoslavia, where it used to be the main entertainment for the male population, especially during the evenings of Ramadan, when the day-long fast was broken. Families in Benin celebrate a happy event – recovery from illness, a welcome visitor, the satisfactory sale of a cash crop – by holding an Ibota, an evening celebration centred on storytelling. It is arranged by the head of the family and everyone gathers near the ancestral shrine to hear stories and songs performed in his honour. Dan Ben-Amos describes these occasions in *Sweet Words: Storytelling Events in Benin*.

Storytelling is popular during *rites of passage*, the ceremonial events which mark a human being's transition from one state of life to another. Thus it was part of the pleasant task of the master of ceremonies to tell stories at a traditional Jewish wedding. Curiously, as it seems to us, it was also customary at wakes for the dead in Europe, South America and the West Indies. An informant remarked to Linda Dégh that to 'put the dead person into the room . . . and leave him alone . . . is a great sin. My God, how nice it is when people assemble for the soul of the deceased!' In Hungary the best storytellers were invited to honour a distinguished man in death. They came with their longest 'vigil tales' and these helped the mourners to stay awake. A tragic death – of a child, for instance – was different. But the death of an old person was not regarded as a cause for great sorrow and a really good wake would be talked about for years after. The same custom obtained in Ireland until very recently. Sean O'Sullivan says the young anticipated the death of the very old as an occasion for fun, especially in areas like Kerry where there was no other form of entertainment. The Hasidim, a pious Jewish sect, tell stories extolling the deeds of an eminent rabbi on *Yohrsait*, the anniversary of his death. It is also a way of passing the short interval between afternoon and evening prayer at *besmedresh*, the house of worship and study, while waiting for the sun to set. Children left to their own devices while their teacher prays with other men, gather round the schoolroom fire and imitate their elders until his return. Smaller children who become restive on the Sabbath are quietened with stories, and tales are told during *melaveh malkeh*, the final repast of the sacred day, taken at the rabbi's table. Men gather for a simple meal to hear legends of their holy men and the rabbi leads the storytelling. It is an activity which plays an exceptionally important role in the culture of the Hasidim, for it is central to the preservation of their religious way of life. Baal Shem Tov, the founder of the sect, used storytelling as a vehicle for his teaching, and his followers, the rabbis, have continued to use the same methods. Storytelling occurs on various social occasions, for it is the main form of entertainment in a community which shuns the theatre, cinema and even secular books. But association with the Sabbath gives it a unique, sacred significance. In *Legends of the Hasidim* Jerome Mintz shows how wonder-working rabbis have used the tales as vehicles of magic and power. If a follower was in distress, the rabbi told him a story, which was intended to help by describing the solution to an identical problem. But the story was more than mere reassurance. A prayer was often concealed in it. Indeed the story itself might be a prayer containing, so it was believed, the power to bring about the desired event.

Telling stories and teaching the faith have always been closely associated for the Jews, following the example of the biblical prophets and kings. Christians are taught the parables of Christ and in many other cultures storytelling is used to present and reinforce the moral precepts of the community. Young Armenian Christians learned wisdom and a sense of duty by listening to stories from parents, teachers, and priests. On the other hand, for Eskimos it meant the difference between life and death. Traditional tales collected by Edwin Hall in Noatak, Alaska, show that certain standards had to be observed in order to survive the harsh arctic climate. A man who stays too long in bed with his wife will not become a good caribou hunter; a lazy person may turn into a porcupine; annoying others can have serious consequences, and so on. Didactic stories are also occasionally used in a legalistic setting. An African parable may be introduced into a case brought before the chief and elders to show an offender that he has done wrong.

There are other practical reasons why stories are told in different cultures. In Eastern Hungary it was a means of getting children to help with the work in the fields: if they stopped, so did the story. We have already seen that it discouraged people from falling asleep at wakes, and Edwin Hall noticed that his elderly Eskimo narrators were rewarded with a meal and small gifts. The Benin storyteller who can play a musical instrument by way of accompaniment sees himself in the role of a psychiatrist who can heal minds and bring happiness. His model is the mythical tragic figure Oba Ewuakpe, who eased his grief by playing the lute. However, just as Limba narrators say that they give the community not only wisdom but enjoyment, so the main purpose of storytellers has always been to entertain.

Who they are varies greatly from one society to another. In Africa they are usually amateurs, though there are some professional narrators in Benin. The Limba say that anyone, even a child, may tell a story to the group and there is no word in their vocabulary which signifies 'professional storyteller'. In much of Europe the storytellers were often itinerants and wanderers: migratory labourers, landless peasants, soldiers, wandering apprentices, beggars and tramps, who told a tale in exchange for a meal and perhaps a night's shelter. There was also a class of trained professional bards and minstrels, who formed an influential elite during the Middle Ages. It seems unlikely that, as the Chadwicks assumed, these people were necessarily seers, though the gift is sometimes linked with a nervous and neurotic personality.

Storytellers could be part of the power structure, like the

court poets of the medieval Celtic lands, who owned estates. But
some occupy an ambiguous position on the fringes of society
and have no clearly defined social status. In Benin the storyteller is associated with night-spirits and witches, which carry
diseases like small-pox. He must placate them with offerings
and hence he is both admired and feared by his people. In
European peasant society the resident storyteller, when there
happened to be one, was usually a gifted member of the community who was offered good tobacco, a seat by the fire, and the
first drink if a bottle was passed round. His was a position of
prestige. The Hasidic storyteller who remembered and told
tales of an esteemed and greatly loved rabbi became revered
himself by association and in time was regarded as a sage who
preserved the history and wisdom of the community.

Usually the attitude towards the stories is one of pleasure,
enjoyment and pride. The Limba love their traditional tales
because they were handed down from the dead and are therefore part of their cultural heritage. Ruth Finnegan was told that
their storytellers are 'taught by the dead and their own heart'.
But throughout the ages there has always been a Puritan
tendency to condemn popular pastimes. The twelfth-century
Hungarian scribe who deplored 'false tales of peasants and
prattling minstrels', and the seventeenth-century Russian Tsar
who condemned the telling of 'events that never happened'
have their counterparts all over the world. American 'tall'
stories form a popular genre today, but the raconteur is generally designated as 'one of the biggest liars'; extreme Protestant
sects in the Bahamas and elsewhere condemn fictional tales as
'lies' and 'trash'. Traditional folk epic in Finland was in danger
of disappearing because the Lutheran clergy tried to stamp out
what they saw as a dangerous, Godless practice. Happily it
survived until comparatively recently, thanks to the more flexible attitude of the Orthodox Church in Karelia.

In many societies, whether unsophisticated or Western in
style, it is customary for tales to 'belong' to certain narrators.
Really good storytellers, who are not interested in competing
with one another, prefer their own stories to anything learned
from a colleague. Linda Dégh found that a Hungarian audience
accepted and respected a narrator's own repertoire. This
served as a form of traditional copyright. Even the same story

learned from a common relative will be presented in a variety of ways by different tellers. Bahamians say that a story does not become 'yours' until you have told it a number of times and so staked your claim. They also make a distinction between the printed and spoken word: a story out of a book is not yours, so you must not tell it!

Like so many other human activities, public storytelling has always been male dominated. Women, limited by their traditional role and place in society, were confined to the home and had no opportunity to go out and enrich their repertoire. In Africa, as we have noted, the traditional time for telling stories is in the evening when women tend to be busy with cooking and other chores. However in the southern part of Africa women tend to be the best narrators. Storytelling in the West Indies is still largely a means of male display before a mixed or female audience. Collecting data among West Indian immigrants in London, I found that my best informants were girls. Perhaps this reflects something of the changed role of women in the more open society of Great Britain.

Storytelling for children has always been one of women's tasks within the home, though naturally there have been exceptions. In parts of Hungary this was regarded as a parental duty. In our own culture we have special children's stories, but this is not a universal practice. Bahamians tell the same stories to adults and children, nor do they remove obscenities if younger listeners are present. We often hear that some children's stories are educational. They are intended to teach proper manners and prepare children for entry into adult society. Certainly many animal stories are in effect a satiric commentary on human mores. But African trickster stories, like the popular cycle featuring Anansi the spider, completely distort accepted behaviour and provide no pattern of guidance. As for the children themselves, they have always loved to hear stories and no doubt always will. In particular, as anyone who has ever performed this task will know, they must be told in the same way, without alterations or omissions. In this manner they serve a reassuring function, providing a firm and stable basis for the maturing personality. As George Orwell expressed it: 'Everything is safe, solid and unquestionable. Everything will be the same for ever and ever.'

Storytelling fulfils different needs and these, to some extent, determine the form that it takes. Myth, which has virtually disappeared from Western society, is sacred narrative set in distant time. It describes the creation of the world and of man, the origins of plant and animal life, and the culture hero who gives to man the knowledge of arts, crafts and fire. Its purpose is to explain to a people its culture and religious beliefs. Myths serve as a foundation charter in the societies in which they are told. They are an important part of the history of the tribe and are used in the education of children.

Legend is also religious in origin. The word is from *legenda*, Latin for 'to be read', because legends, the stories of saints and martyrs were first read aloud at religious services or during monastic meals. Gradually the earlier religious significance broadened and legend came to mean any narrative supposedly based on fact and told as fact about an individual, place or event. Local legends, which repeat the same themes in different parts of the world, are linked to specific sites and explain their geography, names and customs.

The desire to provide an explanation for everything that happens, to discover meaning in our environment and in events is very strong. We like things to be logical and orderly, otherwise we view them as disturbing and a threat. And so we try to find a pattern into which to fit the seeming chaos of existence. This is why legends tend to collect round the puzzling remains of earlier civilisations. Burial mounds used to be associated with fairies; Roman roads, unfinished causeways and other larger-than-life projects were said to be the work of giants or the Devil.

Periods of social upheaval, calamity or unrest, wars, epidemics, destructive freak weather and the like are all characterised by an increase in legend. In times of national danger a link with the past is reassuring. The national hero is not dead but asleep and will return when his country needs him. Legends of this kind were told about Robert the Bruce, King Arthur, Lord Kitchener, Emiliano Zapata and many others.

Legend flourishes today in both urban and rural environments and is one of the most popular forms of storytelling. It occurs in the course of ordinary conversation. No hard and fast distinction is made between narrator and audience; all join in.

One person only has to mention a curious occurrence, like a strange light or an object seen in the sky at night, and this will set off a session of legend-telling, in which one account will be quickly followed by another. Today's legends reflect our twentieth-century way of life. Told in a chatty, informal manner they embrace flying saucers, motor-cars, space satellites and other features of our modern life.

Ghost stories are also very popular. The legend of the Vanishing Hitchhiker – a girl who thumbs a lift, disappears from the car and turns out to have been a spectre – is told all over the British Isles and the United States; it has also been reported from the Far East. Early versions collected in America date back to 1912 and were common in the twenties and thirties, a period when the motor-car was a new invention and the centre of much interest. The narrator nearly always mentions a particular town or city where the event occurred to underline the authenticity of his tale. He will assure the listener that the story is true because it happened to a friend of a friend – though never to himself.

Macabre modern legends circulate on American campuses, especially in women's halls of residence. American students are car-owners and cycles of horror stories highlight the dangers of parking in a dark and lonely spot – the girl whose boy-friend gets out of the car to relieve himself and does not return finds the body hanging from a nearby tree. In a variant of this story of Hangman's Road the lovers are sitting in their car listening to the radio when they learn that a dangerous psychopath has escaped from prison and is in the area. The young man immediately drives his girl-friend home and they arrive safely, but find a sinister, hooked hand dangling from the car-door handle.

Dan Barnes, who collected many of these legends at the University of Kansas, believes that they have two functions. Partly they are told to impress – let's see who knows the most scary story – but they also contain a concealed didactic element. The fact that the majority of Dan's informants heard the stories from hall of residence counsellors and 'big sister' senior students bears this out. Related cycles of legends describe in gruesome detail the fate of any girl who stays on in her hall of residence over the lonely vacation period; a maniac breaks in

and claws her to death. The girl who cuts an official hall of
residence business meeting to visit the vending machines in the
basement meets a similar fate. The story of 'The Pickled Hand'
warns against cruel jokes and initiation stunts. Medical students who hang a cadaver's hand on a room-mate's electric-
light pull, or make a blindfolded freshman hold a dead hand all
night, find their victim in a sorry state: white-haired, insane,
and gnawing at the dead flesh.

Other modern legends are less overtly cautionary. 'The Fatal
Hairdo' was current in the 1960s when 'beehive' hair styles
were in vogue. It describes the agonising death of a girl with
this type of coiffure. She never washes it and keeps the hair
permanently in place with lacquer. Eventually it becomes
infested with cockroaches, which chew a hole in her skull and
enter the brain. Variants describe ant or spider bites which
infect the girl with blood-poisoning. Sometimes prompt treatment saves her life, but this involves shaving off the offending
hair. Underlying this legend-cycle would appear to be a sub-
conscious dislike of extravagant modern fashion, perhaps more
deep-rooted in America with its Puritan background.

In legend we have a vital form of modern narrative which has
displaced the once popular fairy tale. As these were seldom
about fairies, the term seems inappropriate. Professional scholars prefer to call them tales of wonder or magic or *Märchen* –
from the Old German *Mär*, meaning short story. Told as
fictional entertainment, their function has been superseded by
radio, television and the other media.

Just as there has been a shift from one type of genre to
another, so the technique for studying them has altered. The
older method, which ignored the narrator and concentrated on
text, treated the story as if it possessed a life of its own and could
travel from one country or continent to another of its own
volition. A great deal of energy was also expended on systems of
classification of the kind that one finds in botany.

Today it is recognised that the art of storytelling is just as
important as the tales themselves, which need to be studied
within their cultural context. Ruth Finnegan's African research
shows clearly how each narration constitutes a performance in itself. The storyteller makes use of mimicry – perhaps the noise of
a swimming tortoise – gestures to portray the various characters,

and subtle alterations in the timbre of his voice. He will use traditional formulas beloved by his audience, perhaps to describe the hero dressing and mounting his horse. If a singer of Russian heroic epic, the *bliny*, omitted to do this his audience would demand it, crying out: 'Do decorate the man and the horse. You need not pay for it!'

Many traditional storytellers defined the boundaries of their tale with opening and closing formulas, which admit one to the enchanted world and ring down the curtain at the end. *Es war einmal* – once upon a time. 'A story! A story!' cry the Hausa. 'Let it go, let it come.' The music of the Wombles or the Magic Roundabout at the beginning and end of the programme serve the same purpose for the child watching television. Hungarian wood-cutters about to entertain with a story shouted 'bone': the response 'soup' meant that they could begin.

An African audience will respond to the storyteller, clapping their hands, exclaiming and laughing at suitable points in the course of the narrative. Sometimes a member of the audience is specially singled out to do this. The Limba call him 'the answerer'. Audience participation and interested listeners provide encouragement and help the narrator to give a better performance. As a rule he remains seated but, to cite the Limba again, a flamboyant personality will prefer to stand up to tell his tale and will walk about among his hearers.

In many cultures music is an essential part of the story-telling. Story and accompaniment are closely linked among the Limba and their musicians are often the best storytellers. Not every African tale contains a song, but many do and sometimes they serve as its main feature. Bahamians, a distant offshoot of the same culture, call them story-songs. The songs mark out the structure of the story and an African audience will join in the chorus. We had our own cante-fables, as they were called, in England. At the Benin *Okpobhie*, or all-night entertainment, the Edo narrators accompany themselves on the bow-lute or thumb-piano while recounting stories of rural chiefs and heroes. Finnish folk epic, traditionally performed by singers with clasped hands, was accompanied on the *kantele*, a kind of zither, strung in earlier days with horse or human hair. European bards sang their lays and epic poems, like the Yugo-slav storytellers documented by Albert Lord, who accompanied themselves on the *gusla*. Indeed as late as the 1930s the Moslem nobility of that country still possessed their own personal minstrels.

Eminent scholars like the Chadwicks thought in terms of an 'heroic age'; others have written studies of 'ballad society'. The notion of a 'storytelling society' is just as oversimplified and misleading. Much anthropological thinking during the last hundred years has posited a somewhat romantically conceived homogeneous, non-industrial, rural community with its own pure and uncontaminated oral culture. Ruth Finnegan sensibly points out that isolation and self-sufficiency are both relative. It is all too easy to overlook the influence of traders, missionaries, administrators, educators, foreign observers and others. Many cultures described as primitive in the Middle East and Africa have flourished on the borders of a literate tradition: centuries of contact with the world's major religions – Christianity, Hinduism, Islam – are conveniently overlooked. In Europe ethnic communities have become cosmopolitan and oral tradition and literacy continually overlap and borrow from each other.

The oral storyteller and the storytelling society are both romantic constructs. A village is, for a time, noted for story-telling because it has an exceptionally able storyteller – that is all. And the oral storyteller is subjected to outside influences like those already mentioned. It is the exceptional circumstance rather than the sweeping generalisation that is interesting. During the years of Turkish occupation in Christian lands such as Armenia and the Balkans, it was necessary to be circum-spect. To be found in possession of manuscripts praising local heroes who had fought the Turks could be very dangerous. So the tradition of heroic epic went underground and was passed on orally.

Within the somewhat unusual society of Hasidic Jewry, the printed word is regarded with suspicion – or rather, the printing of their own stories is disliked. It is feared that an editor may tamper with the didactic legends, whose function, it will be remembered, is to teach their faith and religious way of life. This was the view of the sect's founder, the Baal Shem Tov, and his disciples, following him in this, have sometimes tried to prevent the stories of their rabbis from being published, lest they become tainted by the supposedly fictional aura of the printed word. Some Hasidic rabbis warn their followers not even to read published legends, on the grounds that they therefore contain untruths.

To what extent does the art of the narrator fulfil the needs of his community? In certain circumstances it may be said to embody the spirit of a nation. Maxim Gorky, a friend of Lenin and doyen of Bolshevik literature, describes in his autobiography *Childhood* the scene in his grandmother's kitchen. The old lady has just finished telling the story of Ivan the Warrior and Miron the Hermit:

> And this, I wist, be a punishment
> That he hearkened so to such evilness,
> That he bent his will to another's will.

Their boarder, a revolutionary nick-named 'That's Fine', is deeply moved:

> He kept making strange convulsive movements with his hands, taking off and putting on his glasses, waving them in rhythm to the verse, nodding his head, pressing his fingers against his eyes, and wiping the sweat pouring off his forehead and cheeks. When grandmother had finished, he jumped up . . . 'That's a wonderful thing! It must be written down by all means! How very true it is' . . . Now I could plainly see that he was crying: his eyes were filled with tears that flowed over and streamed down his cheeks . . . 'It's wrong to let someone else act as your conscience!' he repeated over and over again.

Later he says to the young Gorky: 'That grandmother of yours is a wonderful woman. . . . Can you write?' 'No'. 'Learn. And once you learn, put down what your grandmother recites − that's very important.'*

Storytelling can indeed express the hidden psychological needs of the social group. Melville Jacobs has pointed out that Clackamas Indian tales permit the airing of feelings about

---

* Maxim Gorky, *Childhood* (Moscow, c. 1950, pp. 198, 204.) The original Russian edition appeared in 1913.

those commonplace problematic relationships – with women, grandparents, in-laws – which produce social tension. They thus fulfil a necessity for which their community has provided no other public outlet. This general point is often made by functional anthropologists. At the same time it would be wrong to claim that the storyteller speaks quite literally as the voice of the people. In societies where they serve as court poets, often a hereditary post, the bards are members of a select group, who support and uphold the ruler, and hence the *status quo*.

Stories still continue to be told. There has been a shift from the once popular magic tale to the joke, the anecdote, the legend – and the twentieth century has left its mark. The Hungarian storyteller Zsuzsánna Palkó, exceptional for the excellence of her tales as well as for being a woman, died in 1964 at an advanced age. To the end, she told *Märchen*, remembered from her childhood, but she embellished them with modern details: telephone calls to the castle, the heroine photographed in her coach, the king visiting parliament.

Modern inventions, especially radio and television, have inevitably affected storytelling techniques. Gerald Thomas, investigating a French enclave in Newfoundland several years ago, found that 'soap' operas were increasingly popular. Informants disliked the elaborate structuring of the old *Märchen*, where events follow a pattern occurring in threes for example, preferring instead the unpredictable, rambling presentations of television drama.

Narratives collected by the Irish Folklore Commission in the 1930s illustrate the close link between the Old World and the New. Spectres of Irish emigrants who died in America return to Eire for burial in the family graveyard. A related legend cycle describes the wraith of a friend or relative appearing to the emigrant in San Francisco and warning of an approaching earthquake.

Sokolov, the Russian folklorist, who published the results of his work during Stalin's lifetime, relates storytelling in the Soviet Union to the Five-Year Plans. Here one can clearly see how traditional tales were deliberately altered. He comments on the moral self-consciousness of the storytellers, the curtailment of the old fantastic and miraculous tales, the new stress on realistic satirical narratives of everyday life, and emphasises the role of such stories in revolutionary ideology. Modern details are introduced into old tales of wonder and magic. Korguyev, the White Sea storyteller who 'corrects many of the old concepts' is typical. Contemporary vocabulary like 'comrade' and 'manager' is introduced, and the hero, who uncharacteristically refuses to marry the Tsar's daughter, travels not by eagle but by aeroplane. In their treatment of traditional tales storytellers reflect 'our contemporary Soviet period. They strive to compose new tales . . . expressing . . . their own new world view, their attitude towards the October Revolution and the whole Soviet regime'.

In one such story, which could certainly find many parallels in the contemporary world, three collective farmers wander through the Soviet Union in search of The Most Precious Thing. They discover, after many adventures, that it is the Word of Comrade Stalin. Stories do more than entertain, they instruct, inform, and manipulate.

Profanity in Context

EDMUND LEACH

UNTIL FAIRLY RECENTLY, when it became permissible to print 'four letter words' without restriction, the serious literature on this topic (which everyone finds absorbingly interesting) either took the form of pornography, dressed up as scholarship, or else became buried in specialised dictionaries of argot or journals of linguistics. And even then editors had their problems. As late as 1957 a scholarly journal published by the University of Toronto which printed an item about the difference between vocal and printed versions of bawdy songs carried the footnote: 'The Canadian Criminal Code has made it necessary to delete thirty-six lines of verse from the examples given in this article. These lines, of course, deal with the very thing about which the author writes.'

Things are now rather better, but Edward Sagarin's *The Anatomy of Dirty Words* (1962) has yet to be improved upon. In the present essay I am not so much concerned with 'dirty words' as such as with the relationship between 'dirty words' and other words and with the contexts in which the use of such words comes to be considered a profanity.

Profanity here has the weak general sense of 'the vulgar language of abuse', but there is also a strong sense where it equates with blasphemy. The two meanings are closely related so the surprising prosecution of *Gay News* for publishing a blasphemous libel provides a convenient starting point.*

*In June 1976 the magazine *Gay News* published a poem called *The Love that Dares to Speak its Name* by James Kirkup. The poem was the fantasy of a Roman centurion describing his homosexual love for Jesus. Mrs Mary Whitehouse, self-appointed guardian of decency in Britain, brought a private prosecution against the editor, publisher, and distributor of *Gay News*, charging them with blasphemous libel. The case was heard in July 1977 and the jury returned a verdict of guilty by a majority of ten to two (the smallest majority allowed in English law). The editor was fined £500.00 and given a nine-month prison sentence, suspended for eighteen months. The publisher

Ralph Steadman cover design for *New Scientist*

The verdict evoked a long correspondence in *The Times* which served to confirm my own assessment of the matter. Opinion was very divided. The theologians were mostly put out, they regretted that the prosecution had been started at all. Deities, after all, can presumably look after themselves, so if a human judge and jury feel that they must inflict punishment upon their fellows for insulting the Almighty it must be because they fear that in His indignation He will inflict quite indiscriminate punishment upon the general public if they do not. This view of divine retribution is common enough in primitive society but it is an odd interprctation of the ethics of Christianity!

But leaving the Deity aside, why did the judge and jury feel so shocked? I suggest that it may be relevant that:

1 the offending matter was illustrated poetry and not prose. The mode of expression was thus purportedly metaphoric-synthetic, which is the normal convention for all religious discourse;

2 the poem had an adorational theme which used the metaphor of homosexual relationship to express the love of the poet for his God. But the references to homosexual intercourse were very explicit. They were cast in the metonymic-analytic mode, which is the form of speech in which we ordinarily talk about practical mundane affairs;

3 neither the poet nor the channel of publication could claim special privileged status. *Gay News* was not a 'learned', 'scientific', 'medical' or 'theological' journal; James Kirkup's renown as an established poet was too restricted to allow him to get away with it.

My thesis is that the prosecution's success depended upon the combination of these factors rather than on the content of the poem in isolation. When the present Bishop of Kingston, speaking in plain prose with the authority of a recognised theologian, suggested some years ago that Jesus may have been

---

was fined £1,000.00. The Criminal Division of the Court of Appeal heard their appeal in February 1978 and delivered judgment a month later. It upheld the verdict of the lower court, but quashed the prison sentence. Finally, in February 1979, the House of Lords also upheld the original verdict of guilty, but again by the smallest possible majority of three to two. To reprint the poem here would be to invite a further prosecution for blasphemous libel.

homosexual there was some fluttering of journalistic dove-cots but no major scandal ensued.

The issue then is one of context. Broadly speaking, behaviour which is tabooed in a secular context is behaviour which is characteristic of a sacred context. In secular contexts we endeavour, so far as possible, to keep metaphor and metonymy apart; in sacred contexts we systematically mix them. For the purposes of such analysis sexual intercourse and the associated discourse of lovers is a sacred context. I hope to justify that last, perhaps surprising, proposition during the course of my paper.

This is not the place to elaborate a full-scale framework of structuralist theory but some further explanation of the contrast between metaphor and metonymy may be called for. Metaphor is synthetic; it is the 'unmotivated' assertion of similarity, the associations are arbitrary: 'My love is a rose'. In metaphor quite contradictory assertions are acceptable as equally and simultaneously true. 'God is a Father', 'God is a Son', 'God is a Holy Spirit'. Metonymy is analytic; it is the recognition of association by contiguity; it is a matter of taking things to pieces and showing what is the case by distinguishing one thing at a time, in sequence, as in anatomical dissection or logical demonstration.

In all ordinary vernacular languages normal conversation tends to mix up the metaphoric and metonymic poles of expression, but it is a peculiar feature of our contemporary industrial society that a special type of discourse – logical, mathematical, scientific – from which metaphor is largely excluded has acquired exceptional prestige – and this is discriminated from a complementary field of discourse, that of 'art', from which metonymy is largely excluded.

In this modern context the paradox of the Christian religion, particularly in its Protestant forms, is that it tries to have it both ways. Christians explicitly affirm that the 'truth' of the Gospel story is metonymic and actual (as in science and history), as well as metaphoric and symbolic (as in painting and poetry).

In a formal sense the central mystery of Christianity has always been that Jesus was both an ordinary mortal man capable of ordinary human suffering and also an immortal God born into this world by supernatural means; but, in the context of contemporary society, which separates the metonymic from

the metaphoric to an unprecedented degree, it has become
increasingly difficult to accept this challenge to common sense.
If Jesus was an ordinary mortal he should have had ordinary
human sexual appetites. A variety of Christian mystics, including St Teresa and St John of the Cross, have expanded on this
point, though they have usually done so by resort to metaphor.
Likewise many medieval Christmas carols contain picturesque
references to the sexual attributes of the Deity which Mrs
Whitehouse would almost certainly rate as obscene if she
understood what they meant. But latterly, with our metonymic
insistence on calling spades spades, the theology of educated
laymen has been slipping back from dyophysite orthodoxy
(Christ-Jesus is fully man as well as fully God) into monophy-
site heresy (God and Man are beings of wholly different kinds)
so that the anatomical attributes of Jesus Christ cannot be
thought about. A few professional theologians have used their
privileged position as 'authorities' to discuss such matters, but
for lay Christians, who have usually been taught at school, not
only that logical, metonymic thinking is 'correct', but also that
'sin' equates with 'sex', it seems rather obvious that a sinless
Christ must also be sexless.

This leads back to my earlier point that profanity is always
delimited by social context. Although the verbal content is far
from arbitrary it is only in certain contexts that the relevant
words are thought to be shocking, and it is always the situation
of profanity, rather than the words as such, which generates
excitement. In the vocabularly of verbal expletives all the
words are metaphoric of the same thing . . . whatever that
thing may be. Any one word is the equivalent of any other: fuck,
shit, Christ, bugger, damn and a score of others may all be
evoked by precisely the same situation according to the personal predilection of the speaker.

However there are some interesting and rather puzzling
complications and variations. In any one context and for any
one speaker there is a hierarchy of intensity for such 'swear
words', though the principle on which the hierarchy is based is
not obvious. The facts are difficult to research because of the
lack of reliable literary evidence and the operation of euphem-
ism. Most English males of my own social class and generation
would have felt that the sequence in which the five taboo words

listed above have been arranged places them in declining order of 'badness'. I am told that females of the same species rarely used sexual terms at all; they usually found adequate cathartic release in very attentuated, euphemised, 'religious' terms such as 'hell-(p)', 'Hades'. On the other hand at just this same period (c. 1930) there were workshop situations where all the male operatives used the word 'fucking' as a kind of all purpose adjective to slow down the rate of discourse, for example, 'give me that fucking hammer to drive this fucking nail into this fucking board'. In this context this word, which was still shocking for the middle class and still legally unprintable on grounds of obscenity, carried no 'expletive' quality whatsoever. At the present time differences in such usages as between the sexes, members of particular social classes, and particular local districts have probably been much reduced, but there is still an immense amount of variation. And in any case it is always the situation rather than the lexicon which decides whether or not any particular expression is or is not a profanity and the gravity of that profanity.

And so also in the *Gay News* case, it was the event rather than the content which really mattered. It was quite obvious, for example, that a high proportion of those who felt driven to let off steam by writing to *The Times* had not actually read the offending poem. Moreover nearly all of those who challenged the fairness of the judical verdict relied upon an argument about context rather than content. And this seems very reasonable. It certainly seems likely that at least some of the very restricted readership for whom the poem was originally intended would have seen the author's sexual fantasy as adorational and serious. But in the Establishment Christianity represented by the judiciary, the Deity is male, sexless and authoritarian; consequently, in an English Court of Law, any explicit mixture of human sexuality with divine asexuality constitutes gross disrespect to the Establishment itself.

At this point let me cut a few corners and offer a preliminary definitional hypothesis: 'It is a general principle of human thinking that incongruity of context, "matter out of place", ("dirt" in the language of Lord Chesterfield and Mary Douglas), evokes sentiments of alarm, awe, and respect. Blasphemy-profanity, both in the strong and in the weak sense, is the offence of treating a congeries of incongruities with disrespect and thus blurring the distinction between the religiously awful and the comic.'

Where does comedy come into it? Not perhaps on the surface but underneath. 'Swearing' and laughter are both psychologically cathartic.

Laughter is a very complicated psycho-physical reaction (see Howard Pollio's chapter) and it should not be taken for granted that all situations which are considered to be comic have something in common; but it is very obvious that, in any total inventory of joke stories and practical jokes, two broad categories would be extremely prominent: (1) 'dirty jokes', focused around sexual and excretory activity, and (2) 'role reversal jokes', in which the social persons to whom we are ordinarily expected to defer – policeman, magistrate, business manager, schoolmaster, vicar, mother-in-law, leaders of any kind – are shown up as ridiculous. But if pushed too far this kind of frivolity becomes sacrilege.

Here again fashions change. The extent to which the caricaturists of the Rowlandson era made a mock of the ruling monarch (who in those days exercised genuine political power) would today be considered quite intolerable; on the other hand, over the years, mocking the Deity has become decreasingly dangerous. Even if *Gay News* can still be fined for blasphemy, Mr Kirkup runs no risk of being burnt at the stake for heresy. (I should however make clear that, whatever *The Times* correspondents may have imagined, no intentional mockery of the Deity was in fact involved.)

There are many ways by which the dignity of office may be mocked. Many of them involve the inappropriate use of the uniforms and insignia by which the legitimacy of the office and its authority are ordinarily affirmed. But sexual undertones are usually discernible; fancy dress and music hall or pantomime comedy is very frequently transvestite.

One of the relevant 'incongruities' in such cases is that which comes through in the ambivalent meaning of our English word 'potency' (and its opposite 'impotence'). In common usage potency (= power) is an attribute of God, of persons in authority, of the prime movers of machines, and of males in sexual intercourse. In polite discourse these several meanings are kept apart; so much so that the actual word 'potency' (as distinct from 'power') is now seldom used except in a sexual context. But the fact that very similar metaphors crop up in many different languages shows that the cross-references must be based in some fundamental kind of natural common sense.

The outrage in the *Gay News* case was that the poet pointedly equated sexual potency with divine potency, an equation which Protestant Christianity has declared to be taboo, though in the great majority of human societies this equation is taken for granted. In Saivite Hinduism, for example, the metonymic sign of Deity is a *lingam* which is almost explicitly a human phallus. Half a century ago Katherine Mayo, a Mary Whitehouse of her day, made a proper killing out of this topic and was closely imitated by many others. *Mother India* went through twelve impressions between 1927 and 1930 while Arthur Miles' *The Land of the Lingam* went through four impressions in the course of two months in 1933! It is thus interesting that the plain rectilinear Crusaders' Cross, which is now standard in Protestant Churches, and which was adopted as a Christian symbol relatively late, has historical links with the Egyptian *ankh* (the sign for 'life') which was also, in origin, a stylised phallus.

Let me come clean about what I am saying here. *Power* lies at the interface between separable categories. If 'A' and 'B' are recognised as separate entities in dynamic relationship, then power flows either from A to B or from B to A and the channel through which it flows is the interface boundary which is common to both. The metaphorical equivalence of the potency of sexual intercourse and the potency of Deity thus turns on the fact that in sexual embrace the sensory distinction between 'I' and 'Other' disappears, while in a context of religious worship the distinction between the devotee and his deity disappears, and death becomes life.

Perhaps it will help if I put the same argument in rather a different way. Mystical ideas (such as 'the power of God') are synthetic and metaphorical. They are generated in the first place by the superimposition of a variety of non-congruent ideas which are somehow felt to belong together. At the bottom of all such piled-up metaphors there is always a 'primitive' notion, derived from the thinker's own childhood, which expresses the ultimate category distinction of human consciousness, the difference between I and Other. As the Freudians have very well understood, these primary verbal symbolisations of the I/Other opposition are inextricably entangled with the oral, anal and genital experiences of early childhood. If I am to develop the consciousness of myself as distinct from Other I must learn that my mother's breast is not part of me, that my faecal excretions are not part of me, but also, ultimately and in a very complicated sense, that my genitals are both part of me and part of other.

In our kind of social system we contrast mystical ideas with rational thought. Where mystical ideas are synthetic and metaphoric, one thing piled on top of another in ambiguity and confusion, rational thought depends upon analysis and metonymic association, upon taking complexities to pieces and looking at each of them in turn, one at a time, one after another. The links between the pieces are logical and mechanical like the relationships which bring together the various named components of the human anatomy; by contrast, the links between the component elements of mystical ideas are quite arbitrary and depend simply upon the *assertion* of similarity or identity.

I have already made the point that our literate, high-technology, 'scientific' system attempts, to an unusual degree, to keep the metonymic and metaphoric poles of thinking apart; but, besides that, our modern education leads us to deny that poetic (metaphoric) imagery can lead to any sort of truth. Scientific method is a procedure for eliminating metaphoric error.

Even in less materialistic societies the need to avoid total confusion has always made it necessary to establish conventional rules which will discriminate metonymic relations from metaphoric relations and thus allow the actor to perceive his surroundings as full of separate 'things' rather than just a mess of superimposed sensory stimuli. For we only manage to recognise things as things and events as events by refusing to recognise the spatial and temporal boundaries where one chunk of space-time merges into the next. This is what cultural conventions are all about.

We become aware of the existence of the world around us because of sensory inputs which reach the brain through our eyes, ears, nose, skin, tongue, etc. but we interpret those inputs according to preconceived expectations which are to a large extent determined by the way we have been reared and the way the categories of our language usage cuts things up. We inhabit a *man-made* world, not simply because generations of men have operated upon it by clearing forests, building houses and roads and machines and so on but because we can only recognise the world through the conceptual model which we make with verbal categories in our minds. That world, the model of reality which we hold in our heads and the expression of the model which we have imposed on the world out-there, has to be orderly so that we can understand it and, as it were, find our way about in it. The model world is made orderly by rules; rules which say that certain kinds of verbal and behavioural categories must be kept apart and not mixed up. The rules vary very greatly from one society to another; the infringement of such rules is what constitutes a profanity, a breach of taboo, in the context of that society.

Well that is all very grand and theoretical but what has it really got to do with sexual obscenity, knocking off policemen's helmets or jokes about the mother-in-law?

Perhaps you will begin to see the connection if I draw your attention to another set of verbal associations which crop up repeatedly in all sorts of different linguistic contexts. Cock = Male Bird = Human Penis has been around in various European contexts at least since the Athens of the fourth century BC. In the United States the bird has now become a 'rooster'. Latin *cunnus* is the source of English *cunt* and late Mediaeval French *con*. But French *connil, connin* = English *coney* was the animal we now call a rabbit. In sixteenth-century French love poetry and English Puritan tracts this play on words is explicit, as also in the eighteenth-century term *cunny-house* = brothel. But where coney turned into rabbit for adults, it turned into *bunny* for children, whence it has re-emerged as a title suitable for the ambiguous ladies in *Playboy* magazine's various entertainments for men! Pussy = domestic cat = female pubic hair. In England Ass = Donkey but in various dialects Arse = Buttocks is pronounced Ass; but in the United States *Ass* = Buttocks ≠ Donkey!

A common principle seems to be at work. On the one hand

there is a tendency to use the names of very close and familiar animals as metaphors for the private parts of the human anatomy; on the other we encounter a puritanical sensitivity which vetoes the animal metaphor as well as the sexual organ for which it stands.

A variety of other domestic animals are made to serve a rather similar purpose which is likewise double-faced. It is a rather *mild* form of *derogatory abuse* to identify Other with any of the following: pig, dog, bitch, ass, goat, goose, cat. But another set of 'close' animals are used as epithets of *affection*: chick, lamb, kitten, dove, mouse, duck. A few wild animals which have no legitimate status in the domestic home serve in this way as a rather *severe* form of *abuse*. It is far more offensive to call someone an ape or a reptile or a rat than an ass, a goat, or a goose. There are two intriguing exceptions to this general pattern. Although it is a domestic animal, 'swine' is rather strongly abusive, perhaps because it is felt to be a foreign word (German *Schwein*) rather than normal English. To call someone an owl is the equivalent of goose. But the owl is wild, not tame; furthermore, according to literary tradition, it is linked with Minerva in her capacity as the Goddess of Wisdom! And there are other cases too where the literary ancestry can be traced all the way back to Aesop's Fables. But antiquity is not the point; such usages would not have survived if they did not somehow seem appropriate. I would emphasise again that most of the epithets are *mild*; the abusive variants are scurrilous rather than obscene. Nevertheless they lie right on the boundary of polite speech as is shown by the fact that, at least in American English, *a silly ass* is barely distinguishable from *a silly prick*.

But why do we find this kind of animal imagery 'appropriate'? Appropriate for what? What is at issue, I suggest, is the representation of *power*. As I argued earlier, power lies in the interface of separable categories; but power itself is then an ambiguity, both A and not-A, and when we try to express such ambiguities through the symbolism of language or behaviour we generate a logical contradiction which is emotionally upsetting and which then evokes censorship and taboo. Here is an example. In the course of the evolution of the English language the Old English morpheme *cwene* (woman), which survives in

Dutch as *kween* (a barren cow) and is closely linked with the English four-letter obscenity *quim* (cunt), came to mean (a) a female monarch and (b) a prostitute. This not only constitutes a perfect example of the A/not-A formula but also corresponds to the religious ideology of Catholicism where Mary the Sinless Virgin is a sort of double of Mary Magdalene, the Repentant Sinner. But the overlap of these sensitive religious-sexual-political ideas was intolerable. First *queen* (the monarch) was discriminated from *quean* (the prostitute) by using a different spelling, and then *quean* (the prostitute) was virtually dropped from the lexicon altogether.

The point about domestic animal metaphors is that they allow such paradoxes to be talked about without provoking a drastic sequence of taboo reactions. Sometimes of course the process breaks down – the American rejection of the 'cock' and 'ass' metaphors are cases in point – but on the whole it works. Because we cannot take our domestic animals very seriously – they are, after all, like children, fully under our control – our pets allow us to evoke in permissible form, vicariously and at one remove, the deepest and most private sexual experiences. Pussy on my lap, who is also a vicious cat, is quite safe from prosecution for blasphemy or obscenity. Even the tough-minded Dr Kinsey found it polite to write 'petting to climax' instead of 'mutual masturbation'. But why pets and domestic animals?

The point here is that the basic discrimination which separates I from Other becomes a transform not only of the opposition Man/God but also of Tame/Wild, Humanity/Animality or, in the anthropologist's language, Culture/Nature. Man everywhere has to define himself as a disciplined human being as against the uncontrollable Other, 'Nature in the Wild' out there. But living creatures do not form in this respect a single unitary class; some are close, some are far; some are friends, some are enemies; some we can control, some are beyond our control. Looked at in this way the spectrum represented by the sub-categories: pets, farm animals, game animals, wild animals, places them in a hierarchy 'near' to 'far', 'tame' to 'wild', 'controllable' to 'uncontrollable' and can serve as an 'appropriate' metaphor or transformation for other such spectra. For example:

Word Play

226

	A	B	C	
I				Other
Common Man				God
	pets	farm animals	game animals	wild animals
	members of my domestic family	neighbours	affines	strangers
	incest: unmentionable sex behaviour	illegitimate but recognised sex behaviour	legitimate sex behaviour (marriage)	no sexual relations
	policeman	magistrate	earthly ruler	
	priest	saint	incarnate deity	
	joking coupled with affection	joking coupled with hostility	formalised 'joking relationships'; 'privileged familiarity'	
	weak obscenity	strong obscenity	blasphemy	
	common use of animal joking metaphors	relatively uncommon use of animal joking metaphors	animal metaphors unusual but, when used, regarded as highly offensive	

To read this schema assume that each horizontal line is a transformation (metaphoric substitution) for any other. The three columns A, B, C between them cover the whole of the interface between the opposed major categories I/Other, Common Man/God. Power (potency) is manifested in the sub-categories associated with each of the three columns but the potency gets greater as we move from left to right; likewise attitudes of respect and taboo become intensified as we move from left to right. You can make fun about the *dog* collar worn by the vicar but you come close to blasphemy if you point out that *dog* written backwards reads *god*! When joking behaviour appears in column C it is highly formalised as in a game. Hence we play ritualised games with our *game* animals carefully preserving them at one time of the year and hunting them with elaborate ritual at another. The 'joking relationships' between affines which have repeatedly been described by social anthropologists take on this same formalised unspontaneous form, as do mother-in-law jokes in our own society. A widely syndicated strip cartoon which appears daily in the *Cambridge Evening News* has produced roughly one such joke a week for the past ten years or more!

We can now get back to the original issue of profanity and incongruity. Profanity of the kind which arouses passionate scandal (for example that exhibited in the *Gay News* case) occurs when the conventions implied in my schema are ignored. For example, the ultra-hostile strong obscenity *mother-fucker* implies that I is accusing a neighbourly Column B Other of incest. As Sagarin has noted, this term is 'unique in its ability to incite aggressive anger even among people who have developed an armour of defence against the insults derived from obscenity'. According to the theory I am advancing in this paper the enormous emotive force of this expression, in this particular context, arises because of its interface (potency) position between Columns A and C (given a cultural background impregnated with Christian theological ideas).

In Column A, according to Freud, accusations of incest with the mother are constantly thought about but never mentioned, while in Column C the incest of the Deity with His own mother constitutes the inexpressible essence of the mystery of the Incarnation.

And this takes us back to the *Gay News* case. James Kirkup's poem nowhere employs the language of obscenity but the images evoked by the poem may well have evoked echoes of such obscene language in the minds of the judge and jury. In particular, verse four, which has come in for special denunciation, may have evoked the crudely sexual, though not particularly emotive, Column B obscenity *cocksucker*. In that case the jury may have felt completely outraged that such language, even by implication, should be shifted to Column C.

But if this is a valid interpretation of what happened then it would seem that the members of the jury were not very well informed about the finer contextual nuances of obscene language! Earlier on I recorded the use of *fucking* as an all-purpose adjective which is entirely devoid of emotive content, and similarly Sagarin notes of *cocksucker* that 'a man addicted to the use of this word may find it handy thirty or forty times during an evening of conversation'; it is applicable to members of either sex, to 'any reprobate, any contemptible person, anyone who is to be insulted or defamed, anyone crossing one's path'. I admit that many English people do find this term peculiarly offensive though just why this should be so is far from clear; it is not self-evident that it is any 'worse' than its inverse, the adjective *henpecked*! Although Kirkup did not in fact use the word (or any other obscenity) comparison of his text with what has been written about it by the legal pundits (for example M. S. Samuels in *The Times* correspondence of 25 July 1977) suggests that it was only because he *might* have so used it that the jury could conclude that the poem was 'so obscene or scurrilous as to vilify the Christian religion and be calculated or tend to arouse strong feelings of resentment which could lead to a breach of the peace'.

Robert Graves once told the story of how a patient in a military hospital when asked by the lady visitor where he had been wounded could only reply: 'I'm sorry, Ma'am; I don't know: I never learnt Latin.' Perhaps if blasphemy by verbal association becomes a general fashion we shall need, in common prudence, to amend the well-known formula to 'The Law is a Derrière'.

CONCLUSION

CONCLUSION

Images of Man

PETER LOIZOS

THE ANTHROPOLOGICAL JOURNAL *Man* recently published a paper by Bill McGrew and Caroline Tutin, two ethologists who argued that chimpanzees could be said to have culture, in a sense of the word usually reserved for humans. Predictably, two anthropologists wrote a letter of protest stressing that unlike any other animals, 'human social behaviours depend on language (cognitive abilities and speech). The human brain is so constituted that human beings not only learn language with the greatest of ease, but such learning can only be prevented under the most extreme conditions' (Washburn and Benedict 1979). They did not need to tell their audience that speech enables humans to do lots of other things which ethologists have not claimed for animals – loving, laughing, crying, reflecting on death, inventing gods, the whole range of artistic, scientific and other practices which were once called cultural, and are now often called 'symbolic'.

We are continually presented with models of human nature, variously stressing different aspects of our behaviour. It is claimed we are 'fundamentally' selfish, altruistic, aggressive, pacifistic, ascetic, acquisitive, and a lot more besides. Often, such arguments conceal a desire to sell a particular view of society, and in any pub one can hear socialists and conservatives, vegetarians and carnivores arguing that the philosophies of their opponents violate our 'natural' psychology.

This collection of essays is our most recent attempt to break out of a particular view of ourselves which is perhaps largely the product of urban, industrial society, a view in which we are shaped, if not distorted by preoccupations with work, survival, philosophy and politics, the Serious Sides of Life. Rodin's

famous sculpture of a ponderous, brooding human form could sum up this image: Man the Thinker.

But in 1938 Johan Huizinga, a Dutch historian, sought to persuade us of a very different model of our nature. He very deliberately called his book *Homo Ludens*, which can only lamely be rendered 'Man the Player', and he meant to supplement the dominant view of Man the Maker, *Homo Faber*, that rather serious hard-working character who had been credited till then with building civilisation.

Turning first to language, Huizinga writes: 'Behind every abstract expression there lie the boldest metaphors, and every metaphor is a play upon words.'

And a little later he makes his major claim:

Now in myth and ritual the great instinctive forces of civilised life have their origin: law and order, commerce and profit, craft and art, poetry, wisdom and science. All are rooted in the primeval soil of play.

Huizinga wished us to rethink the history of civilisation, and discover a rather wide-ranging play-instinct, as the seeds of (almost) everything.

For much of this century we have been accumulating histories, sociologies, psychologies and anthropologies of art, religion, sexuality, games, sport and leisure. If the anthropology of 'play', in a narrow sense, has been rather neglected, then in the wider sense, the work of Mauss and Malinowski has led to a solid body of data on a range of related topics. This work almost never refers to the chosen activity – feasting, fighting, competitive games or other exchanges – as 'play'. (One also notes in passing that children's games, and indeed children themselves have been virtually absent from anthropological writing.) But since the very category of 'play' is a rather curious and ambiguous one (a point this essay will argue) that is not in itself either surprising, or the sign of a problem. In one sense a more basic problem is why the idea of work dominates so much of our thinking. And there is the more general problem of how to divide up the varieties of our activities, to make sense of them. I have no answers to either of these puzzle-questions, merely a belief in their importance.

Even though some ethologists have tried to approach human behaviour via a short cut from studies of other animal species, many have expressed great caution about such an approach. It is not at all clear that we can directly learn very much about our own behaviour from considering animal play.

In a recent review of play behaviour in higher primates we are informed that 'the subject of play, probably more than any other area of animal behaviour, is open to confusion, misinterpretation and armchair theorising' (C. Loizos 1967). The first problem is that 'Play is a human concept, used of activity that is other than, or even opposed to work. By analogy the word has come to be applied to behaviour in animals which cannot be seen to have any immediate biological end, any obvious survival value. . . . But for animals, of course, it is different. Since they do not work, at any rate in our sense of the word, they cannot really be said to play – in our sense of the word.'

The reviewer then suggests that for understanding play in animals, it might be more fruitful to assume that the behaviour does have survival value, but that by the time it occurs in humans, it has become divorced from its original functions. The briefest reflection suggests that we must not *assume* that any common ground is covered by the word *play*, in any of the three following situations: (1) between animal 'play' and human play; (2) between children's play, and adult 'play'; (3) between different cultures, in how or what they 'play'.

For the rest of this essay, I shall be concerned only with adult activities in human societies, as discussed in some of the essays in this collection, and I shall not try to include Leach's essay on profanity.

The essays do seem to have a loose, 'family' resemblance. They describe behaviour which is *voluntary, rule-governed, non-routine* and which is *intrinsically rewarding*, that is, people do it mainly for its own sake, for the pleasures or excitements it yields. This, then, is one result of having selected activities which are all negatively defined as not-work, not-survival. We note that the arts are represented (theatre, storytelling) but in no sense exhaustively, and this points ahead to a major difficulty in deciding what is being called to our attention. The four characteristics just listed all fit another huge area of human activity, which is also not-work, and, arguably, not-survival, that is, religion. To distinguish 'play' from 'religion' we would then have to add that religion (like science) has a fifth attribute, that it is concerned with existential truths.

Further reflection also raises the question of sexual behaviour. Normally it too is voluntary, rule-governed, non-routine, and rewarding in itself; (one can see special cases in which it is none of these things, but those *are* special cases, and point to another problem which plagues the play issue – any piece of human behaviour can be twisted, given another meaning by the quirks of individual motive, perception or context). To think about sexual behaviour, and how far it should be included in the framework of this book is to face the survival issue yet again: while sexual reproduction is essential for the survival of the human species, most sexual acts are not performed with procreation 'in mind'. (Would a biologist wish to say that an evolutionary reproductive force is present 'in body'?) Like everything else we do, we can make what we like of sex, we can have a view of it which, whatever its biological substratum, makes it have *varied* meanings for us.

Obviously, sex can for some people at some times, be 'play'; and a religious procession or ritual may contain 'playful' elements. Play clearly spills over into several other areas of human activity which are not directly concerned with survival.

> Thousands have lived without love,
> None without water . . .   W. H. AUDEN

One answer to the question of what humans need for survival says little more than food and water. Another view, which is almost Huizinga's, argues that artistic, religious, spiritual activities are, for some people at some times, almost equally necessary. The trouble partly comes from asking about survival-in-general as if all humans at all times could be accounted for in a quick list. Some people have gone to the stake for their religious or political beliefs, so for them self-respect was more important than physical survival. Some small groups with complex cultural systems have found their belief systems shattered by intrusive change, and stopped reproducing themselves. 'Survival' at first sight seems a more clear-cut criterion for dividing up different human activities than it later proves to be. Almost anything may play a crucial role in somebody's survival. Otherwise, one is forced back to the bread-and-water view. A formulation is sometimes possible in a very abstract way: 'children need to be brought up by adults, if a group is to reproduce' but every first year anthropology student could immediately explain that 'the family' so familiar from industrial society is just one of dozens of ways of producing upbringing, so *in itself* 'the family' is not essential for survival.

Before leaving the question of survival, it is worth noting that even in the most basic things humans do, which seem responses to survival-needs, there are always the 'unnecessary' elaborations of culture: food is *dressed, deliberately varied* and *cooked*, even though for survival we could eat it raw and probably be healthier. Cooking utensils are almost invariably decorated, and so are our bodies. As Terence Turner's chapter shows, we do not simply 'cover' our bodies for 'protection' but we clothe them in our cultures.

We approach the idea of not-work largely with the prejudices which 'work' has imprinted in us. Hannah Arendt showed that 'work' itself contained a prior and instructive ambivalence: classical Greek, Latin, English, French and German all contain words which distinguish *labour* (painful, compulsory drudgery to keep alive) from *work* (a creative construction beyond immediate survival needs). A citizen of a Greek city-state was thought to need property and slaves in order to be free himself to concentrate on civic matters. In Britain today, supporters of the *Labour* Party are prone to describe themselves as wage-*slaves*, we talk of doing creative work, but not creative labour. The creativity of childbirth, because it is lengthy and tiring, is termed labour. The distinction seems, ambiguously, to persist.

All this is set aside when we contrast 'work' and 'play' in everyday speech. That is, both 'labour' and 'work' are understood together, as *work*, in order to make the strong black and white contrast so characteristic of our common-sense categories, and so misleading as a guide to reality. Let me suggest that very often when speakers of standard English use the key terms, they wish to imply some or all of the following contrasts (note that work is 'naturally' on the left, the 'sinister' or negative side):

Work	*Play*
obligatory	voluntary
tiring	refreshing
disciplined	spontaneous
hierarchical	egalitarian
serious	not serious
formal	informal
done for others	done for ôneself
etc.	etc.

In fact, the contrasts are highly misleading. People with a high degree of work satisfaction would stress the voluntary, refreshing and self-directed nature of what they do, and pick out the moments of spontaneity. Someone with a boring, repetitive job would probably agree to all the suggestions of the left hand column; for others work is unreal and play is real, work the non-serious way of filling up time between serious bouts of play. We see the basic terms very much through our own experiences, and the peculiarities of advanced industrial societies, in which so many tasks lack any intrinsic reward, and (unlike food production in pre-industrial societies) do not seem directly and immediately related to meeting one's immediate needs.

The contrasts are misleading for another reason. We know from the sociology of work, and our own experiences, that 'at work' a great deal of what goes on is *not* work. That is, it is joking, horse-play, courtship, making friends, relieving boredom and so on. Even in some jobs where the worker must keep up a formal and disciplined public style (as with waiters, who are expected to control their bodies, not sing, pick their noses, whistle or audibly break wind, etc. while serving customers) there is usually an 'off-stage' situation (out in the kitchen) away from the customers, where a very different set of behaviours takes place. We are not always at work, at work.

This same point is made by many of the writers in this collection: we work in play and play in work. Gerald Mars, an anthropologist, reported (Mars 1972) that in Newfoundland, a man who normally worked in a longshore gang had to join the gang for long drinking sessions, even when he was off sick, in order to keep his standing with his friends, and so, his job. This is just one example of the interpenetration of the two fields. In fact, there are many others.

The amounts of time and energy committed to 'play' are greater than in 'work' when we read about Olympic athletes in training, the bank-clerk who is a marathon runner. Perhaps we are less prepared for the competitive world of the Melanesians who enter into the *abutu* food exchanges, when a challenge followed by a response, focusing personal honour, may take years to conclude, with the commitment of time and energy to additional cultivation. Although *abutu* seems to be a substitute for a form of fighting now illegal, that fighting was probably less about survival, or material resources, than the wish to prove local superiority, a very long way from 'necessary labour'.

Games are often hierarchical in their internal organisation, with captains, and expert specialists for particular tasks, which make them like 'work-teams' (although some games, like volley-ball, characteristically avoid such organisation). However, several papers here point up the various connections between games and leadership, as in the Afghan game *buzkashi*. But the very participation of leaders in the games may be a way of reinforcing their own leadership. The Kennedy family games of touch football at Hyannisport were undoubtedly important in creating images of youth and vitality which contrasted strongly with the golf games of Eisenhower and Nixon. Heath's yachting exploits may have had a similar consequence in politics (while his ability to conduct a choir would appeal to yet other constituencies). There is an excellent 'grass-roots' example from a classic of urban sociology, William Whyte's *Street Corner Society*, a study of young men who stood about on a street corner in downtown Boston. Whyte observed that Doc, the informal but undisputed leader of the gang, used to win remarkably often when the group went to the bowling alley; while this was partly a matter of personal skill, it was also influenced by the way his lieutenants and he himself behaved when junior members of the group were taking their turns. A good deal of caustic mockery was directed at the subordinates, which made it psychologically a lot harder for them to bowl well, whereas when Doc bowled, the group not only *expected* him to do well, *and* refrained from catcalling, but actually *cheered him on*. To him that hath . . .

Except under conditions of the most extreme deprivation, we have always found time and energy for non-essential activities. Anthropologists celebrating variety stress that the things done, or made, always reflect the cultures that have shaped them. Essential tasks have sometimes been demanding and monotonous but at other times have left large amounts of free time; and it seems unlikely that any attempt to explain the immense range of non-work activities in terms of any single principle (such as 'creativity' or 'surplus energy') will be adequate. We need a good deal of order, predictability and certainty, but too much of these produces a condition popularly called boredom, with its accompanying frustrations; too little of them, that is, a series of chaotic experiences, seems to produce great anxiety, and to be the enemy of play, but may also be the catalyst for great art. Somewhere between these shifting compass points, we know from these essays (and the vast literature which precedes them) that human nature contains a playful and inventive aspect, and that it is as plastic and susceptible as many of our other attributes – our altruism, egotism, aggressiveness, pacificism and so on. If the modern world and its problems leave few of us inclined to describe our species as *Homo Ludens*, it is well to remind ourselves from time to time that it is still in us to be something *more* than mere survivors. In 1979 the BBC broadcast the first British performance of *Emperor of Atlantis*, an opera composed by inmates of a concentration camp. The factor which psychiatrist Victor Frankl (himself a camp survivor) described as the 'will to meaning' is *one* of the distinctive features of 'human nature'.

BIBLIOGRAPHY

ABOUT THE AUTHORS

INDEX

Bibliography

An Introduction to Affluence
C. Geertz, *The Interpretation of Cultures*, Hutchinson, London (1975).
R. Leakey & R. Lewin, *People of the Lake*, Collins, London (1979).
R. B. Lee & I. DeVore (eds), *Man the Hunter*, Aldine, Chicago (1968).
M. Sahlins, *Stone Age Economics*, Tavistock, London (1974).

The Purpose of Play
J. S. Bruner, A. Jolly and K. Sylva (eds), *Play: Its Role in Development and Evolution*, Penguin, Harmondsworth (1976).

Infant Games and the Creation of Culture
J. S. Bruner *et al.* (1976) *op. cit.*
C. Garvey, *Play*, Fontana, London (1977).
R. E. Harran & B. Sutton-Smith, *Child's Play*, Wiley, New York (1971).
B. Tizard & D. Harvey, *Biology of Play*, Heinemann, London (1976).
C. Trevarthen, 'Conversations with a two-month-old', in R. Lewin (ed), *Child Alive*, Maurice Temple Smith, London (1974).

It's Only a Game
M. Avedon & B. Sutton-Smith (eds), *The Study of Games*, Wiley, New York (1971).
A. Dundes, 'A Study of the Structure of Non-Verbal Folklore', *New York Folklore Quarterly*, vol 20, pp 276–288 (1964).
A. Milberg, *Street Games*, McGraw-Hill, New York (1976).

244   *Bibliography*

I. Opie & P. Opie, *The Lore and Language of Schoolchildren*, Clarendon Press, Oxford (1959).
——, *Children's Games in Street and Playground*, Clarendon Press, Oxford (1969).

Playing with Aggression

W. Arens, 'The Great American Football Ritual', *Natural History*, vol 84, pp 72–81 (1975).
D. W. Ball, 'Failure in Sport', *American Sociological Review*, vol 41, pp 726–739 (1976).
M. R. Real, 'Super Bowl: Mythic Spectacle', *Journal of Communication*, vol 25, pp 31–43 (1975).
R. G. Sipes, 'War Sports and Aggression', *American Anthropologist*, vol 75, pp 64–86 (1973).

Gambling: Mirror of Society

C. Geertz, 'Deep Play: Notes on the Balinese Cockfight', *Daedalus*, vol 101, pp 1–38 (1972).
J. von Neumann & O. Morgenstern, *Theory of Games and Economic Behaviour*, Princeton, New Jersey (1944).
D. Riches, 'Cash, Credit and Gambling in a Modern Eskimo Economy', *Man*, vol 10, pp 21–33 (1975).
M. Sahlins (1974) *op. cit.*
J. Woodburn, *The Material Culture of the Nomadic Hadza*, British Museum, London (1970).

Institutions of Violence

A. Balikci, 'Village Buzkashi', *Afghanistan Journal*, vol 5, no 1 (1978).
R. Gardner & K. G. Heider, *Gardens of War: Life and Death in the New Guinea Stone Age*, New York (1968).
K. G. Heider, *The Dugum Dani: A Papuan Culture in the Highlands of West New Guinea*, Viking Fund Publication No 49, Wenner-Gren Foundation, New York (1970).
S. Jones, *Men of Influence in Nuristan: A Study of Social Control and Dispute Settlement in Waigal Valley, Afghanistan*, Academic, London (1974).
M. Young, *Fighting with Food: Leadership, Values and Social Control in a Massim Society*, Cambridge UP, Cambridge (1971).

The Social Skin

Q. Bell, *On Human Finery*, A. A. Wyn, New York (1949).

M. Sahlins, *Culture and Practical Reason*, University of Chicago, Chicago (1976).

T. S. Turner, 'The Kayapo of Central Brazil', in Anne Sutherland (ed), *Face Values*, BBC, London (1978).

What's So Funny?

A. J. Ambrose, 'Development of the smiling response in early infancy', in B. Foss (ed), *Determinants of Infant Behaviour*, vol 1, Wiley, New York (1961).

L. H. Charles, 'The clown's function', *Journal of American Folklore*, vol 58, pp 25–34 (1945).

R. J. Coser, 'Laughter among colleagues', *Psychiatry*, vol 23, pp 81–95 (1960).

A. M. Ludovici, *The Secret of Laughter*, Constable, London (1932).

L. A. Sroufe & J. P. Wunsche, 'The development of laughter in the first year of life', *Child Development*, vol 43, pp 1326–1344 (1972).

R. W. Washburn, 'A study of the smiling and laughing of infants in the first year of life', *Genetic Psychology Monographs*, vol 6, pp 397–537 (1929).

Fighting Words

R. D. Abrahams, 'Playing the Dozens', *Journal of American Folklore*, vol 75, pp 209–220 (1964).

——, 'Joking: the training of the man of words in talking broad' in T. Kochman (ed), *Rappin' and Stylin' Out*, University of Illinois Press, Urbana (1972).

M. R. Ayoub & S. A. Barnett, 'Ritualised verbal insult in white high school culture', *Journal of American Folklore*, vol 78, pp 337–344 (1965).

A. Dundes, J. W. Leach & B. Özkök, 'The Strategy of Turkish boys' verbal duelling rhymes', in J. Gumperz & D. Hymes (eds), *Directions in Sociolinguistics: the Ethnography of Speaking*, Holt, Rinehart & Winston, New York (1972).

G. H. Gossen, 'Verbal duelling in Chamula', in B. Kirschenblatt-Gimblett (ed), *Speech Play*, University of Philadelphia Press, Philadelphia (1976).

W. Labov, 'Rules for ritual insults', in D. Sudnow (ed), *Studies in Social Interaction*, Free Press, New York (1972).

Drama: Aristotle in Indonesia

Aristotle, *Poetics*, translated by Leon Golden, commentary by O. B. Hardison, Jr, Prentice-Hall, New Jersey (1968).

F. Dukore, *Dramatic Theory and Criticism: Greeks to Grotowski*, Holt, Rinehart and Winston, New York (1974).

L. Peacock, *Rites of Modernisation: Symbolic and Social Aspects of Indonesian Proletarian Drama*, University of Chicago Press, Chicago (1968).

Plato, *The Republic*, translated by A. D. Lindsay, introduction and notes by Renford Rambrough, J. M. Dent & Sons, London (1976).

Tell us a Story

V. Newall, *An Egg at Easter: a folklore study*, Routledge, London (1971).

Profanity in Context

E. R. Leach, *Culture and Communication: The logic by which symbols are connected*, Cambridge University Press, Cambridge (1976).

E. Sagarin, *The Anatomy of Dirty Words*, Lyle Stuart, New York (1962).

Images of Man

H. Arendt, *The Human Condition*, University of Chicago Press, Chicago (1969).

V. S. Frankl, *Will to Meaning: Foundations and Applications of Logotherapy*, Souvenir Press, London (1971).

J. Huizinga, *Homo Ludens: a study of the play element in culture*, 1970 ed, Introduction by George Steiner, Maurice Temple Smith, London (1970).

C. Loizos, 'Play behaviour in higher primates: a review', in D. Morris (ed), *Primate Ethology*, Weidenfeld and Nicolson, London (1967).

G. Mars, 'An anthropological study of longshoremen and of industrial relations in the port of St John's Newfoundland, Canada', unpublished PhD thesis, University of London (1972).

W. C. McGrew & C. E. G. Tutin, 'Evidence for a social custom in wild chimpanzees?', *Man*, vol 13, pp 234–251 (1978).

S. L. Washburn & B. Benedict, 'Non-human primate culture', *Man*, vol 14, pp 163–164 (1979).

About the Authors

WILLIAM ARENS is an Associate Professor of Anthropology at State University of New York, Stony Brook. He did his doctorate fieldwork in Tanzania, and spent 1978 in the Sudan. He co-edited *The American Dimension*, and has just published *The Man-eating Myth*, a book on human cannibalism.

LAURENCE G. AVERY is Professor of English and Director of Graduate Study at the University of North Carolina at Chapel Hill. His most recent book is *Dramatist in America: Letters of Maxwell Anderson, 1912–1958.*

DONALD BRENNEIS is an Associate Professor of Anthropology at Pitzer College in California. He received his PhD from Harvard for his work in Fiji and has published several papers in *Language and Society*.

JEREMY CHERFAS obtained his PhD for work on the role of experience in learning, and is currently Biological Sciences Editor of *New Scientist* magazine.

DOROTHY EINON is Pinsent Darwin Fellow in Mental Pathology at the University of Cambridge. She obtained a PhD for her work on partial reinforcement and has been studying play and isolation for the past five years.

FIONA GRANT is a graduate student at Edinburgh University. She is working on the development of the conventional, symbolic use of objects by young children.

SCHUYLER JONES is University Lecturer in Ethnology, and Assistant Curator of the Pitt Rivers Museum in Oxford. He has done fieldwork in Afghanistan, Pakistan, and much of Africa. With Lennart Edelberg, he has just completed a major book, *Nuristan.*

Sir EDMUND LEACH is Professor of Social Anthropology and was Provost of King's College, Cambridge. His most recent book is *Culture and Communication*.

ROGER LEWIN is Deputy Editor of *New Scientist* magazine. He has written extensively on the evolution of man, including *Origins* and, more recently, *People of the Lake*.

PETER LOIZOS is a lecturer in Social Anthropology at the London School of Economics. His doctorate fieldwork was on politics in a Cypriot village, and he has recently completed a book on Greek Cypriot refugees. He is currently editor of *Man*, the journal of the Royal Anthropology Institute.

VENETIA NEWALL is an Honorary Research Fellow in Folklore at University College, London and Honorary Secretary of the Folklore Society. The University of Chicago awarded her the International Folklore Prize for her book *An Egg at Easter*.

JAMES L. PEACOCK is Professor of Anthropology at the University of North Carolina, Chapel Hill. His fieldwork has been largely in Indonesia, and he has published extensively. His latest book is *Purifying the Faith: 'Muhammadijah', an Indonesian Reformation*.

HOWARD R. POLLIO is the Distinguished Service Professor in Psychology at the University of Tennessee. He has spent time teaching at the University of London and Cambridge University and is very interested in the uses of language. His book *Psychology and the Poetics of Growth* is a study of figurative language and development, and he is busy completing *Behaviour and Existence*, a rewriting of psychology from existential and phenomenological viewpoints.

DAVID RICHES is a lecturer in Social Anthropology at Queen's University, Belfast. He spent eighteen months among the Canadian East Arctic eskimos at Port Burwell collecting data for his PhD, and has contributed two articles to Robert Paine's book *The White Arctic*, a study of the influence of the white man in the far north.

COLWYN TREVARTHEN is Reader in Psychology at
Edinburgh University. He began his research working on
split-brain patients with Roger Sperry, but is now more
interested in the development of human understanding and
interpersonal relationships. Babies are especially important
in this, as they must obtain cooperation without benefit of
language.

TERENCE S. TURNER is Associate Professor of Anthropology
at the University of Chicago. He worked for his doctorate
among the Amazonian Indians.

Index